# Cloud Native Infrastructure with Azure

*Building and Managing
Cloud Native Applications*

*Nishant Singh and Michael Kehoe*

Beijing · Boston · Farnham · Sebastopol · Tokyo

**Cloud Native Infrastructure with Azure**

by Nishant Singh and Michael Kehoe

Published by O'Reilly Media, Inc., 1005 Gravenstein Highway North, Sebastopol, CA 95472.

O'Reilly books may be purchased for educational, business, or sales promotional use. Online editions are also available for most titles (*http://oreilly.com*). For more information, contact our corporate/institutional sales department: 800-998-9938 or *corporate@oreilly.com*.

**Acquisitions Editor:** Jennifer Pollock
**Development Editor:** Rita Fernando
**Production Editor:** Christopher Faucher
**Copyeditor:** Audrey Doyle
**Proofreader:** Kim Cofer

**Indexer:** Ellen Troutman-Zaig
**Interior Designer:** David Futato
**Cover Designer:** Karen Montgomery
**Illustrator:** Kate Dullea

February 2022:     First Edition

**Revision History for the First Edition**

2022-02-09:     First Release

See *http://oreilly.com/catalog/errata.csp?isbn=9781492090960* for release details.

978-1-492-09096-0

[LSI]

# Table of Contents

# Preface

Cloud computing has been widely adopted as a model of next-generation digital business transformation that drives growth and innovation. Nowadays, customers look for an ecosystem and experience that is fast and that seamlessly integrates with their existing services. From an enterprise perspective, the cloud delivers services for consumers and businesses in a way that is scalable, highly reliable, and available. From an end-user perspective, the cloud provides a simple model for acquiring computing services without needing to fully understand the underlying infrastructure and technology.

To take full advantage of the speed and agility of cloud services, many existing applications have been transformed into cloud native applications, and new solutions are being built for the cloud first. Cloud native applications are built from the ground up to embrace rapid change, large scale, and resilience. By default, the underlying infrastructure for cloud native applications plays a critical role in efficiently serving a business's needs. If the underlying infrastructure is not architected with the correct practices, even the best cloud native applications will fail in production environments.

This book explores how modern cloud native infrastructures on Azure can be built and managed in a production environment, along with various requirements and design considerations of cloud native applications.

## Who Should Read This Book

This book provides a simple yet comprehensive introduction to the cloud native landscape and all the major technologies that engineers use to build such reliable environments. The book is for site reliability engineers (SREs), DevOps engineers, Solution architects, Azure enthusiasts, and anyone who is involved in building, migrating, deploying, and managing the day-to-day operations of a cloud native workload.

The book assumes that you possess basic knowledge of the cloud and DevOps culture in general. But even if you don't, and you want to better understand the buzz around cloud native and other fancy technologies, this book is still the right place for you to get started.

## Goals of This Book

By the end of this book, you will be able to follow and build your own infrastructure on Microsoft Azure. We present a sequential introduction to the major components of the cloud native world and how to use, deploy, and maintain them over Azure. Additionally, you will be introduced to the need for cloud native technologies in today's brave new world, the problems they solve, and hands-on best practices.

In this book, you will:

- Learn how to build cloud native infrastructure over Azure following the path of the Cloud Native Computing Foundation's (CNCF) cloud native landscape
- Ascertain which technologies to use at different stages of design
- Discover how to address the problems you may face while managing and operating cloud native infrastructure, as well as the technologies that help solve them

## Navigating This Book

This book is organized as follows:

- Chapter 1 provides a basic introduction to the cloud and the need for cloud native technology and its adaptations.
- Chapter 2 covers the fundamentals of infrastructure as code (IaC) with Terraform and Packer, and introduces Azure and Ansible as provisioners/configuration managers.
- Chapter 3 introduces containers, and container runtimes such as containerd, Docker, and CRI-O. Different types of container registries are also discussed.
- Chapter 4 discusses Kubernetes and includes the details necessary to use the infrastructure in upcoming chapters.
- Chapter 5 deals specifically with the Azure Kubernetes Service and the Helm package manager.
- Chapter 6 focuses on how modern cloud native infrastructure can be made observable.
- Chapter 7 is all about service discovery and service mesh. We introduce the CoreDNS DNS server and the Istio service mesh in this chapter.

- Chapter 8 covers network and policy management, including the Calico, Flannel, Cilium, Azure Policy, and Open Policy Agent container networking interfaces.
- Chapter 9 discusses how persistent storage systems are deployed on cloud native infrastructure, with a focus on Azure Storage, Vitess, Rook, TiKV, and etcd.
- Chapter 10 is primarily focused on messaging and streaming platforms such as NATS and Azure messaging services.
- Chapter 11 is a simple introduction to the serverless side of things in the cloud native landscape.
- Chapter 12 serves as a wrap-up of everything we discussed in the preceding chapters.

## Conventions Used in This Book

The following typographical conventions are used in this book:

*Italic*
: Indicates new terms, URLs, email addresses, filenames, and file extensions.

`Constant width`
: Used for program listings, as well as within paragraphs to refer to program elements such as variable or function names, databases, data types, environment variables, statements, and keywords.

**`Constant width bold`**
: Shows commands or other text that should be typed literally by the user.

 This element signifies a tip or suggestion.

 This element signifies a general note.

 This element indicates a warning or caution.

# Using Code Examples

Supplemental material (code examples, exercises, etc.) is available for download at *https://github.com/stormic-nomad-nishant/cloud_native_azure*.

If you have a technical question or a problem using the code examples, please send email to *bookquestions@oreilly.com*.

This book is here to help you get your job done. In general, if example code is offered with this book, you may use it in your programs and documentation. You do not need to contact us for permission unless you're reproducing a significant portion of the code. For example, writing a program that uses several chunks of code from this book does not require permission. Selling or distributing examples from O'Reilly books does require permission. Answering a question by citing this book and quoting example code does not require permission. Incorporating a significant amount of example code from this book into your product's documentation does require permission.

We appreciate, but generally do not require, attribution. An attribution usually includes the title, author, publisher, and ISBN. For example: "*Cloud Native Infrastructure with Azure* by Nishant Singh and Michael Kehoe (O'Reilly). Copyright 2022 Nishant Singh and Michael Kehoe, 978-1-492-09096-0."

If you feel your use of code examples falls outside fair use or the permission given above, feel free to contact us at *permissions@oreilly.com*.

# O'Reilly Online Learning

 For more than 40 years, *O'Reilly Media* has provided technology and business training, knowledge, and insight to help companies succeed.

Our unique network of experts and innovators share their knowledge and expertise through books, articles, and our online learning platform. O'Reilly's online learning platform gives you on-demand access to live training courses, in-depth learning paths, interactive coding environments, and a vast collection of text and video from O'Reilly and 200+ other publishers. For more information, visit *http://oreilly.com*.

# How to Contact Us

Please address comments and questions concerning this book to the publisher:

O'Reilly Media, Inc.
1005 Gravenstein Highway North
Sebastopol, CA 95472
800-998-9938 (in the United States or Canada)
707-829-0515 (international or local)
707-829-0104 (fax)

We have a web page for this book, where we list errata, examples, and any additional information. You can access this page at *https://oreil.ly/cloud-native-azure*.

Email *bookquestions@oreilly.com* to comment or ask technical questions about this book.

For news and information about our books and courses, visit *http://oreilly.com*.

Find us on Facebook: *http://facebook.com/oreilly*.

Follow us on Twitter: *http://twitter.com/oreillymedia*.

Watch us on YouTube: *http://youtube.com/oreillymedia*.

# Acknowledgments

We would like to thank Rita Fernando, Nicole Taché, and Jennifer Pollock, our editors at O'Reilly who were supportive and awesome as they guided us through the writing process. We would also like to thank our tech reviewers for their valuable contributions to the book. This book would not have been possible without the thorough and amazing reviews and feedback from Matt Franz, Peter Jausovec, Liudmila Sinkevich, Steve Machacz, and Alexander Kabonov.

In addition, we would like to highlight Matt Franz for his thorough reviews, suggestions, and contributions to improve the quality of the book. Matt gave extensive feedback on chapters and contributed Chapter 10.

Nishant would like to thank his mom, his dad, and his wife, Mahek, for being so patient and supportive while he was working on the book. He would also like to thank the O'Reilly team and his peers at LinkedIn who supported the idea from the very beginning.

Michael would like to thank his family, who encouraged him to follow his dreams and never give up. He would also like to thank his best friend, Jennifer, for her support and patience while he was working on this book, the O'Reilly staff for helping to bring the book from idea to reality, and all of the reviewers for their time.

# CHAPTER 1

# Introduction: Why Cloud Native?

Even though using the cloud provides a way to solve problems with the scalability, availability, and reliability of our applications, it is not a silver bullet. We cannot put our applications in the cloud and expect them to be up and running forever, nor can we package our applications in containers to turn them into microservices that can run smoothly in the cloud. To take full advantage of what the cloud has to offer, we need to develop infrastructures and services with the cloud at the forefront of our minds.

To truly understand the cloud native journey and its importance, we need to first look back at what the world of infrastructure and services looked like during the early days of the internet. So, let's embark on this journey.

## The Journey to the Cloud

Back in the early days of the internet, the overall web application infrastructure was hosted using physical servers that needed to be procured and prepared before applications could be served from them. IT teams had to physically buy the servers and set them up on premises, install relevant server operating systems, prepare the environments, and then deploy applications on top of them. There were many problems with this approach: for example, you'd have underutilized servers (since you'd never end up fully using them), it was difficult to run multiple applications, and setup and maintenance costs were high. *Virtualization* was developed to allow more efficient utilization of physical servers. Virtualization creates an abstraction layer over physical hardware that allows underlying resources, such as processors, memory, and storage, to be divided and shared.

Virtualization solved many problems with resource utilization and multitenancy, but you still needed to own the hardware to deploy your application and you still needed to maintain all the overhead of running your data center. This gave rise to the need to run infrastructure as a service (IaaS), where the servers are owned by third parties that are responsible for your applications' underlying infrastructure. This was the beginning of the cloud computing era, and it allowed companies to focus on their applications and underlying environments without worrying about hardware, overhead, or configuration issues. IaaS was followed by platform as a service (PaaS), which focused on reducing the toil further by separating the underlying software environment and runtime. This meant developers only had to focus on writing their applications and defining the dependencies, and the service platform would be completely responsible for hosting, running, managing, and exposing the applications. PaaS led the way to fully managed cloud services with the advent of software as a service (SaaS), popularly known as "on-demand software," which provides consumers with the application as a service on a pay-as-you-go basis.

As cloud computing gained in popularity, so did the idea of having cloud native technologies that would use the cloud more efficiently while harnessing the full potential of cloud infrastructure and its various offerings. This gave rise to the development of cloud native infrastructure and cloud native application development. Cloud native infrastructure creates an abstraction on the cloud provider's underlying infrastructure and exposes the infrastructure with APIs. This infrastructure management philosophy makes it very easy to scale and reduce underlying complexity, which indirectly improves availability, resiliency, and maintainability. Similarly, cloud native applications fortify the bridge between the application and infrastructure by incorporating supporting features such as health checks, telemetry and metrics, resiliency, a microservices environment, and self-healing.

Let's now take a look at challenges in the cloud computing environment.

# Challenges in the Cloud

Public cloud providers have become a dominant enterprise solution for a lot of growing industry needs and business requirements. They give you advantages such as higher availability and scalability along with the flexibility to design your applications in a way that utilizes cloud services. When cloud solutions were first introduced, numerous challenges including security, effective cost management, compliance, and performance concerned potential customers. Those early challenges are now a thing of the past for the majority of cloud consumers, as they have been overcome with advances in both cloud provider technologies and the way enterprises deploy solutions on the cloud.

Even though we have come a long way, this does not mean the cloud is perfect. There are still challenges in the cloud landscape, but they look very different from the ones we faced back when the cloud was still new. Customers today now have to consider the following challenges:

*Too many choices*

There are plenty of cloud providers out there with an extensive array of services to choose from. This means you need to hire expert architects and engineering teams who know how to operate the services and use them according to your business use case. Not only is hiring these engineers difficult, but finding engineers who are experts in a specific field requires a significant time investment.

*Rapid growth and development of cloud services and technologies*

A huge number of new cloud services are being released by cloud provider giants like Amazon, Microsoft, and Google. This results in a greater need to train engineers in these new services and a greater need to maintain these services in the future as the applications grow. Often, the level of investments in these services also indirectly causes vendor lock-in, resulting in a spiral of future constraints in application design.

*Multiple generations of technology*

As we have moved into the cloud era, we have also lifted and shifted our application stacks from various generations of infrastructure solutions, ranging from virtual machines to containers to serverless technologies. This migration of applications requires a significant amount of effort to understand the underlying technologies and support them in the future.

*Growing operational complexity*

These rapidly growing technologies, combined with accelerated migration of workloads to the cloud, have given rise to operational complexity and an ever-growing list of factors to look out for, including storage systems, security models, governance models, and management platforms, among others.

*Evolution of business needs and technologies*

New areas of technology and cultural change have also rapidly evolved the enterprise architecture. For instance, with the advent of the DevOps culture, a new application that once took weeks or months to develop can now be rolled out in a couple of minutes. More advanced areas, such as data science and machine learning, have also come into the picture, increasing business needs and overall engineering maturity.

So, despite the power of cloud computing, businesses had to wade through numerous complexities. Eventually, it became clear that businesses wanted to have the speed, scale, and margin of the cloud but none of the overhead. To accomplish this, it was necessary to embrace the cloud native approach of application building, which would help companies take full advantage of the cloud.

# Cloud Native Computing Foundation

As more companies are adopting cloud native technologies, creating software in-house, and closely partnering with other businesses to quickly bring products to market, strides are being made to improve the cloud native domain. One organization that is helping to lead the way in this effort is the Cloud Native Computing Foundation (CNCF) (*https://cncf.io*). Its mission is as follows:

> Cloud native technologies empower organizations to build and run scalable applications in modern, dynamic environments such as public, private, and hybrid clouds. Containers, service meshes, microservices, immutable infrastructure, and declarative APIs exemplify this approach.
>
> These techniques enable loosely coupled systems that are resilient, manageable, and observable. Combined with robust automation, they allow engineers to make high-impact changes frequently and predictably with minimal toil.
>
> The Cloud Native Computing Foundation seeks to drive the adoption of this paradigm by fostering and sustaining an ecosystem of open-source, vendor-neutral projects. We democratize state-of-the-art patterns to make these innovations accessible for everyone.

CNCF has compiled an interactive cloud native landscape (*https://landscape.cncf.io*) that shows the full extent of today's cloud native solutions. The CNCF landscape acts like a map to cloud native technologies and provides guidelines for building successful cloud native applications. Though the cloud native landscape provides a lot of information on how to build services, it can be challenging, especially for beginners, to work their way through it as it includes a number of services that are used together. In this book, we have chosen the best of the available technology while following the CNCF guidelines to better navigate the cloud native world.

# Adopting a Cloud Native Infrastructure with Azure

Now that you understand the origins of cloud computing, the challenges of operating in the cloud, and how cloud native offerings aimed to change the way services were being developed and delivered, let's discuss how this book can help you moving forward.

If you take a look at the cloud native movement and begin plotting its story from the beginning, the first technology that comes up is Kubernetes, and you'll find plenty of people who have adopted it. On the surface, you might observe that many companies have Kubernetes in the middle of their stack. This gives the impression that Kubernetes is an essential tool that can solve all your problems and magically make your environment self-healable and fault tolerant. This misconception has pushed a lot of people to explore Kubernetes as a silver bullet without fully understanding the deeper meaning. It's important to understand the need for such solutions and gain insight to the full ecosystem while looking at the bigger picture.

In the chapters that follow, we provide guidance on how to build cloud native environments following the guidelines suggested by CNCF. We wrote this book as a primer for engineers and enthusiasts who are just starting out with cloud native transformations and want to explore the overall need for cloud native architectures. You'll learn practical ways to create cloud native infrastructures over Microsoft Azure by navigating the CNCF landscape. You'll also learn the principles of cloud native infrastructure from a beginner's perspective, and you'll deploy mature solutions over Azure.[1] As Azure is one of the key players in the public cloud ecosystem, it provides a mature understanding of the infrastructure stack. We will take you through cloud infrastructure basics and explain how to become cloud native through various technologies while highlighting why these technologies are necessary. We will give an extensive overview of cloud native technologies and Azure services through a practical application, and we will showcase the advantages of being cloud based (with Azure) versus cloud native. Our end goal is to give you a book that showcases all the major cloud native technologies and their importance so that you can understand the logical reasoning behind the advantages of using these technologies.

## Summary

In this introductory chapter, we laid the foundation of what cloud computing is and how cloud native technologies help improve cloud adoption. You learned how the cloud became popular and how cloud computing evolved from physical hardware to a serverless environment. You also learned about the challenges with cloud computing and the growing need to adapt to cloud native technologies. We explained what cloud native means and how the rest of the book will follow the path to cloud native on Azure. We hope you find the journey ahead to be interesting and that this effort will help you adapt cloud native technologies more effectively.

---

1 Azure also gives plenty of architectural guidelines, which showcase best practices for building services on Azure: see *https://docs.microsoft.com/en-us/azure/architecture* and *https://azure.microsoft.com/pt-br/blog/azure-application-architecture-guide*.

# CHAPTER 2

# Infrastructure as Code: Setting Up the Gateway

The cloud, with its rich assortment of solutions offering everything from effortless networking to "planet-scale" computing, is becoming the de facto home for most organizations regardless of their size. The ecosystem of most cloud providers is now larger than ever and includes simple virtual machines, complicated managed clusters, and even highly sophisticated infrastructure. Microsoft Azure, for example, offers a variety of well-built services for end users. These solutions are built on top of infrastructure that is resilient by nature, and they have well-defined service-level agreements (SLAs)[1] to meet the needs of all customers, from small start ups to large enterprises.

While the dynamic nature of cloud computing is a boon for organizations, it can be challenging to maintain services in cloud environments as your organization grows. As you leverage more and more cloud-based services to support your growing business needs, you quickly realize you can no longer maintain your applications and underlying infrastructure by simply clicking into the web console each time you want to perform a new action. The evolutionary design of the cloud was built upon previous generations of hardware and virtualized infrastructure with a programmable control plane that provides flexibility in the form of API layers. These APIs are leveraged by infrastructure-as-code (IaC) tooling to enable cloud practitioners to easily maintain their environments.

When you want to build a production-grade infrastructure from the ground up, you have to start treating your infrastructure definitions the same way you treat your

---

1 An SLA is an agreement between the cloud provider and the client (you) about measurable metrics such as uptime, responsiveness, and responsibilities.

code. Provisioning and scaling your infrastructure manually is not only cumbersome and time consuming; it is also an error-prone process—you cannot build the same infrastructure twice with the same level of confidence. When you treat your infrastructure as code, you also inherit software engineering principles such as version control, testability, automation, and speed of development as part of the DevOps strategy. IaC ensures that your infrastructure can be built in a consistent and repeatable manner. As more software development teams have adopted Agile methodologies, they are now required to move features and solutions more frequently and more quickly into the cloud. As such, infrastructure has become closely attached to applications, and teams are required to manage applications and infrastructure through a seamless process. Also, teams need to iterate and repeatedly deploy new features and underlying infrastructure more frequently. A quick way to implement IaC is to use the prewritten templates that are offered by cloud providers, which give instructions on how to create an infrastructure. Azure natively supports Azure Resource Manager (ARM) templates, which are used to define and create infrastructure resources that shed light directly on the IaC philosophy. This combination of the cloud and IaC allows organizations to introduce changes more quickly and more efficiently.

This chapter serves as a foundation for developing a rich understanding of IaC and Azure. First, we will introduce the IaC concept and its importance in building cloud native infrastructure. Then we will introduce Microsoft Azure, which is the cloud provider we will use throughout the book.

Next, we'll dive into Terraform as a tool for implementing IaC. We will also cover Packer, which is primarily a tool for building machine images, and Ansible, to introduce you to configuration management while building cloud native applications. Finally, we'll touch on Azure DevOps before we close the chapter. Let's get started.

# Infrastructure as Code and Its Importance in the Cloud Native World

In the old days, when an IT team wanted to procure new hardware for application deployment, they first had to initiate a hardware procurement request, which would take days or even weeks to complete. Even after the hardware was finally delivered on premises, it would take a few more days to get it in a working state before applications could be deployed on it. Today, with the growth of DevOps and the cloud, these slow processes have vanished. Release cycles have become shorter, and the speed with which business requirements can be delivered has increased.

However, even with the introduction of the cloud, managing infrastructure is still a problem. Although physical servers were replaced by virtual servers and the management of complex infrastructure became the responsibility of the cloud vendor, growing and scaling infrastructure was still a hard and error-prone task. Engineering teams needed to consistently build new infrastructures and software stacks while continuing to maintain the old infrastructure. To alleviate the tedium and fatigue associated with these tasks, the building and management of cloud-based systems became automated, resulting in a robust infrastructure and application environment.

Eventually, as code was adapted to provision the compute, networking, and storage layers of the stack, the benefits of treating infrastructure as code became evident. This led to the movement of adapting IaC in cloud environments.

*Infrastructure as code* is the philosophy of treating your infrastructure as programmable instructions. Just as you check in source control files, you check in your infrastructure definitions. Treating your infrastructure as code provides numerous advantages, including the following:

- The ability to check in a version of your infrastructure definitions and roll back to a particular version in case of an issue
- Idempotence, which enables you to reproduce the exact same infrastructure with minimal effort
- Standardized logging, monitoring, and troubleshooting across your stack
- Reducing single points of failure in your engineering teams (i.e., where only one engineer knows how to build a particular type of system)
- Increased developer productivity (the site reliability engineers [SREs] and/or DevOps engineers can focus on writing code that developers can use to build a test environment)
- Minimal manual interaction, which leads to less error-prone infrastructure
- Drastically reduced mean time to recover (MTTR) from failures
- The ability to test your infrastructure even before it's created

With the benefits of IaC, it becomes evident that such tooling plays an important role in modern cloud native environments where applications must be changed on the fly. Changes can be minor, such as adding a new configuration tag, or major, such as adding new clusters to keep up with capacity requirements. A reliable IaC strategy helps developers manage these changes with ease without compromising the speed of the software development process. Once IaC is embedded into the core of your infrastructure build process, it also helps build antifragile infrastructure.

### Antifragile Infrastructure

Antifragile infrastructure are systems that can endure stress and showcase elasticity along with resiliency. Antifragile aims to build infrastructure that can handle unpredictable and irregular events while growing stronger.

Today's cloud native applications are considered to be applications in motion since the underlying infrastructure also keeps changing and upgrading. The cloud enables you to treat your infrastructures as short-lived entities rather than permanent entities. The cloud native approach promotes building infrastructure that is replaceable as opposed to fixing infrastructure that is broken. Since the cloud native approach decouples applications from your infrastructure, it gives engineers the control and confidence to make changes to the infrastructure, knowing that they can roll back and move forward with ease.

**Cloud Native Infrastructure Philosophy**

While building cloud native infrastructure, always treat your underlying infrastructure as short-lived entities rather than long-living, maintainable systems. This means that if a server goes down, it will be easy to kill it and bring up a new server instantly, rather than trying to fix it.

The shift from monolithic architecture to microservices also helped IaC gain momentum by ensuring that modern applications were able to follow the "twelve-factor app" methodology (*https://12factor.net*), which allows infrastructure decisions to be made independent of application development. Another important advantage of IaC in building cloud native infrastructure is that it enables immutable infrastructure; that is, once the infrastructure is deployed, it can't be changed or configured. In a typical mutable application deployment scenario, an application is developed, then it's deployed on underlying infrastructure, and finally it's configured on the underlying infrastructure (Figure 2-1). This process introduces *configuration drift*, which gives rise to infrastructure that starts to transition away from the initial state. Immutable infrastructure, on the other hand, focuses on redeployment of infrastructure and applications each time a new change is pushed, which tightly holds the infrastructure to its exact state. Immutability is achieved by developing and configuring your application in a prebaked (e.g., machine image) state and then deploying it (Figure 2-2).

*Figure 2-1. The mutable flow*

*Figure 2-2. The immutable flow*

The main advantages of building immutable infrastructure are:

- Predictable infrastructure/systems rather than reactive infrastructure/systems
- Deployments that are now atomic in nature
- More control of your infrastructure, which leads to better telemetry

Now that we have discussed IaC and its value when building cloud native infrastructure, let's look at how you can use Microsoft Azure in your cloud native infrastructure.

# Getting Started with Azure and Setting Up the Environment

Microsoft Azure is a cloud provider with tens of regions across the globe. Azure allows you to quickly create and deploy infrastructure via both manual and automated means, as we'll discuss throughout this book. Azure as a PaaS (platform as a service) gives a lot of flexibility to the developer community to innovate, create, and deploy applications. We chose Azure as our cloud environment because of its speed, flexibility, security, disaster recovery, and simple learning curve.

In this section, we'll explain basic concepts around Azure and how to create an Azure account.

## Azure Fundamentals and Preparing Your Azure Environment

Before we get started with Azure, it's important to understand some of its basic constructs (*https://oreil.ly/4XZ1K*). Understanding these concepts will help inform policy decisions in the future:

*Tenant*
An Azure tenant is an Azure Active Directory (AAD) representation of an organization. You are likely already familiar with traditional Active Directory (AD) services. When an organization creates an account with Microsoft, an AAD instance will be created.

All AAD instances are completely separated from each other, as are all identities (user or service accounts). If you have an existing Microsoft tenant (e.g., for Office 365), you can utilize it for your Azure footprint. You can also create your own AAD tenant via the Azure Portal (*https://oreil.ly/4bqpi*). Remember to enable multifactor authentication (*https://oreil.ly/9VoEI*) (MFA)[2] on your tenant.

---

2 MFA adds a layer of protection to the sign-in process. When accessing accounts or apps, users provide additional identity verification, such as scanning a fingerprint or entering a code they receive on their phone.

*Subscriptions*

Azure subscriptions are essentially a billing container for your resources. You can also set specific Azure policies at the subscription level.

*Management groups*

Azure management groups provide a means for organizing and managing subscriptions. You can use management groups to apply policy/governance to all the resources (including subscriptions) inside the management group. All subscriptions within the management group will inherit the management group policy by default.

*Resource groups*

A resource group is a container that holds related resources for an Azure solution. The resource group includes those resources that you want to manage as a group. You decide which resources belong in a resource group based on what makes the most sense for your organization. Moreover, resources can be located in different regions from the resource group.

*Regions*

An Azure region contains two or more availability zones. An availability zone is a physically isolated data center in a geographic region.

Figure 2-3 depicts how these basic constructs are associated with each other.

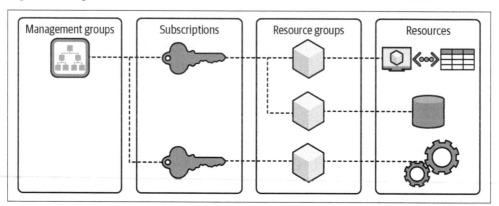

*Figure 2-3. Azure basic constructs*

## Creating an Azure Account

You can create an Azure account by navigating to *https://azure.microsoft.com* and using the free plan. You will need to sign in with a Microsoft account; a Hotmail, Outlook, or Office 365 account will work, though we highly recommend using MFA as well. Follow the instructions on the Azure website to create your account. To continue, click the My Account link at the top-right corner or go straight to the Microsoft Azure portal (*https://portal.azure.com*).

Now let's discuss how to use the Azure CLI.

## Installing the Azure CLI

The Azure CLI is a set of commands that can be used to create and manage Azure resources. You can use the CLI on the web browser in the Azure portal, or you can download an appropriate version (*https://oreil.ly/O4cIJ*) to be installed locally on your machine. For example, on macOS you can install the Azure CLI with the command `brew install azure-cli`.

You can interact with Azure through the portal using the `az` command as follows:

```
$ az account show
{
  "environmentName": "AzureCloud",
  "id": "b5627140-9189-4305-a94c-3b199afe86791",
  "isDefault": true,
  "name": "Visual Studio Enterprise",
  "state": "Enabled",
  "tenantId": "baeb0498-d28a-41cd-a20d-d9409814a06k",
  "user": {
    "name": "cloudnative@xyz.com",
    "type": "user"
  }
}
```

You can even use the Azure CLI to declaratively script your cloud infrastructure. These scripts can be executed in PowerShell or Bash. Though Azure scripts work well for tasks such as the creation, teardown, and fresh redeployment of infrastructure, tasks such as updating an existing environment are not straightforward due to lack of idempotency in Azure CLI commands.

In addition to Azure, other tools are available for creating and managing cloud environments. We'll look at some of the more prominent ones next.

## Prominent IaC Tools

As mentioned previously, additional tools can be used to build cloud native infrastructure by following the IaC approach. Here we will focus on three of the more popular open source tools that can be used with a variety of cloud providers:

- Terraform, a CLI-based IaC tool
- Packer, a CLI tool for building machine images
- Ansible, a configuration management tool

You can use all of these tools in continuous integration/continuous deployment (CI/CD) setups as well; in this scenario, as soon as you write a new configuration it can be continuously integrated into your deployment pipeline.

## Terraform

Terraform is an open source IaC tool from HashiCorp, written in the Go programming language. The word *terraform* means transforming a planet's environment to closely resemble earth's atmosphere such that the human species is able to live on it. This analogy holds true when you look at cloud providers as environments that need to be transformed into a manageable infrastructure to help your application take full advantage of the cloud and reach its true potential.

Terraform helps you build, change, and version infrastructure in the cloud in a safe and efficient manner. It uses a declarative syntax, which means you just have to tell it *what* you want to build rather than *how* you want to build it. A major advantage of Terraform is its support for an easy-to-understand domain-specific language (DSL) called HashiCorp Configuration Language (HCL), which is relatively easy for humans to interpret. Alternatively, you can use JSON for the same purpose. Moreover, Terraform is cloud agnostic, and hence supports multiple cloud providers, which makes it really easy to learn since you don't have to learn the language (HCL/JSON) again for a different cloud provider. In this section, we will discuss how Terraform can be leveraged to build infrastructure over Azure using IaC philosophy.

For you to understand how Terraform works, first we have to review some basic terminology:

*Providers*
> A provider in Terraform is generally (but not always) a cloud provider. The provider's responsibility is to expose the resources (e.g., cloud resources) and interpret the API. Some of the providers supported by Terraform are Azure, Amazon Web Services (AWS), Google Cloud Platform (GCP), and PagerDuty.

*Plan*
> When you are creating your infrastructure using the command `terraform plan`, Terraform creates an execution plan for you that is based on the code you write via the Terraform config (*.tf*) files. The execution plan includes the steps Terraform will take to build the requested infrastructure.

*Apply*
> When you are satisfied with the plan Terraform has created, you can use the `terraform apply` command to create the infrastructure, which will eventually reach the desired state (if there are no conflicts or errors).

*State*

Terraform requires a way to store the state of your infrastructure so that it can manage it. The states are stored in text-based *state files* that hold the mapping of your cloud resources to your configuration. There are generally two ways Terraform can store the state of your infrastructure: locally on the system where you initialize it, or remotely. Storing state remotely is the recommended method because it keeps your infrastructure state backed up, and more engineers can come together to build infrastructure since now there is a single source of truth that makes it possible to know the infrastructure's current state. State files should not be checked in a Git repository as it can contain secrets; you can utilize Azure blob storage instead. Terraform also supports locking by default for state files.

*Module*

A terraform module is a group of many resources that are used together. Modules help to create reusable infrastructure by abstracting the resources that are configured once and used multiple times. One of the main advantages of using modules is that they allow you to reuse code that can be shared later across teams for various projects.

*Backend*

A backend describes how a state will be loaded. It's where your state file will be stored eventually. You can use local file storage or Azure blob storage for this purpose.

Figure 2-4 shows the *provider* and *resource* blocks. The provider block mentions the version of the Azure resource manager while the two resource blocks create the Azure resource group and virtual network.

```
provider "azurerm" {
  version = "2.0.0"
  features {}
}

resource "azurerm_resource_group" "example" {
  name     = "dummy-resource-group"
  location = "West Europe"
}

resource "azurerm_virtual_network" "example" {
  name                = "example-network"
  resource_group_name = azurerm_resource_group.example.name
  location            = azurerm_resource_group.example.location
  address_space       = ["10.0.0.0/16"]
}
```

*Figure 2-4. A simple Terraform file depicting resource creation and the Azure provider*

Now that we've introduced the fundamentals of Terraform, let's see how they all come together to provision cloud native infrastructure in Azure. Figure 2-5 depicts the general workflow.

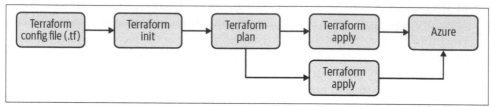

Figure 2-5. Terraform workflow

To start using Terraform, follow these steps:

1. Initialize Terraform with the `terraform init` command. You cannot run `plan` and `apply` if you haven't initialized the directory.

2. After you have successfully initialized Terraform, create the execution plan or a dry run using the `terraform plan` command.

3. When you are satisfied with the output of the plan, create your infrastructure using the `terraform apply` command.

Depending on the provider you use, the infrastructure will be provisioned in the corresponding cloud provider's environment (in our case, it's Microsoft Azure). If you want to destroy your infrastructure, you can simply issue the `terraform destroy` command, which will delete the infrastructure corresponding to the current directory. It's very important to be extremely careful while deleting your infrastructure with Terraform.

 Be extremely careful while deleting your infrastructure with Terraform. Once an infrastructure is deleted, the state file is updated with the updated values. Before deleting your infrastructure, visually check the output of `terraform destroy` so that you don't accidentally delete important information.

Now that you have a general understanding of the workflow and operational details, let's get more hands-on with Terraform.

## Installing Terraform

To install Terraform on your machine,[3] first you must find the appropriate binary package (*https://oreil.ly/EXXrX*) for your operating system. If you are using Azure Cloud Shell, the latest version of Terraform will be present by default. As of this writing, the current version of Terraform is 0.12.28. To find the appropriate binary package:

```
# For Linux-based systems:
$ wget https://releases.hashicorp.com/terraform/0.12.28/terraform_0.12.28_linux_amd64.zip

# For macOS-based systems:
$ wget https://releases.hashicorp.com/terraform/0.12.28/terraform_0.12.28_darwin_amd64.zip
```

Once you grab the ZIP file, unzip the binary and move the single binary to */usr/local/ bin*. You can verify that Terraform is installed by using Terraform's help from the shell:

```
$ ~ terraform --version
Terraform v0.12.28
$ ~ terraform --help
Usage: terraform [-version] [-help] <command> [args]

The available commands for execution are listed below.
The most common, useful commands are shown first, followed by
less common or more advanced commands. If you're just getting
started with Terraform, stick with the common commands. For the
other commands, please read the help and docs before usage.

Common commands:
    apply              Builds or changes infrastructure
    console            Interactive console for Terraform interpolations
    destroy            Destroy Terraform-managed infrastructure
    env                Workspace management
    fmt                Rewrites config files to canonical format
    get                Download and install modules for the configuration
    graph              Create a visual graph of Terraform resources
    import             Import existing infrastructure into Terraform
    init               Initialize a Terraform working directory
    login              Obtain and save credentials for a remote host
    logout             Remove locally-stored credentials for a remote host
    output             Read an output from a state file
    plan               Generate and show an execution plan
    providers          Prints a tree of the providers used in the configuration
    refresh            Update local state file against real resources
    show               Inspect Terraform state or plan
    taint              Manually mark a resource for recreation
    untaint            Manually unmark a resource as tainted
    validate           Validates the Terraform files
    version            Prints the Terraform version
    workspace          Workspace management
```

---

3 Azure Cloud Shell comes with the latest version of Cloud Shell. For information on how to get started with Terraform on Cloud Shell, visit *https://docs.microsoft.com/en-us/azure/developer/terraform/get-started-cloud-shell*.

```
All other commands:
    0.12upgrade        Rewrites pre-0.12 module source code for v0.12
    debug              Debug output management (experimental)
    force-unlock       Manually unlock the terraform state
    push               Obsolete command for Terraform Enterprise legacy (v1)
    state              Advanced state management
$  ~
```

## Setting up Terraform access to a Microsoft Azure account

Now that you have set up your Azure account and set up Terraform locally, you can configure Terraform to access your Azure account:

1. Click the Cloud Shell icon at the top-right corner in your Azure portal account and then click "Create storage." This will create a new storage account for you, which will take a few minutes.

2. After selecting Cloud Shell, you can choose either Bash or PowerShell. You can also change the shell later if you want. Throughout this book, we will be using the Bash shell. Once setup has completed, you will be presented with the following:

   ```
   Requesting a Cloud Shell.Succeeded.
   Connecting terminal...

   Welcome to Azure Cloud Shell

   Type "az" to use Azure CLI
   Type "help" to learn about Cloud Shell

   $
   ```

3. Now you must get a list of subscription ID and tenant ID values. To do this, run the following command in Cloud Shell to list all Azure account names, subscription IDs, and tenant IDs:

   ```
   $ az account list --query "[].{name:name, subscriptionId:id, tenantId:tenantId}"

   [
     {
       "name": "Visual Studio Enterprise",
       "subscriptionId": "b1234567-89017-6135-v94s-3v16ifk86912",
       "tenantId": "ba0198-d28a-41ck-a2od-d8419714a098"
     }
   ]
   $
   ```

4. Note the subscriptionId value from the returned JSON output. Then, while still in Cloud Shell, replace the subscriptionId with the following command:

   ```
   $ az account set --subscription="b1234567-89017-6135-v94s-3v16ifk86912"
   ```

   The preceding command should execute without any return output.

---

5. Create a service principal[4] for use with Terraform using the following command on Cloud Shell:

```
$ az ad sp create-for-rbac --role="Contributor" \
  --scopes="/subscriptions/b1234567-89017-6135-v94s-3v16ifk86912"

Creating a role assignment under the scope of \
  "/subscriptions/b1234567-89017-6135-v94s-3v16ifk86912"
  Retrying role assignment creation: 1/36
{
  "appId": "b0b88757-6ab2-3v41-1234-23ss224vd41e",
  "displayName": "azure-cli-2020-07-03-18-24-17",
  "name": "http://azure-cli-2020-07-03-18-24-17",
  "password": "aH2cK.asfbbashfbjafsADNknvsaklvQQ",
  "tenant": "ba0198-d28a-41ck-a2od-d8419714a098"
}
$
```

This command returns the `appId`, `displayName`, `name`, `password`, and `tenant`.

6. Use the following data to configure Terraform environment variables on the local machine:

```
ARM_SUBSCRIPTION_ID=<subscription>
ARM_CLIENT_ID=<appId>
ARM_CLIENT_SECRET=<password>
ARM_TENANT_ID=<tenant>
```

7. In your *.bash_profile* (or, if you prefer, *envvar.sh*), replace the variables in the preceding code as follows:

```
#!/bin/sh
echo "Setting environment variables for Terraform"
export ARM_SUBSCRIPTION_ID=b1234567-89017-6135-v94s-3v16ifk86912
export ARM_CLIENT_ID=b0b88757-6ab2-3v41-1234-23ss224vd41e
export ARM_CLIENT_SECRET=aH2cK.asfbbashfbjafsADNknvsaklvQQ
export ARM_TENANT_ID=ba0198-d28a-41ck-a2od-d8419714a098

# Not needed for public, required for usgovernment, german, china
export ARM_ENVIRONMENT=public
```

8. Do a `source .bash_profile` on your terminal to read and execute commands from the file to the current shell environment.

Now you can use Cloud Shell to interact with Azure resources or, if you prefer, use the Azure CLI on your local machine to interact with Azure.

---

4 An Azure service principal is an identity created for use with applications, hosted services, and automated tools to access Azure resources. This access is restricted by the roles assigned to the service principal, giving you control over which resources can be accessed and at which level.

At this point, you need to log in to Azure using the command line, which will redirect you to the browser to authenticate yourself. After successful authentication, you will be able to log in:

```
$ ~ az login
You have logged in. Now let us find all the subscriptions to which you have access...
[
  {
    "cloudName": "AzureCloud",
    "id": "b1234567-89017-6135-v94s-3v16ifk86912",
    "isDefault": true,
    "name": "Visual Studio Enterprise",
    "state": "Enabled",
    "tenantId": "ba0198-d28a-41ck-a2od-d8419714a098",
    "user": {
      "name": "nishant7@hotmail.com",
      "type": "user"
    }
  }
]
```

Now that you have successfully logged in and authenticated with Azure, you can check the *~/.azure* directory, which contains the authentication and authorization information:

```
$ ls -al
total 44
drwxr-xr-x 1 nsingh nsingh  270 Apr 13 21:13 .
drwxr-xr-x 1 nsingh nsingh  624 Apr 13 21:13 ..
-rw------- 1 nsingh nsingh 7842 Apr 13 21:13 accessTokens.json
-rw-r--r-- 1 nsingh nsingh    5 Apr 13 21:13 az.json
-rw-r--r-- 1 nsingh nsingh    5 Apr 13 21:13 az.sess
-rw-r--r-- 1 nsingh nsingh  420 Apr 13 21:21 azureProfile.json
-rw-r--r-- 1 nsingh nsingh   66 Apr 13 21:21 clouds.config
-rw-r--r-- 1 nsingh nsingh 5053 Apr 13 21:13 commandIndex.json
drwxr-xr-x 1 nsingh nsingh  318 Apr 13 21:21 commands
-rw------- 1 nsingh nsingh   51 Apr 13 21:13 config
drwxr-xr-x 1 nsingh nsingh   26 Apr 13 21:13 logs
drwxr-xr-x 1 nsingh nsingh   10 Apr 13 21:13 telemetry
-rw-r--r-- 1 nsingh nsingh   16 Apr 13 21:13 telemetry.txt
-rw-r--r-- 1 nsingh nsingh  211 Apr 13 21:13 versionCheck.json
```

## Basic usage and infrastructure setup with Terraform

Now that you have successfully set up Terraform to communicate with Azure, you can build some basic infrastructure. As you work your way through these steps, you will be able to connect the dots and use Terraform effectively.

All the Terraform code related to this chapter is available in the book's GitHub repository (*https://bit.ly/3GRlnx7*), which you can clone onto your local machine.

Go to the *Test* directory, and you will find a file named *test.tf*. Example 2-1 shows the contents of this file. In this example, we are using a local state file to store the current state of the infrastructure.

*Example 2-1. The test.tf file*

```
provider "azurerm" {
}
resource "azurerm_resource_group" "rg" {
  name = "testResourceGroup"
  location = "westus"
}
```

The code will create a resource group named testResourceGroup in westus.

To run this file, follow these steps:

1. Run terraform init to initialize Terraform and download the AzureRM Provider:

```
$ Test git:(master) terraform init

Initializing the backend...

Initializing provider plugins...
- Checking for available provider plugins...
- Downloading plugin for provider "azurerm" (hashicorp/azurerm) 2.17.0...

The following providers do not have any version constraints in configuration,
so the latest version was installed.

To prevent automatic upgrades to new major versions that may contain breaking
changes, it is recommended to add version = "..." constraints to the
corresponding provider blocks in configuration, with the constraint strings
suggested below.

* provider.azurerm: version = "~> 2.17"

Terraform has been successfully initialized!

You may now begin working with Terraform. Try running "terraform plan" to see
any changes that are required for your infrastructure. All Terraform commands
should now work.

If you ever set or change modules or backend configuration for Terraform,
rerun this command to reinitialize your working directory. If you forget, other
commands will detect it and remind you to do so if necessary.
```

2. After successful initialization, run terraform plan:

```
$ Test git:(master) ✗ terraform plan
Refreshing Terraform state in-memory prior to plan...
The refreshed state will be used to calculate this plan, but will not be
persisted to local or remote state storage.

------------------------------------------------------------------------

An execution plan has been generated and is shown below.
Resource actions are indicated with the following symbols:
  + create
Terraform will perform the following actions:
```

```
# azurerm_resource_group.rg will be created
+ resource "azurerm_resource_group" "rg" {
    + id       = (known after apply)
    + location = "westus"
    + name     = "testResourceGroup"
  }

Plan: 1 to add, 0 to change, 0 to destroy.
------------------------------------------------------------------------
Note: You didn't specify an "-out" parameter to save this plan, so Terraform
can't guarantee that exactly these actions will be performed if
"terraform apply" is subsequently run.
```

3. As you can see in the preceding output, we are trying to create a resource group with the name testResourceGroup. Now you can finally create the resource by issuing terraform apply. Remember that you need to explicitly type yes in order to continue:

```
$  Test git:(master) ✗ terraform apply

An execution plan has been generated and is shown below.
Resource actions are indicated with the following symbols:
  + create

Terraform will perform the following actions:

  # azurerm_resource_group.rg will be created
  + resource "azurerm_resource_group" "rg" {
      + id       = (known after apply)
      + location = "westus"
      + name     = "testResourceGroup"
    }

Plan: 1 to add, 0 to change, 0 to destroy.

Do you want to perform these actions?
  Terraform will perform the actions described above.
  Only 'yes' will be accepted to approve.

  Enter a value: yes

azurerm_resource_group.rg: Creating...
azurerm_resource_group.rg: Creation complete after 3s
[id=/subscriptions/b5627140-9087-4305-a94c-3b16afe86791/resourceGroups/ \
  testResourceGroup]

Apply complete! Resources: 1 added, 0 changed, 0 destroyed.
$  Test git:(master) ✗
```

This should create a resource group, as shown in Figure 2-6. You can verify it by checking the Azure portal.

*Figure 2-6. Creating a simple resource group with Terraform*

You should also view it from the CLI. Note that the shell operation is *not* region specific. You can see resources across multiple locations. Use the following command to list the resource group:

```
$ az group list --output table
Name                       Location    Status
-------------------------  ----------  ---------
testResourceGroup          westus      Succeeded
```

In your *Test* directory, you might notice a file named *terraform.tfstate* that was created after the resource group was provisioned. This is the state file holding the current state of the infrastructure.

## Exploring the Azure infrastructure with Terraform

Now that we've created a basic infrastructure with Terraform, let's dig deeper and create additional infrastructure.

In Example 2-1, we showed you how to store your state locally. Though this is not a recommended process, it is sufficient for basic usage, as in the case of the resource group creation example (*test.tf*). It is better to use remote storage, like Azure blob storage, which provides both durability and safety for your infrastructure configurations.

 Terraform states are the source of truth and should always be stored in a backend such as Consul or Amazon DynamoDB Azure storage because this will safely store your infrastructure state along with version control for easier management or rollback in case of a disaster. States should not be checked in the Git version control system, because Git contains secrets.

In the following subsections, we will create blob storage in our Azure account to store all our infrastructure states. We will also follow the "Don't repeat yourself" (DRY) principle by ensuring that we make use of Terraform's module. We will be going over the creation of virtual networks and virtual machines. You can find the modules in this chapter's GitHub repo (*https://bit.ly/2ZSvSze*).

**Creating Azure blob storage.**    To create Azure blob storage, you need to use the following module: *https://bit.ly/3bM6jCx*.

Now, follow the steps outlined in "Basic usage and infrastructure setup with Terraform" on page 20 to deploy the storage account. Once you issue the command `terraform plan`, you will see a lot of information regarding the plan intertwined with modules. You will also notice that the modules (e.g., `Storage_accounts`) are abstracted, while the resource file looks like this:

```
module "CloudNativeAzure-strg-backend" {
  source = "../Modules/Services/Storage_accounts"
  resource-grp-name = "CloudNativeAzure-group"
  storage-account-name = "cnabookprod"
  azure-dc = "westus"
  storage-account-tier = "Standard"
  storage-replication-type = "LRS"
  storage-container-name = "cloud-native-devs"
  storage-container-access = "private"
  blob-name = "cloud-native-with-azure"
}
```

This demonstrates the power of abstracting the repeatable infrastructure behind the modules. Once you use `terraform apply`, the program will run, and after a few minutes you will see a storage account named `cnabookprod` and a blob named `cloud-native-with-azure`:

```
.
.
module.CloudNativeAzure-strg-backend.azurerm_storage_container.generic-container: Creation
complete after 3s [id=https://cnabookprod.blob.core.windows.net/cloud-native-devs]
module.CloudNativeAzure-strg-backend.azurerm_storage_blob.generic-blob: Creating...
module.CloudNativeAzure-strg-backend.azurerm_storage_blob.generic-blob: Creation complete
after 4s [id=https://cnabookprod.blob.core.windows.net/cloud-native-devs/cloud-native-with-
azure]
Apply complete! Resources: 4 added, 0 changed, 0 destroyed.
Outputs:
Blob-ID = https://cnabookprod.blob.core.windows.net/cloud-native-devs/cloud-native-
with-azure
Blob-URL = https://cnabookprod.blob.core.windows.net/cloud-native-devs/cloud-
native-with-azure
Primary-Access-Key =
Bfc9g/piV3XkJbGosJkjsjn13iLHevR3y1cuPyM8giGT4J0vXeAKAKvjsduTI1GZ45ALACLAWPAXA==
```

Figure 2-7 shows the Azure storage account and blob.

*Figure 2-7. Azure storage account and blob*

Note the output from the `terraform apply` operation in the previous step and copy the primary access key's value. You will need to update the value of the primary key in the same *.bash_profile* in your local machine as follows:

```sh
#!/bin/sh
echo "Setting environment variables for Terraform"
export ARM_SUBSCRIPTION_ID=b1234567-89017-6135-v94s-3v16ifk86912
export ARM_CLIENT_ID=b0b88757-6ab2-3v41-1234-23ss224vd41e
export ARM_CLIENT_SECRET=aH2cK.asfbbashfbjafsADNknvsaklvQQ
export ARM_TENANT_ID=ba0198-d28a-41ck-a2od-d8419714a098

# Not needed for public, required for usgovernment, german, china
export ARM_ENVIRONMENT=public
export
ARM_ACCESS_KEY=Bfc9g/piV3XkJbGosJkjsjn13iLHevR3y1cuPyM8giGT4J0vXeAKAKvjsduTI1GZ45AL
ACLAWPAXA==
```

Now we can safely create further infrastructure and store the state of the infrastructure in blob storage.

**Creating an Azure virtual network and instances..**   Now we will create a virtual network on Azure following the Terraform configuration in *https://bit.ly/3bHE342*.

We will also explain the syntactic flow of the virtual network module, which will give you a better understanding of the simplicity of the code.

Take a closer look at the `Virtual_network` module in the directory */Modules/Services/Virtual_network* and you'll see the step-by-step process of virtual network creation:

1. Create a network security group using `azurerm_network_security_group`.
2. Add the security rule and attach it to the security group in step 1.
3. Create a DDoS protection plan.
4. Create a virtual network.
5. Create four different subnets inside the virtual network.
6. Create a network interface and attach it to a subnet (private).
7. Create public IPs.
8. Create a public subnet by attaching a public IP to it.

The final `apply` result by Terraform looks like this:

```
Apply complete! Resources: 12 added, 0 changed, 0 destroyed.
Releasing state lock. This may take a few moments...
Outputs:

private-nic-id = /subscriptions/b5627140-9087-4305-a94c-3b16afe86791/resourceGroups/
CloudNativeAzure-group/providers/Microsoft.Network/networkInterfaces/private-nic
private-subnet-a-id = /subscriptions/b5627140-9087-4305-a94c-3b16afe86791/resourceGroups/
CloudNativeAzure-group/providers/Microsoft.Network/virtualNetworks/cna-prod/subnets/
linkedin-private-a
private-subnet-b-id = /subscriptions/b5627140-9087-4305-a94c-3b16afe86791/resourceGroups/
CloudNativeAzure-group/providers/Microsoft.Network/virtualNetworks/cna-prod/subnets/
linkedin-private-b
pub-nic-id = /subscriptions/b5627140-9087-4305-a94c-3b16afe86791/resourceGroups/
CloudNativeAzure-group/providers/Microsoft.Network/networkInterfaces/public-nic
public-subnet-a-id = /subscriptions/b5627140-9087-4305-a94c-3b16afe86791/resourceGroups/
CloudNativeAzure-group/providers/Microsoft.Network/virtualNetworks/cna-prod/subnets/
linkedin-public-a
public-subnet-b-id = /subscriptions/b5627140-9087-4305-a94c-
3b16afe86791/resourceGroups/CloudNativeAzure-group/providers/Microsoft.Network/
virtualNetworks/cna-prod/subnets/linkedin-private-b
vpc-id = /subscriptions/b5627140-9087-4305-a94c-3b16afe86791/resourceGroups/
CloudNativeAzure-group/providers/Microsoft.Network/virtualNetworks/cna-prod
```

In Figure 2-8, you can see the virtual network being created in the Azure portal.

Figure 2-8. Virtual network creation

As shown in Figure 2-9, Terraform has stored the state of the virtual network on the blob storage account we created earlier.

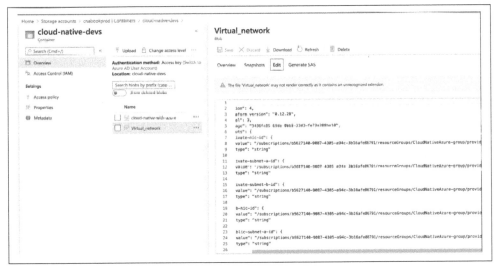

Figure 2-9. Virtual network state uploaded by Terraform on storage account

Similarly, you can follow the preceding steps and launch a virtual machine inside one of the subnets by using the Terraform module at *https://bit.ly/3bQjTEV*.

 After you are done creating the resources in this example, make sure you destroy them using the command `terraform destroy` inside each resource directory in case you have billing enabled for your Azure account.

## Terraform and ARM templates

Before we move on to the next section, let's take a look at what Azure natively offers to implement infrastructure as code. As noted earlier, Azure uses ARM templates to implement infrastructure as code for Azure-based workloads. The ARM templates come in a JSON[5] file that defines the infrastructure and configuration for your project. The file uses a declarative syntax similar to Terraform, which lets you state your intended infrastructure configuration. In addition to declarative syntax, ARM templates also inherit idempotency; that is, you can deploy the same template multiple times and get the same resource types in the same state. The resource manager is responsible for converting the ARM template into a REST API operation. For example, if you deploy the following ARM template:

```
"resources": [
  {
    "type": "Microsoft.Storage/storageAccounts",
    "apiVersion": "2019-04-01",
    "name": "teststorageaccount",
    "location": "eastus",
    "sku": {
      "name": "Standard_LRS"
    },
    "kind": "StorageV2",
    "properties": {}
  }
]
```

the resource manager will convert the JSON into a REST API operation, which will be sent to the Microsoft.Storage resource provider as follows:

```
PUT
https://management.azure.com/subscriptions/{subscriptionId}/resourceGroups/ \
  {resourceGroupName}/providers/Microsoft.Storage/storageAccounts/ \
  teststorageaccount?api-version=2019-04-01
REQUEST BODY
{
  "location": "eastus",
  "sku": {
    "name": "Standard_LRS"
  },
  "kind": "StorageV2",
  "properties": {}
}
```

You can also use Terraform to deploy ARM templates using the resource azurerm_resource_group_template_deployment for the AzureRM Provider.

---

5 Azure offers JSON (JavaScript Object Notation) by default for writing ARM templates. Azure also offers a domain-specific language called Bicep that also uses declarative syntax to deploy Azure resources. You can use Bicep instead of JSON since it reduces complexity and improves the overall development/management experience.

# Packer

At the beginning of this chapter, we introduced the term *immutable infrastructure*, which represents the shift in provisioning and deployment of cloud native applications. One of the most widely used tools for building a prebaked[6] machine image is Packer. Machine images are primarily compute resources that have all the configurations, metadata, artifacts, and related files preinstalled/configured. Packer (*https://packer.io*) is an open source tool from HashiCorp that is used to create machine images from a defined configuration. It automates the whole process of machine image creation, which increases the speed of infrastructure deployment. Just like Terraform is used to build infrastructure, Packer assists in building machine images by baking all the essential software, binaries, and so forth, into the machine image.

Moreover, since all the software on the machine image is installed and configured before the image is built, Packer helps improve the overall stability of the infrastructure. It also supports different cloud providers, which eventually create identical machine images across multiple platforms. Let's dive a bit deeper into how Packer can be used to build images in Azure.

## Installing Packer

To get started with Packer, download the appropriate Packer binary (*https://oreil.ly/Sprhk*) for your local machine[7]. Unzip the binary and move it to */usr/local/bin*. This should set up Packer on your machine; you can verify this by running `packer --help` on your shell:

```
$ ~ packer --help
Usage: packer [--version] [--help] <command> [<args>]

Available commands are:
    build       build image(s) from template
    console     creates a console for testing variable interpolation
    fix         fixes templates from old versions of packer
    inspect     see components of a template
    validate    check that a template is valid
    version     Prints the Packer version
```

## Building a Linux image on Azure

Packer uses a configuration file that defines the machine image. The configuration file is called a Packer *template* and is written in JSON. The template includes *builders* and *provisioners*. Builders create a machine image for a platform by reading the configuration and authentication keys. Provisioners are responsible for installing and

---

6 *Prebaked* is a term used to refer to preinstalling software onto a machine image, which can be used later to spin more instances or containers.

7 Packer is available on Azure Cloud Shell by default.

configuring software on top of the machine image prior to the image becoming immutable. Figure 2-10 depicts the Packer image creation process.

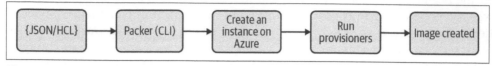

*Figure 2-10. Image creation process using Packer*

You can find the code related to Packer machine image creation at *https://bit.ly/3GRgswf*. To run this code, first you must update the code with the authentication details in the *example.json* file. You can use the authentication details for your Azure account from the *bash_profile* file. The output of the run should look like this:

```
$  1.2.2.2 git:(master) X packer build example.json
azure-arm: output will be in this color.

==> azure-arm: Running builder ...
==> azure-arm: Getting tokens using client secret
==> azure-arm: Getting tokens using client secret
    azure-arm: Creating Azure Resource Manager (ARM) client ...
==> azure-arm: WARNING: Zone resiliency may not be supported in East US, checkout the
docs at https://docs.microsoft.com/en-us/azure/availability-zones/
==> azure-arm: Creating resource group ...
==> azure-arm:   -> ResourceGroupName : 'pkr-Resource-Group-k9831ev1uk'
==> azure-arm:   -> Location          : 'East US'
==> azure-arm:
.
.
.
.
.
==> azure-arm:
Build 'azure-arm' finished.

==> Builds finished. The artifacts of successful builds are:
--> azure-arm: Azure.ResourceManagement.VMImage:

OSType: Linux
ManagedImageResourceGroupName: CloudNativeAzure-group
ManagedImageName: myfirstPackerImage
ManagedImageId: /subscriptions/b1234567-89017-6135-v94s-3v16ifk86912/resourceGroups/
   CloudNativeAzure-group/providers/Microsoft.Compute/images/myfirstPackerImage
ManagedImageLocation: East US
```

Figure 2-11 shows the image we created in the Azure portal. You can verify that the image will have the Nginx web server and the HAProxy load balancer and proxy server baked into it by spinning virtual machines using the image.

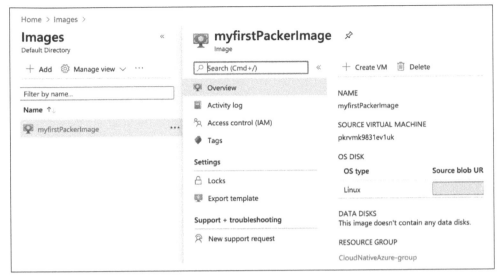

*Figure 2-11. Machine image creation with Packer*

Now that you understand Packer's role as an image building tool, let's look at Ansible, which is a huge add-on in the management of complex cloud native environments.

## Ansible

Ansible is a simple configuration management tool that allows you to provision, configure, and manage servers. Ansible makes it really easy to manage servers that have no preinstalled agent running on them, though you can configure Ansible as an agent-based system as well. Also, you can leverage Ansible as a tool once you have created the infrastructure using Terraform and prebaked machine images using Packer.

The basic concepts of Ansible are as follows:

*Playbooks*

Ansible playbooks are a list of tasks or *plays* that need to be executed on an instance. A simple example would be:

- Add the Nginx repository.

- Install Nginx.

- Create the root directory.

This ordered list can be converted into an Ansible playbook as follows:

```
---
- hosts: local
  vars:
    - docroot: /var/www/serversforhackers.com/public
```

```
tasks:
  - name: Add Nginx Repository
    apt_repository: repo='ppa:nginx/stable' state=present

  - name: Install Nginx
    apt: pkg=nginx state=installed update_cache=true

  - name: Create Web Root
    file: dest=/etc/nginx
          mode=775
          state=directory
          owner=www-data
          group=www-data
    notify:
      - Reload Nginx
```

*Control node*

This is usually the node from which you will be executing the Ansible playbook. This could be any node where Ansible is installed. To run an Ansible playbook, you can execute the following command in your terminal:

```
ansible-playbook -vi path_to_host_inventory_file playbook.yaml
```

*Managed nodes*

The nodes or the hosts that you want to manage are referred to as managed nodes. These nodes are usually the remote servers. The best part about Ansible is that you don't need to install an agent on the remote instances to manage them. All you need is a Secure Shell (SSH) daemon that is listening and Python installed on the hosts. Ansible creates an SSH connection to execute the playbooks.

*Inventory file*

The inventory file holds the list of all the hosts Ansible is managing. The inventory usually holds IP addresses, hostnames, the SSH username, and keys to connect to the remote machine. The following is an example of the inventory:

```
mail.example.com

[webservers]
foo.example.com
bar.example.com

[dbservers]
one.example.com
two.example.com
three.example.com

[midtierrservers]
10.0.1.2
10.2.3.4
```

Since Ansible does not require a lot of overhead and is written in YAML, it serves as a great post-configuration tool. We will be using Ansible in this book at times to provision parts of the services.

Before we wrap up this chapter, let's take a quick look at Azure DevOps, which helps us combine all of these tools in an automated fashion to create a CI/CD pipeline.

# Azure DevOps and Infrastructure as Code

Azure offers *Azure DevOps,* which provides an end-to-end DevOps toolchain for developing and deploying applications and is primarily a hosted service for deploying CI/CD pipelines. You can use Terraform, Ansible, and Packer together as well, and build multistaged pipelines for your projects. Azure DevOps has a bunch of services, including *Azure Pipeline,* which is primarily used for building, testing, and deploying the CI/CD pipelines. We will not take a deep dive into Azure DevOps since it's beyond the scope of this book, but you can read more about setting up Azure DevOps in the official documentation (*https://oreil.ly/9sRem*).

# Summary

In this chapter, we introduced the steppingstones for building a modern cloud native environment using Azure. You created an Azure account, which will come in handy in upcoming chapters as you gain a deeper understanding of cloud native technologies. You were also introduced to Terraform, Packer, and Ansible: three helpful cloud native orchestrators that will assist you in deploying and managing your cloud infrastructure. Terraform is a cloud-agnostic tool for developing infrastructure as code from the ground up, Packer is used to create machine images for development of immutable artifacts, and Ansible is a configuration management tool.

With this basic understanding of Azure and related technologies under your belt, we can move on to the next chapter, where we will talk about containers, the container registry, and containerizing your application.

# CHAPTER 3

# Containerizing Your Application: More Than Boxes

Over the past several years, containers have grown in popularity. Not only do they offer low overhead, high security, and high portability, they also follow best-practice cloud principles such as immutability, ephemerality, and autoscaling.

In this chapter, we'll explain what containers are and discuss the popular containerization platforms. In addition, we'll look past the general industry hype and explain why you might want to use containers. We'll also highlight some of their benefits, especially when it comes to the cloud.

## Why Containers?

Containers run on top of the host operating system and usually are orchestrated using software like Docker (as we'll discuss later in this chapter) or Kubernetes (see Figure 3-1).

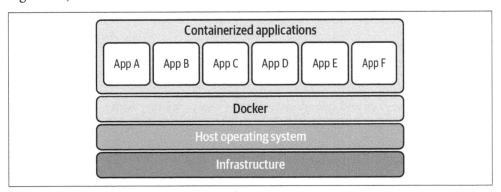

*Figure 3-1. The container operating paradigm*

One of the most important benefits of containers is that they provide virtual-machine-like isolation, but without the overhead of running an instance of the host operating system for each container. At scale, this can save a significant amount of system resources.

## Isolation

Containers provide isolation via a number of methods in a flexible manner that is configured by the administrator. Containers can be isolated in the following ways:

*System resources*
Isolation is achieved via the CPU, memory, and disk cgroups.

*Namespaces*
Isolation is achieved by allowing separate namespaces for each container.

*POSIX limits*
Isolation with this method allows you to set rlimits on your container.

These mechanisms allow you to safely run numerous workloads together without worrying about resource contention or one system disturbing another. If you have a container orchestrator that is workload aware, you can efficiently utilize all of the resources on a host machine without performance degradation (known as *bin packing*). Done well at scale, this can create significant cost savings as you increase your infrastructure efficiency.

## Security

Building off the container isolation features, the OCI container runtime specification (*https://oreil.ly/dZ6GT*) (discussed later in this chapter) provides a number of run-time security-related features that ensure that if an application inside a container is compromised, the risk of lateral movement throughout your network is significantly reduced.

Some of these features include:

*Linux capabilities*
These reduce the container's access to kernel APIs.

*User/group attributes*
These set the user and group attributes of the container, which can then limit access to filesystem resources.

*Devices*
These control which devices a container has access to.

*SELinux labels*
> Like other components of a Linux system (files, processes, pipes), SELinux labels can be applied to containers.

*Sysctl*
> This adds (limited) additional controls to the container.

These layers of runtime security features provide a deterministic, managed way to deploy applications with significantly diminished risk to the host infrastructure and neighboring applications. Within the container ecosystem there is also a suite of artifact security paradigms, which we will cover later in this chapter.

Note that if you want to apply system policy via an orchestration mechanism (Puppet/Chef, etc.), it is much more work to implement it on a per-application basis than it would be to just use the features the container provides.

## Packaging and Deployment

As we'll discuss later in this book, the standardization of container images and the portability of those images is extremely useful. It is relatively straightforward to take a container that's running on your desktop and deploy it to production without significant operational overhead or having to perform extra configuration and administration steps. Docker's mantra is "Build, ship, and run," which highlights the desktop-to-production mentality that containerization brings to the software development lifecycle.

Furthermore, given the OCI specification of images, as we'll discuss later in this chapter, you can feel confident that the deployment system will succeed without issue as long as your container registry is available.

# Basic Container Primitives

You may be surprised to know that containers are not a first-class concept within Linux. In fact, there was no formal definition of a container until the creation of the OCI specification in 2017 (*https://oreil.ly/77ITn*) (we'll talk more about specifications later in this chapter). A basic container is generally made up of the following primitives:

- Cgroups
- Namespaces
- Copy on write (CoW)
- Seccomp-BPF

Linux containers are a natural evolution of similar technologies such as FreeBSD jails, Solaris zones, and virtual machines. In many ways, containers bring together the best of these technologies.

Because containers are not a primitive concept, a number of container software platforms are available. We'll explore them later in this chapter. For now, let's go through each of the basic container primitives.

## Cgroups

A control group (cgroup) is a Linux primitive that provides the ability to limit the resources a group of programs within a cgroup can access/allocate. This provides protection against the "noisy neighbor" problem. The following is a list of controls that cgroups provide:

*CPU*
> The CPU subsystem control allows you to allocate a certain amount of CPU time (cpuacct) or a certain number of cores (cpuset) to a cgroup, so you can ensure that one process doesn't overwhelm all the CPU resources on a physical machine.

*Memory*
> The memory subsystem allows you to report and set limits for memory usage in a cgroup. This works for both user memory and swap memory.

*Blkio*
> The blkio (pronounced block-i-o) controller subsystem provides a mechanism to limit the input/output operations per second (IOPS) or bandwidth (bps) from a cgroup to a block device.

*PID*
> The PID (process identifier) controller sets the maximum number of processes that can run in the cgroup.

*Devices*
> Applicable only to cgroups v1, this control allows the administrator to set allow/ deny lists for what devices a cgroup can access on the host machine.

*Network*
> The network classifier (net_cls) cgroup provides an interface to tag network packets with a class identifier (classid).

The network priority (net_prio) cgroup provides an interface to dynamically set the priority of network traffic generated by various applications.

For the most part, network control functionality is better provided by eBPF (*https:// ebpf.io*) in newer Linux kernel versions.

# Namespaces

Namespaces (*https://oreil.ly/zG7JO*) are a feature in Linux that allows you to limit noncompute resources so that one group of processes will see one set of resources and a second group of processes will see a different set of resources. At the time of this writing, Linux contains a set of namespace types as follows:

*Mount (*mnt*)*
> Controls the filesystem mounts that are available to the container. This means processes in different mount namespaces see different views of a directory hierarchy.

*PID (*pid*)*
> Provides the container with an independently numbered set of PIDs. This means the first process within a container with its own PID namespace will have a PID of 1. Any descendants of PID 1 will act like a regular Unix system.

*Network (*net*)*
> An exceptionally useful feature that allows you to virtualize your network infrastructure. Each namespace will have a private set of IP addresses (*https://oreil.ly/eVndv*) and its own routing table (*https://oreil.ly/lddmv*), socket (*https://oreil.ly/tI1Bd*) listing, connection tracking table, firewall (*https://oreil.ly/yA7gF*), and other network-related resources.

*Interprocess communication (*ipc*)*
> Isolates processes from Linux interprocess communication (IPC). Examples include pipes and signals.

*Unix Time Sharing (*uts*)*
> Allows a single system to appear to have different host (*https://oreil.ly/ZGBIF*) and domain names (*https://oreil.ly/5hnkt*) for different processes.

*User ID (*user*)*
> Similar to the PID namespace; allows you to have elevated privileges within the container but not the overall system. The user namespace provides user identification segregation between namespaces. The user namespace contains a mapping table converting user IDs from the container's point of view to the system's point of view. This allows, for example, the root user to have user ID 0 in the container but to be treated as user ID 1,400,000 by the system for ownership checks.

*Control group (*cgroup*)*
> Hides the identity of the control group (*https://oreil.ly/rrv3c*) of which the process is a member (this is separate from the cgroup primitive).

*Time (time)*

> Allows processes to see different system times in a way similar to the UTS namespace.

## Copy on Write

Copy on write (CoW) is a memory management technique that only copies memory when a resource is modified (or written). This technique reduces the amount of memory required.

## Capabilities

Linux capabilities allow the administrator to more tightly control what capabilities the process or cgroup has on the host system. You can find a list of capabilities in the capabilities(7) manpage (*https://oreil.ly/VMEN4*). For example, if you wanted to run a web server on port 80, you would only need to give the cgroup/process the CAP_NET_BIND_SERVICE capability. If the web server is compromised, the attacker's actions would be limited as the process does not have system permissions to perform other administrative commands.

## Seccomp-BPF

Seccomp (SECure COMPuting) is useful for creating absolute restrictions across systems. Seccomp-BPF allows for granular control on a per-application basis. Seccomp-BPF offers per-thread granularity (in strict mode). It was added to the kernel in version 3.5 (2012).

Seccomp-BPF allows Berkeley Packet Filter (BPF) programs (programs that run in kernel space) to filter syscalls (and their arguments) and return a value on what should happen after the Seccomp-BPF program exits.

# Components of Running a Container

As we discussed earlier in this chapter, containers are not a first-class concept in Linux (there is no Linux container primitive), which makes them slightly difficult to define—meaning that in the past, it was difficult to make containers portable. Nevertheless, to run a container there needs to be some kind of defined interface between the container construct and the operating system software (or host software).

In this section, we'll discuss the finer points of container software, including container runtimes (the software that runs the container), container platforms, and container orchestrators.

First, let's quickly look at the layers of abstraction in the container ecosystem (Figure 3-2).

*Figure 3-2. The layers of container abstraction*

In this section, we will walk through these abstraction layers from top to bottom to see how we work from neatly orchestrated containers to the low-level Linux concepts that enable containers to operate.

## Container Orchestrators

At the topmost layer are the container orchestrators that perform the magic of managing the autoscaling, instance replacement, and monitoring of a container ecosystem that makes containers as a concept so attractive. As we'll discuss in Chapter 4 and Chapter 5, Kubernetes is the Cloud Native Computing Foundation's (CNCF) graduated scheduling and orchestration platform.

Container orchestrators generally provide the following functionality:

- Autoscaling of cluster instances depending on instance load
- Provisioning and deployment of instances
- Basic monitoring functionality
- Service discovery

Other CNCF container orchestrators include:

- Azure Kubernetes Service (AKS)
- Azure Service Fabric
- Amazon Elastic Container Service (ECS)
- Docker Swarm
- Apache Mesos
- HashiCorp Nomad

Good container orchestrators make it simple to build and maintain compute clusters. At the time of this writing, there is no standard configuration for container orchestrators.

## Container Software

Container daemons, located just below the orchestrators, provide the software to execute a daemon. Depending on what orchestrator you are using, this may be transparent to you. Essentially, container daemons manage the lifecycle of the container runtime. In many cases, this will be as simple as starting or stopping the container or as complicated as interacting with plug-ins like Cilium (which we'll discuss in Chapter 8).

Common container software platforms include:

- Docker
- Mesos agent (Mesos)
- Kubelet (Kubernetes)
- LXD (LXC)
- Rkt

As we will discuss later in this chapter, Docker allows you to take an image and then create container instances of it, essentially providing the user interface as a nonorchestrated action. Mesos agents or kubelets are slightly different as they are driven by CLIs or REST APIs.

## Container Runtimes

Container runtimes provide an interface in order to run container instances. Industry-wide, there are two standard categories of interfaces:

- Container runtime (runtime-spec)
- Image specification (image-spec)

The container runtime specifies the configuration of the container (e.g., capabilities, mounts, and network configuration). The image specification contains information about the filesystem layout and contents of the image.

While each container daemon or orchestrator has its own configuration specification, the container runtime is one area that does have standardization across the image.

Three of the most prominent container runtimes are:

- Containerd
- CRI-O
- Docker (until Kubernetes v1.2)

### Containerd

Containerd is an OCI-compliant container runtime that is used in Docker. Containerd acts as a layer of abstraction between all the Linux syscalls that make a container operate and the standard OCI configuration that configures a container. Containerd

---

has an events subsystem that allows other systems like etcd to subscribe to system changes and act accordingly. Notably, containerd supports both OCI and Docker image formats. "What is containerd?" (*https://oreil.ly/X6tog*) is an excellent blog post with further information.

### CRI-O

CRI-O is an implementation of the Kubernetes Container Runtime Interface (CRI) (*https://oreil.ly/ew1G5*) that enables OCI-compatible runtimes. It is considered to be a lightweight alternative to using Docker and containerd. CRI-O also supports running Kata Containers (a virtual-machine-like container created by VMware) and is extensible to any other OCI-compliant runtime. This makes it an attractive runtime to use for a number of use cases.

### Docker

Not to be confused with the complete Docker platform, Docker actually contains a runtime engine that ironically is essentially containerd. Kubernetes supported Docker as a container runtime until the v1.20 release of Kubernetes (*https://oreil.ly/1jUM1*).

## Containers

The container instance is the deployment and operation of software as defined by a container specification. The container runs the defined software (usually provided by an image) contained by a number of settings and limits.

## Operating System

The operating system is the lowest of the constructs, which is what our containers run on. In most container runtimes, the kernel is shared among all container instances.

# Open Container Initiative (OCI) Specification

As mentioned earlier, containers were not a well-defined concept in the beginning. The Open Container Initiative (*https://opencontainers.org*) (OCI) was established in 2015 to formalize the aforementioned runtime (*https://oreil.ly/QNMkq*) and image (*https://oreil.ly/ZHY8z*) specifications.

A container's runtime configuration is specified in a *config.json* file that is used by the container runtime to configure the container's operational parameters. The use of an OCI-compliant container allows the same container image/configuration to be run on multiple container orchestrators (e.g., Docker and rkt) without the need to modify anything.

## OCI Image Specification

The OCI image specification (*https://oreil.ly/ZHY8z*) outlines how the layers of the container are defined. Some of the properties of the image include:

- Author
- Architecture and operating system
- User/group to run the container as
- Ports that are exposed outside the container
- Environment variables
- Entry points and commands
- Working directory
- Image labels

The following is an example of a container image:

```
{
    "created": "2021-01-31T22:22:56.015925234Z",
    "author": "Michael Kehoe <michaelk@example.com>",
    "architecture": "x86_64",
    "os": "linux",
    "config": {
        "User": "alice",
        "ExposedPorts": {
            "5000/tcp": {}
        },
        "Env": [
            "PATH=/usr/local/sbin:/usr/local/bin:/usr/sbin:/usr/bin:/sbin:/bin",
        ],
        "Entrypoint": [
            "/usr/bin/python"
        ],
        "Cmd": [
            "app.py"
        ],
        "Volumes": {
            "/var/job-result-data": {},
            "/var/log/my-app-logs": {}
        },
        "WorkingDir": "/app,
        "Labels": {
            "com.example.project.git.url": "https://example.com/project.git",
            "com.example.project.git.commit": "45a939b2999782a3f005621a8d0f29aa387e1d6b"
        }
    },
    "rootfs": {
      "diff_ids": [
        "sha256:c6f988f4874bb0add23a778f753c65efe992244e148a1d2ec2a8b664fb66bbd1",
        "sha256:5f70bf18a086007016e948b04aed3b82103a36bea41755b6cddfaf10ace3c6ef"
      ],
      "type": "layers"
    },
```

```
    "history": [
      {
        "created": "2021-01-31T22:22:54.690851953Z",
        "created_by": "/bin/sh -c #(nop) ADD file:a3bc1e842b69636f9df5256c49c5374fb4eef1e28
          1fe3f282c65fb853ee171c5 in /"
      },
      {
        "created": "2021-01-31T22:22:55.613815829Z",
        "created_by": "/bin/sh -c #(nop) CMD [\"sh\"]",
        "empty_layer": true
      }
    ]
}
```

# OCI Runtime Specification

At a high level, the runtime config specification provides control of the following container attributes:

- Default filesystems
- Namespaces
- User ID and group ID mappings
- Devices
- Control group configuration
- Sysctl
- Seccomp
- Rootfs mount
- Masked and read-only paths
- Mount SELinux labels
- Hook commands
- Other specialized attributes (e.g., personality, unified, and Intel RDT)

The OCI specification also covers (*https://oreil.ly/QNMkq*) how the state of a container is defined and the lifecycle of the container. The state of the container can be queried by a `state` function (in containerd, in and `runc`) and returns the following attributes:

```
{
    "ociVersion": "0.2.0",
    "id": "oci-container1",
    "status": "running",
    "pid": 4422,
    "bundle": "/containers/redis",
    "annotations": {
        "myKey": "myValue"
    }
}
```

The lifecycle of the OCI container (*https://oreil.ly/bJWIg*) brings together all the runtime specifications, including how the runtime specification interacts with the image specification. It defines how the container is started and configured, and then how it interacts with the image start/stop hooks.

# Docker

Docker (*https://docker.com*) provides a platform as a service (PaaS) that enables users to run containerized applications on a desktop in a simplified and standardized manner. Docker runs images that are OCI compliant and is often a means to test a code deployment before deploying in a production environment. Furthermore, Docker's general availability of desktop software provides developers an easy mechanism to test the packaging and deployment of their code, which has made it an attractive system for developers.

## Building Your First Docker Image

Docker images by themselves are non–OCI-compliant images (their structure is different from the OCI specification) that run on Docker and on systems that support the Docker runtime (containerd). The beauty of Docker images is in how quick and simple they are to create. Each container image is defined by a Dockerfile. This file consists of properties and commands for building the image, running the application, exposing it to the network, and performing health checks. It defines what dependencies and files are copied into the container image as well as what commands are executed to start the applications within the container. This approach of building the Docker image with a simple (imperative) shell-script-like format (running command after command) was preferred by developers who were dealing with painful package management or bundling applications in RPM or DEB (or tarballs).

Docker provides a full configuration reference (*https://oreil.ly/0vUIt*) that may assist you in building your own container.

**Building Your Own Container**

A great way to understand how containers work is to build your own basic container. We recommend trying the rubber-docker workshop (*https://oreil.ly/3DfJe*). It walks through the basic components of a container and shows how they are implemented.

While the Dockerfile allows for complex setups, it is exceptionally easy to create an image in just a few lines. In the following example, we'll run a Python Flask web application and expose port 5000:

1. Create a *requirements.txt* file:

   ```
   Flask >2.0.0
   ```

2. Create an *app.py* file:

   ```
   from Flask import flask

   app = Flask(__name__)

   @app.route('/')
   def index():
       return "Hello, World"
   ```

3. Create your Dockerfile, called *Dockerfile*:

   ```
   FROM ubuntu:18.04        ❶
   COPY . /app              ❷
   WORKDIR /app             ❸
   RUN pip3 install -r requirements.txt    ❹
   ENTRYPOINT ["python3"]        ❺
   CMD ["app.py"]           ❻
   EXPOSE 5000              ❼
   ```

❶ We take a base image to use. In this case, we're going to use Ubuntu 18.04 from the Docker Hub registry.

❷ We copy the current directory into a new image directory called *app*.

❸ We set the current working directory to */app*.

❹ We use pip to install the application's defined dependencies.

❺ We set the entrypoint application as python3 (this is a Docker/Python best practice).

❻ We start the application by running *app.py*.

❼ We expose port 5000 services outside the container.

In its entirety, this container image copies over our application and then installs the application's requirements, starts itself, and allows network connections on port 5000 (the default Flask port).

To allow users or other applications to access your container, the Dockerfile contains a directive, EXPOSE (*https://oreil.ly/orq5d*), that allows the container network stack to listen on the specified port at runtime. We'll discuss network connectivity in Chapter 8.

A Dockerfile is technically a mix of both a container runtime and an image specification since it provides semantics about the contents of the image as well as how it is run (i.e., CPU or memory cgroup limitations).

Once you have created your Dockerfile, you can build your container image using the docker build command. This is typically done with the current file path (e.g., docker build), but you may also use a URL (e.g., docker build https:// github.com/abcd/docker-example). You can find a full reference on how to use docker build in the documentation (*https://oreil.ly/uCDIy*).

You should create a tag for your image so that you can reference it quickly and easily in the future when you build the image. You can do this by adding the --tag option when you build:

```
docker build --tag example-flask-container
```

When you run docker build you will see output similar to the following:

```
[internal] load build definition from Dockerfile
=> transferring dockerfile: 203B
[internal] load .dockerignore
=> transferring context: 2B
[internal] load metadata for docker.io/library/ubuntu:18.04
[1/6] FROM docker.io/libraryubuntu:18.04
[internal] load build context
=> transferring context: 953B
CACHED [2/6] WORKDIR /app
[3/6] COPY requirements.txt requirements.txt
[4/6] RUN pip3 install -r requirements.txt
[5/6] COPY . .
[6/6] CMD [ "python3", "app.py"]
exporting to image
=> exporting layers
=> writing image sha256:8cae92a8fbd6d091ce687b71b31252056944b09760438905b726625831564c4c
=> naming to docker.io/library/example-flask-container
```

## Best Practices While Using Docker

The twelve-factor app (*https://12factor.net*) tracks a number of characteristics of Dockerized and cloud-based applications. This means the application should be able to be deployed, started, stopped, and destroyed without causing problems. While we will talk about container storage solutions later in this book, you should try to avoid persisting data as much as is practically possible unless you're reading data from a persistent volume or using a cloud native data service (see Chapter 9 for more on this).

There are a few more best practices that you should follow:

- Utilize the `docker build` options (*https://oreil.ly/RqjNp*). These options allow you to customize your Docker image to add features such as cgroup controls, tags, network configurations, and more.
- Utilize a *.dockerignore* file. Similar to *.gitignore*, a *.dockerignore* will ensure that certain files or folders are not included in the image build.
- To reduce complexity, dependencies, file sizes, and build times, avoid installing extra or unnecessary packages.
- Use multistage builds (*https://oreil.ly/ONlyS*). If you need to install dependencies to compile your application, you can do this during the build process of your image, but *only* copy the output into the container image. This reduces the size of your image build.

You can find more information on Dockerfile best practices on the Docker website (*https://oreil.ly/PeUBE*).

# Other Container Platforms

While the Docker platform and OCI images remain industry leaders, there are still a number of other container offerings available.

## Kata Containers

Kata Containers are OCI-compliant containers that aim to enhance security. Kata Containers have the following lightweight container features:

- Cgroups
- Namespaces
- Capability filters
- Seccomp filtering
- Mandatory access control

Kata Containers also possess some virtual machine concepts, particularly a separate guest kernel per container and better hardware isolation. The `kata-runtime` process controls the instantiation of the OCI-compliant container. The largest difference is that there is a separate guest kernel per container instead of a shared kernel between container instances.

## LXC and LXD

LXC (Linux Containers) (*https://oreil.ly/lj7Gc*) is one of the earliest container mechanisms to be released. LXC mainly uses the kernel's cgroup and namespace capabilities as well as a standard set of library APIs to control the containers.

LXD (*https://oreil.ly/lYXYP*) is the container management software and tools that help orchestrate the LXC APIs. The LXD daemon provides a REST API over a Unix socket/network that allows you to use the provided command-line tools or build your own.

The ecosystem of both LXC and LXD is more oriented toward running infrastructure than application development due to a lack of development and deployment tooling.

# Container Registries

After building your container images, you will need places to store them and serve them. These are known as *container registries*. Container registries have grown in popularity due to their easy deployment mechanisms and their built-in replication mechanisms, which replace the challenging rsync setups required for DEB and RPM package repositories.

When deploying a container, the container deployment system will download the image from the registry to the host machine. Essentially, a container registry acts as a highly available container image file server (with some protections). All of the common containerization platforms allow you to configure a public or private repository as a source for the container images.

While these responsibilities sound reasonably Vanal, there are a lot of overlooked features of container registries that are important parts of secure container deployments. Such features include:

*Image replication*
    Replicating the images to other container registries (globally)

*Authentication*
    Only allowing authorized users to access the registry and its contents

*Role-based access control*
    Restricting who can modify images and data within the registry

*Vulnerability scanning*
    Checking images for known vulnerabilities

*Garbage collection*
    Removing old images regularly

*Auditing*
> Providing trusted information on changes to the container registry for information security purposes

Current cloud native products include (see the CNCF landscape (*https://oreil.ly/nzdGw*) for more):

- Harbor
- Dragonfly
- Alibaba Container Registry
- Amazon Elastic Container Registry (Amazon ECR)
- Azure Registry
- Docker Registry
- Google Container Registry
- IBM Cloud Container Registry
- JFrog Artifactory
- Kraken
- Portus
- Quay

Many of these systems are tied to specific vendors. However, Harbor is one of the most popular open source container registry systems, so we'll explore it further.

## Securely Storing Images with Harbor

Harbor is the premier open source cloud native container registry platform. Created in 2016, Harbor stores container images and provides signing and security scanning functionality. Furthermore, Harbor supports high availability and replication functionality as well as a number of security functions, including user management, role-based access control, and activity auditing. The beauty of Harbor is that it provides top-tier features even though it is open source, which makes it a great platform to utilize.

### Installing Harbor

When you utilize Harbor, it essentially becomes a critical component of your build and deploy pipelines. You should run it on a host that meets these recommended specifications:

- Quad-core CPU
- 8 GB of memory

- Minimum 160 GB disk
- Ubuntu 18.04/CentOS7 or later

 You will want to evaluate the performance of the disk SKU or configuration to match the performance you desire. Harbor is essentially a file server, and the performance of the disk will significantly affect your build and deploy times.

Harbor supports multiple installation methods, including Kubernetes and Helm. As we haven't yet explored Kubernetes, we are going to install Harbor manually.

Harbor has two releases (or types of installations): an online installer and an offline installer. The online installer is smaller in size and relies on an internet connection to download the full image from Docker Hub (directly off the internet). The offline installer is larger in size and does not require an internet connection. If your security posture is restrictive, the offline installer may be a better option.

The Harbor releases are listed on GitHub (*https://oreil.ly/1BRQz*).

---

## Verifying the Installer

It is recommended that you verify the integrity of the downloaded package. You will need to open outbound internet access to port TCP/11371 in order to reach the GPG keyserver. To verify the installer:

1. Download the corresponding *.asc* file for your installer version.
2. Obtain the public key for Harbor releases:

   ```
   gpg --keyserver. hkps://keyserver.ubuntu.com --receive-keys 644FF454C0B4115C
   ```

3. Verify the package by running:

   ```
   gpg -v -keyserver hkps://keyserver.ubuntu.com -verify <asc-file-name>
   ```

You should see `gpg: Good signature from "Harbor-sign (The key for signing Harbor build)` in the output of the preceding command.

---

### Configuring Harbor for installation

Before configuring Harbor, you should enable HTTPS by installing a Secure Sockets Layer (SSL) certificate via your own certificate authority (CA) or through a public CA like Let's Encrypt. More information on how to do this can be found in the Harbor documentation (*https://oreil.ly/39ISm*).

---

All the installation parameters for Harbor are defined in a file called *harbor.yml*. The parameters defined in this file configure Harbor for its first use or when it is being reconfigured via the *install.sh* file. Details on all the configuration options can be found on GitHub (*https://oreil.ly/x9TsD*). To get started, we will use the following required parameters (*https://oreil.ly/86JTs*):

```
hostname: container-registry.example.com

http:
  # port for http, default is 80. If https enabled, this port will redirect to https port
  port: 80

https:
  port: 443
  certificate: /your/certificate/path
  private_key: /your/private/key/path

harbor_admin_password: Harbor12345

# DB configuration
database:
  password: root123
  max_idle_conns: 50
  max_open_conns: 100

# The default data volume
data_volume: /data

clair:
  updaters_interval: 12

jobservice:
  max_job_workers: 10

notification:
  webhook_job_max_retry: 10

chart:
  absolute_url: disabled

log:
  level: info
  local:
    rotate_count: 50
    rotate_size: 200M
    location: /var/log/harbor

proxy:
  http_proxy:
  https_proxy:
  no_proxy: 127.0.0.1,localhost,.local,.internal,log,db,redis,nginx,core,portal, \
    postgresql,jobservice,registry,registryctl,clair
```

## Building a Packer image

Using our knowledge from Chapter 2, we are going to build a Packer image to deploy Harbor. You can use the following *harbor.json* file:

```json
{
  "builders": [{
    "type": "azure-arm",

    "client_id": "<place-your-client_id-here>",
    "client_secret": "<place-your-client_secret-here>",
    "tenant_id": "<place-your-tenant-id-here>",
    "subscription_id": "<place-your-subscription-here>",

    "managed_image_resource_group_name": "CloudNativeAzure-group",
    "managed_image_name": "harborImage",

    "os_type": "Linux",
    "image_publisher": "Canonical",
    "image_offer": "UbuntuServer",
    "image_sku": "16.04-LTS",

    "azure_tags": {
        "env": "Production",
        "task": "Image deployment"
    },

    "location": "East US",
    "vm_size": "Standard_DS1_v2"
  }],
  "provisioners": [{
    "execute_command": "chmod +x {{ .Path }}; {{ .Vars }} sudo -E sh '{{ .Path }}'",
    "inline": [
      "apt-get update",
      "apt-get upgrade -y",
      "/usr/sbin/waagent -force -deprovision+user && export HISTSIZE=0 && sync"
    ],
    "inline_shebang": "/bin/sh -x",
    "type": "shell"
  },
  {
  {
      "type": "shell",
      "inline": [
        "wget https://github.com/goharbor/harbor/releases/download/v2.1.3/ \
          harbor-online-installer-v2.1.3.tgz -O /tmp/harbor-online-installer-v2.1.3.tgz",
        "tar -xvf /tmp/harbor-online-installer-v2.1.3.tgz"
      ]
  },
  {
      "type": "file",
      "source": "{{template_dir}}/harbor.yml",
      "destination": "/tmp/harbor"
    },
    {
      "type": "shell",
      "inline": [
        "sudo chmod 0777 /tmp/harbor/install.sh",
        "sudo  /tmp/harbor/install.sh"
      ]
    }
  ]
}
```

When you run `packer build harbor.json` your image will build with Harbor installed and configured. If you're using HTTPS (and you should), you will need to modify the Packer file to include copying the certificate and private key files.

## Securely Storing Images with Azure Container Registry

Azure provides its own container registry, known as Azure Container Registry. Since the registry is provided by Azure, the initial setup and ongoing maintenance requirements are much less time consuming than when running software like Harbor.

### Installing Azure Container Registry

Deploying a container instance is exceptionally simple:

1. Log in to the Azure portal and click "Create a resource," as shown in Figure 3-3.

*Figure 3-3. Azure portal home page*

2. Search for "container registry" in the search bar, and click the Container Registry offering from Microsoft (see Figure 3-4).

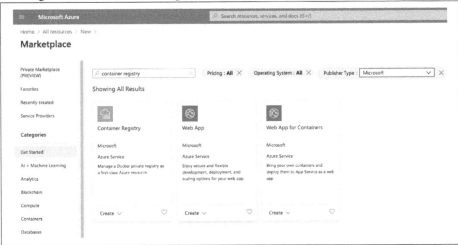

*Figure 3-4. Searching for Azure Container Registry*

You will see a form to fill out with the basic information about the registry you will be creating (Figure 3-5).

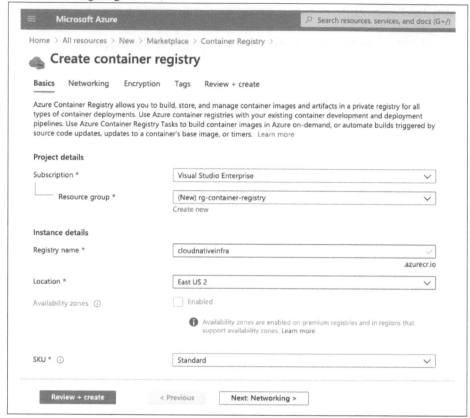

*Figure 3-5. First page for creating a container registry*

3. Provide the following basic details of the container registry:

*Subscription*
Pick the subscription that you want to deploy into.

*Resource group*
You can use an existing resource group or create a new one. In this case, we're going to create a new one called rg-container-registry.

*Registry name*
This will configure the URL used to access the registry. We're going to use *cloudnativeinfra.azurecr.io*. This is globally unique, so you will need to pick your own and ensure you don't get an error message stating that it is already taken.

*Region*

Choose your region. We are going to deploy in the East US 2 region.

*SKU*

Three tiers are available. You can find a comparison on the Container Registry pricing page (*https://oreil.ly/smNPa*). We're going to use the Standard tier.

4. Choose your Networking configuration (Figure 3-6). Since we're using the Standard tier, we cannot make any configuration changes here. Therefore, the container registry that will be created is available over the internet and not just within our Azure network.

*Figure 3-6. Container registry networking configuration*

5. Choose your Encryption configuration (Figure 3-7). The Standard tier provides encryption-at-rest for stored data, while the Premium tier allows users to set their own encryption keys.

*Figure 3-7. Container networking registry encryption*

6. Click "Review + create" to create your container registry. This should take less than two minutes to deploy.

**Private Endpoints**

Private endpoints are an Azure concept that allows cloud resources to be available via the RFC1918 address space instead of a public IP. This means your resource is available only through a locally connected network and not over the internet.

If you would like to deploy your container registry via Terraform, the following code will allow you to do so:

```
resource "azurerm_resource_group" "rg" {
    name = "example-resources" location = "West Europe"
}

resource "azurerm_container_registry" "acr" {
    name = "containerRegistry1"
    resource_group_name = azurerm_resource_group.rg.name
    location = azurerm_resource_group.rg.location
    sku = "Premium"

    identity {
        type = "UserAssigned"
        identity_ids = [ azurerm_user_assigned_identity.example.id ]
    }
```

```
    encryption {
        enabled = true
        key_vault_key_id = data.azurerm_key_vault_key.example.id
        identity_client_id = azurerm_user_assigned_identity.example.client_id
    }
}

resource "azurerm_user_assigned_identity" "example" {
    resource_group_name = azurerm_resource_group.example.name
    location = azurerm_resource_group.example.location name = "registry-uai"
}

data "azurerm_key_vault_key" "example" {
    name = "super-secret"
    key_vault_id = data.azurerm_key_vault.existing.id
}
```

# Storing Docker Images in a Registry

As we discussed previously, you need to be able to store and serve container images reliably. Once you've built your custom image, you need to push it to the registry. Also, and as we discussed previously, there are numerous options for storing images, including the Docker Registry and the container registries of the various cloud providers (e.g., Azure Container Registry). In this case, we are going to utilize the Harbor registry we created earlier in this chapter.

First we will log in to the registry:

```
$ docker login <harbor_address>
```

For example:

```
$ docker login https://myharborinstallation.com
```

Now we'll tag the image:

```
$ docker tag example-flask-container <harbor_address>/demo/example-flask-container
```

And now we'll push it:

```
$ docker push <harbor_address>/demo/example-flask-container
```

Once this completes, Harbor will be able to serve our image to any container software that is downloading it.

# Running Docker on Azure

In Azure, there are two ways you can run your Docker container image: using Azure Container Instances or running your own virtual machine with Docker installed. In this section, we will demonstrate both of these methods.

## Azure Container Instances

Azure Container Instances (ACI) allows you to quickly spin up a container instance in Azure without having to manage underlying infrastructure. This provides a Docker-like service, but in the public cloud. ACI allows the deployment of Azure Container Registry images or Docker images from either private or public repositories.

ACI also allows these instances to be placed in private or public networks depending on the use of the container images.

Some additional features of ACI include:

- No need to configure an OCI runtime specification
- The ability to pass environment variables to the container
- Basic firewall management
- Managed container restart policies

Simply put, ACI is the easiest way to start running containers in Azure! ACI also gives you the ability to test new container images without creating a totally separate environment.

There are some important caveats to note when running an ACI:

- There is a quad-core/16 GB limit to any single container instance.
- The ACI settings for CPU and memory will override any runtime setting you applied to your container image.

# Deploying an Azure Container Instance

Deploying an Azure container instance is exceptionally simple. First, log in to the Azure portal and then click "Create a resource," as shown in Figure 3-8.

*Figure 3-8. Azure portal home page*

Click down to Containers on the lefthand side and you'll see an offering of container-related products (see Figure 3-9). Click the Container Instances link.

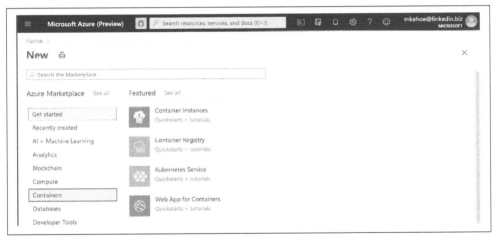

*Figure 3-9. Searching for container products*

You will be presented with a form to fill out the basic information about the container instance you will be creating (Figure 3-10).

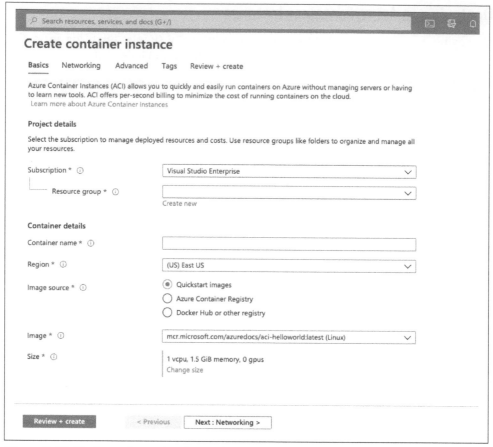

*Figure 3-10. Basic configuration for an Azure container instance*

Fill in the following fields:

*Subscription*
Pick the subscription that you want to deploy into.

*Resource group*
You can use an existing resource group or create a new one. In this case, we're going to create a new one called rg-aci-test.

*Container name*
Name your container instance. We are going to call ours aci-demo.

*Region*
Choose your region. We are going to deploy in the East US region.

*Image source*

This is where you pick your container image. You are presented with three options:

- Use a demo quickstart image that Azure provides.
- Use an image that has been uploaded to the Azure Container Registry.
- Use an image that is uploaded to Docker Hub or another registry. If you have deployed Harbor, you can configure this here. In this case, we're going to pick the Nginx quickstart image (*https://oreil.ly/dOCN9*).

*Size*

Here you pick what kind of virtual machine you want. Keep in mind that the larger the virtual machine is, the more you will need to pay to run it. In this case, we are going to run a configuration of "1 vcpu, 1.5GiB memory, 0 gpus". This means we have one virtual core, 1 GB of memory, and no graphics card.

Once this has been configured, click the Next: Networking button to configure the networking (Figure 3-11).

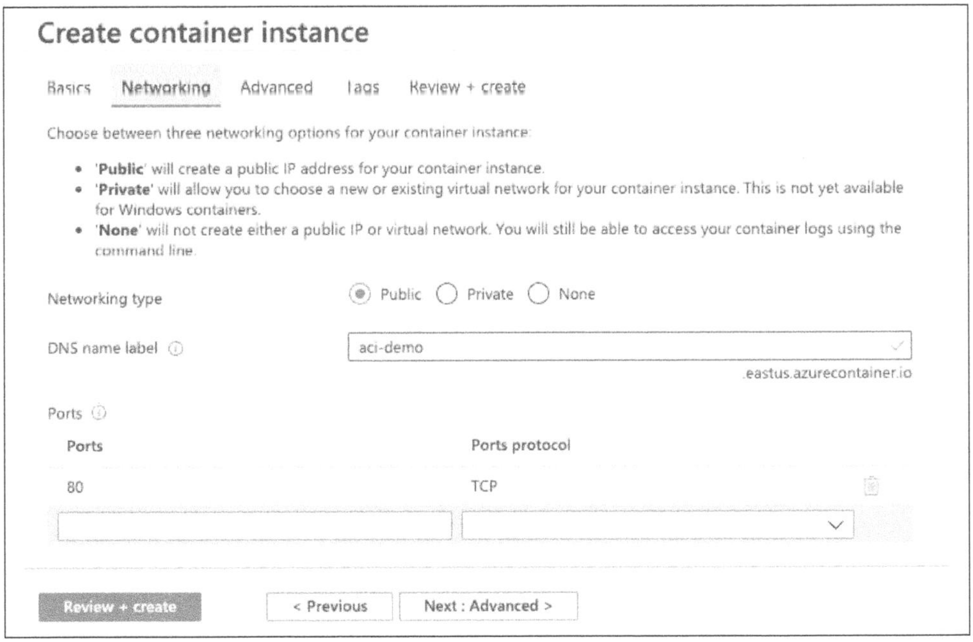

*Figure 3-11. Network configuration for an Azure container instance*

In this demo, we are going to assign a public IP to our container instance (so that we can access it from the internet) and then give the IP address a DNS name of *aci-demo.eastus.azurecontainer.io* (you will want to use a unique name for this). We then have the option to make TCP or UDP ports available from outside the container.

As we are using an Nginx container, port 80 is automatically opened. You can also create a virtual network (or use an existing one) and subnet if you're using private IP addressing.

If you click the Next: Advanced button, you'll see there are some other settings you can apply to deal with failure policies and environment variables. For this instance, we're not going to make any changes (Figure 3-12).

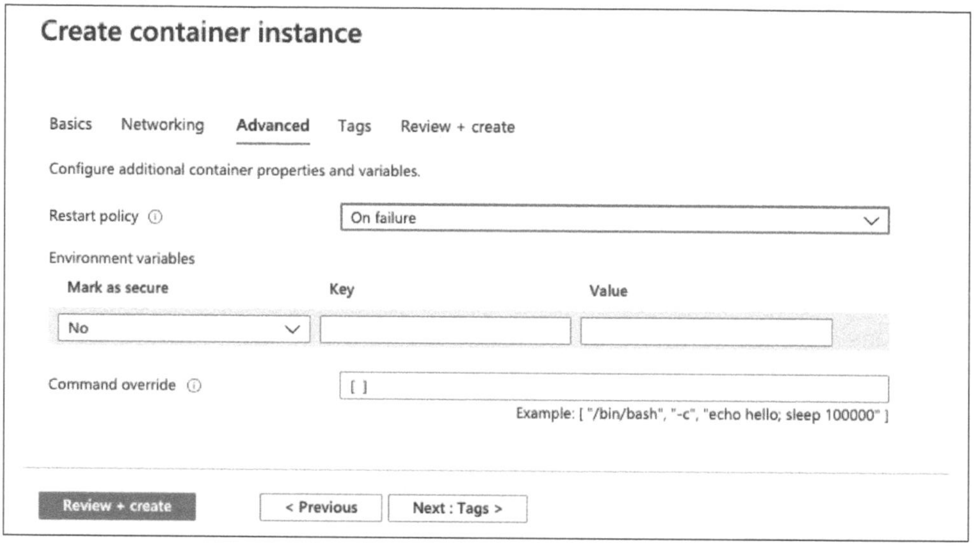

*Figure 3-12. Advanced configuration for an Azure container instance*

Finally, click "Review + create" and the container image will be created. It will take about two minutes for a quickstart image to deploy.

Once your container is deployed, you will be able to go to the DNS name of your container in an internet browser and see the "Welcome to nginx!" banner (see Figure 3-13). Via the Azure portal, you can also get a console connection to the instance.

# Welcome to nginx!

If you see this page, the nginx web server is successfully installed and working. Further configuration is required.

For online documentation and support please refer to nginx.org.
Commercial support is available at nginx.com.

*Thank you for using nginx.*

*Figure 3-13. Nginx default welcome page*

You can find more information on deploying ACI in the Microsoft documentation (*https://oreil.ly/AoP7u*).

## Running a Docker Container Engine

If you want finer control of your container environment, running your own Docker container engine (CE) is also an option. This comes with a trade-off of having to manage the underlying virtual machine that Docker is running on.

1. Install the Docker CE on an Azure virtual machine:

   Centos/Red Hat:

   ```
   $ sudo yum install -y yum-utils

   $ sudo yum-config-manager \
       --add-repo \
       https://download.docker.com/linux/centos/docker-ce.repo
   $ sudo yum install docker-ce docker-ce-cli containerd.io
   ```

   Debian/Ubuntu:

   ```
   $ sudo add-apt-repository \
       "deb [arch=amd64] https://download.docker.com/linux/ubuntu \
       $(lsb_release -cs) \
       stable"

   $ sudo apt-get update
   $ sudo apt-get install docker-ce docker-ce-cli containerd.io
   ```

   Another option may be to install the Docker CE via a Packer image. The following is an example Packer configuration:

   ```
   {
     "builders": [{
       "type": "azure-arm",
       "client_id": "<place-your-client_id-here>",
       "client_secret": "<place-your-client_secret-here>",
       "tenant_id": "<place-your-tenant-id-here>",
       "subscription_id": "<place-your-subscription-here>",
       "managed_image_resource_group_name": "CloudNativeAzure-group",
       "managed_image_name": "DockerCEEngine",

       "os_type": "Linux",
       "image_publisher": "Canonical",
       "image_offer": "UbuntuServer",
       "image_sku": "16.04-LTS",

       "azure_tags": {
           "env": "Production",
           "task": "Image deployment"
       },

       "location": "East US",
       "vm_size": "Standard_DS1_v2"
     }],
     "provisioners": [{
       "execute_command": "chmod +x {{ .Path }}; {{ .Vars }} sudo -E sh '{{ .Path }}'",
   ```

```
    "inline": [
      "apt-get update",
      "apt-get upgrade -y",
      "/usr/sbin/waagent -force -deprovision+user && export HISTSIZE=0 && sync"
    ],
    "inline_shebang": "/bin/sh -x",
    "type": "shell"
  },
  {
      "type": "shell",
      "inline": [
        "sudo apt-get remove docker docker-engine",
        "sudo apt-get install apt-transport-https ca-certificates curl \
          software-properties-common",
        "curl -fsSL https://download.docker.com/linux/ubuntu/gpg | sudo apt-key add \
          -sudo apt-key fingerprint 0EBFCD88",
        "sudo add-apt-repository "deb [arch=amd64] https://download.docker.com/ \
          linux/ubuntu      $(lsb_release -cs) stable",
        "sudo apt-get update",
        "sudo apt-get -y upgrade",
        "sudo apt-get install -y docker-ce",

        "sudo groupadd docker",
        "sudo usermod -aG docker ubuntu",
        "sudo systemctl enable docker"
        ]
  }]
}
```

2. Once your Docker CE is running, start your container by running:

```
$ docker run -d <container-name>
```

3. Using our Flask example from earlier, you could start your container by running:

```
$ docker run -d -p 5000:5000 http://myharborinstallation.com/demo/ \
  example-flask-container
```

4. If you run curl localhost:5000/, you will see "Hello, world" returned.

# Summary

In this chapter, we briefly discussed the layers of abstraction that make up the container ecosystem. As the container ecosystem is now firmly centered on the OCI specification and Kubernetes, it is thriving and we're seeing a proliferation of security and network products that are built on the OCI standard. In Chapter 8, we will explore another container standard, the Container Network Interface (CNI), and look at how to leverage it for your container networking setup.

# CHAPTER 4

# Kubernetes: The Grand Orchestrator

As monolithic applications were broken down into microservices, containers became the de facto housing for these microservices. Microservices are a cloud native architectural approach in which a single application is composed of many smaller, loosely coupled, and independent deployable components or services. Containers ensure that software runs correctly when moved between different environments. Through containers, microservices work in unison with other microservices to form a fully functioning application.

While breaking monolithic applications into smaller services solves one problem, it creates bigger problems in terms of managing and maintaining an application without significant downtime, networking the various microservices, distributed storage, and so on. Containers help by decoupling applications into fast-moving, smaller codebases with a focus on feature development. However, although this decoupling is clean and easy at first since there are fewer containers to manage, as the number of microservices in an application increases it becomes nearly impossible to debug, update, or even deploy the containerized microservices safely into the stack without breaking something or causing downtime.

Containerizing applications was the first big step toward creating self-healable environments with zero downtime, but this practice needed to evolve further, especially in terms of software development and delivery in cloud native environments. This led to the development of schedulers and orchestrator engines like Mesos, Docker Swarm, Nomad, and Kubernetes. In this chapter and the next, we will focus on Kubernetes due to its maturity and wide industry adoption.

Google introduced Kubernetes to the world in 2014, after spending almost a decade perfecting and learning from its internal cluster management system, *Borg*. In simple terms, Kubernetes is an open source container orchestration system. The term *container orchestration* primarily refers to the full lifecycle of managing containers in dynamic environments like the cloud, where machines (servers) come and go on an as-needed basis. A container orchestrator automates and manages a variety of tasks, such as provisioning and deployment, scheduling, resource allocation, scaling, load balancing, and monitoring container health. In 2015, Google donated Kubernetes to the Cloud Native Computing Foundation (CNCF).

Kubernetes (aka K8s) is one of the most widely adopted pieces of a cloud native solution since it takes care of deployment, scalability, and maintenance of containerized applications. Kubernetes helps site reliability engineers (SREs) and DevOps engineers run their cloud workload with resiliency while taking care of scaling and failover of applications that span multiple containers across clusters.

### Why Is Kubernetes Called K8s?

Kubernetes is derived from a Greek word that means *helmsman* or *pilot of a ship*. Kubernetes is also called K8s. This numeronym was derived by replacing the eight letters between K and S ("ubernete") with an 8.

Following are some of the key features that Kubernetes provides right out of the box:

*Self-healing*
One of the most prominent features of Kubernetes is the process of spinning up new containers when a container crashes.

*Service discovery*
In a cloud native environment, the containers move from one host to another. The process of actually figuring out how to connect to a service/application that is running in a container is referred to as *service discovery*. Kubernetes exposes containers automatically using DNS or the containers' IP address.

*Load balancing*
To keep the deployed application in a stable state, Kubernetes load-balances and distributes the incoming traffic automatically.

*Automatic deployments*
Kubernetes works on a declarative syntax, which means you don't have to worry about how to deploy applications. Rather, you tell what needs to be deployed and Kubernetes takes care of it.

*Bin packing*
To make the best use of compute resources, Kubernetes automatically deploys the containers on the best possible host without wasting or impairing overall availability for other containers.

In this chapter, we will dive into the major components and the underlying concepts of Kubernetes. Though this chapter doesn't aim to teach Kubernetes in full, as there are already a wide array of books[1] that cover the topic at length, we want to build a strong foundation. This hands-on approach will help you better understand the nitty-gritty of the overall environment. Let's start with a discussion of how the Kubernetes cluster works.

# Kubernetes Components

The Kubernetes cluster contains two types of node components:

*Control plane*
> This is the governing component of the Kubernetes cluster. It ensures that a couple of important services (e.g., scheduling, starting up new Pods[2]) are always running. The core purpose of the control plane node is to make sure the cluster is always in a healthy and correct state.

*Worker nodes*
> These are the compute instances that run your workload on your Kubernetes cluster, which hosts all your containers.

Figure 4-1 depicts the high-level components of Kubernetes. The lines signify the connections, such as worker nodes accepting a connection talking to the load balancer, which distributes traffic.

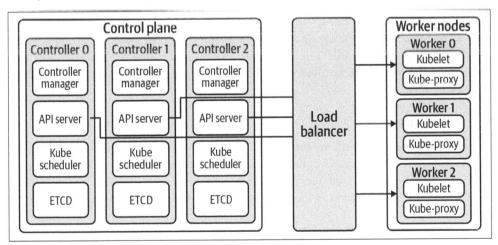

*Figure 4-1. Kubernetes components*

---

1 *Managing Kubernetes* by Brendan Burns and Craig Tracey (O'Reilly, 2019); *Kubernetes in Action* by Marko Lukša (Manning, 2018).

2 Pods are the smallest deployable units of computing that you can create and manage in Kubernetes.

Now let's take a detailed look at each component.

## Control Plane

The control plane is primarily responsible for making global decisions about the Kubernetes cluster, such as detecting cluster state, scheduling Pods on nodes, and managing the lifecycle of the Pods. The Kubernetes control plane has several components, which we describe in the following subsections.

### kube-apiserver (API server)

The API server is the frontend of the Kubernetes control plane and the only component with direct access to the entire Kubernetes cluster. As you saw in Figure 4-1, the API server serves as the central point for all the interactions between the worker nodes and the controller nodes. The services running in a Kubernetes cluster use the API server to communicate with one another. You can run multiple instances of the API server because it's designed to be scalable horizontally.

### Kube scheduler

The Kube scheduler is responsible for determining which worker node will run a Pod (or basic unit of work; we will explain Pods in more detail later in this chapter). The Kube scheduler talks to the API server, that determines which worker nodes are available to run the scheduled Pod in the best possible way. The scheduler looks for newly created Pods which are yet to be assigned to a node, and then finds *feasible* nodes as potential candidates and scores each of them based on different factors, such as node resource capacity and hardware requirement, to ensure that the correct scheduling decision is made. The node with the highest score is chosen to run the Pod. The scheduler also notifies the API server about this decision in a process referred to as *binding*.

### Kube controller manager

Kubernetes has a core built-in feature that implements the self-healing capabilities in the cluster. This feature is called the Kube controller manager and it runs as a daemon. The controller manager executes a control loop called the reconciliation loop, which is a nonterminating loop that is responsible for the following:

- Determining whether a node has gone down, and if so, taking action. This is done by the Node controller.
- Maintaining the correct number of Pods. This is done by the Replication controller.
- Joining the endpoint objects (i.e., servicers and Pods). This is done by the Endpoint controller.

- Ensuring that default accounts and endpoints are created for new namespaces. This is done by the Service Account and Token controllers.

The reconciliation loop is the driving force behind the self-healing capability of Kubernetes. Kubernetes determines the state of the cluster and its objects by continuously running the following steps in a loop:

1. Fetch the user-declared state (the *desired state*).

2. Observe the state of the cluster.

3. Compare the observed and desired states to find differences.

4. Take actions based on the observed state.

### etcd

Kubernetes uses etcd as a data store. etcd is a key-value store that is responsible for persisting all the Kubernetes objects. It was originally created by the CoreOS team and is now managed by CNCF. It is usually spun up in a highly available setup, and the etcd nodes are hosted on separate instances.

## Worker Nodes

A Kubernetes cluster contains a set of worker machines called worker nodes that run the containerized applications. The control plane manages the worker nodes and the Pods in the cluster. Some components run on all Kubernetes worker nodes; they are discussed in the following subsections.

### Kubelet

Kubelet is the daemon agent that runs on every node to ensure that containers are always in a running state in a Pod and are healthy. Kubelet reports to the API server about the currently available resources (CPU, memory, disk) on the worker nodes so that the API server can use the controller manager to observe the Pods' state. Since kubelet is the agent that runs on the worker nodes, the worker nodes handle basic housekeeping tasks such as restarting containers if required and consistently conducting health checks.

### Kube-proxy

Kube-proxy is the networking component that runs on each node. Kube-proxy watches all Kubernetes services[3] in the cluster and ensures that when a request to

---

3 In Kubernetes, services are a way of exposing your Pods so that they can be discovered inside the Kubernetes cluster.

a particular service is made, it gets routed to the particular virtual IP endpoint. Kube-proxy is responsible for implementing a kind of virtual IP for services.

Now that you've got the basics of Kubernetes components under your belt, let's dig a bit deeper and learn more about the Kubernetes API server.

# Kubernetes API Server Objects

The API server is responsible for all the communication inside and outside a Kubernetes cluster, and it exposes a RESTful HTTP API. The API server, at a fundamental level, allows you to query and manipulate Kubernetes objects. In simple terms, Kubernetes objects are stateful entities that represent the overall state of your cluster (Figure 4-2). To start working with these objects, we need to understand the fundamentals of each.

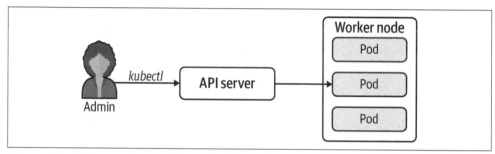

*Figure 4-2. API server interaction with cluster objects*

# Pods

In Kubernetes, Pods are the smallest basic atomic unit. A Pod is a group of one or more containers that get deployed on the worker nodes. Kubernetes is responsible for managing the containers running inside a Pod. Containers inside a Pod will always end up on the same worker node and are tightly coupled. Since the containers inside a Pod are co-located, they run in the same context (i.e., they share the network and storage). This shared context is characteristic of Linux namespaces, cgroups, and any other aspects that maintain isolation (as we explained in Chapter 3). Pods also get a unique IP address.

In typical scenarios, a single container is run inside a Pod, but in some instances, multiple containers need to work together in a Pod. This latter setup is usually referred to as a *sidecar* container. One of the most common examples of running a sidecar container is running a logging container for your application that will ship your logs to external storage, such as an ELK (Elasticsearch, Logstash, and Kibana) server, in case your application Pod crashes or a Pod is deleted. Pods are also smart in that if a process in a container dies, Kubernetes will instantly restart it based on the health checks defined at the application level.

Another characteristic of Pods is that they allow horizontal scaling by replication implemented through ReplicaSets. This means that if you want your application to scale horizontally, you should create more Pods by using ReplicaSets.

Pods are also ephemeral in nature, which means that if a Pod gets killed, it will be moved and restarted on a different host. This is also accomplished by using ReplicaSets.

## ReplicaSets

Reliability is a chief characteristic of Kubernetes, and since no one would be running a single instance of a Pod, redundancy becomes important. A *ReplicaSet* is a Kubernetes object that ensures that a stable set of replica Pods are running to maintain a self-healing cluster. All of this is achieved by the reconciliation loop, which keeps running in the background to observe the overall state of the Kubernetes cluster. ReplicaSets use the reconciliation loop and ensure that if any of the Pods crash or get restarted, a new Pod will be started in order to maintain the desired state of replication. In general, you should not directly deal with ReplicaSets, but rather, use the `Deployment` object, which ensures zero-downtime updates to your application and has a declarative approach toward managing and operating Kubernetes.

## Deployments

Kubernetes is primarily a declarative syntax-focused orchestrator. This means that in order to roll out new features, you need to tell Kubernetes what you need to do and it's up to Kubernetes to figure out how to perform that operation in a safe manner. One of the objects that Kubernetes offers in order to make the release of new versions of applications smoother is `Deployment`. If you go on manually updating Pods, you will need to restart the Pods, which will cause downtime. While a ReplicaSet knows how to maintain the desired number of Pods, it won't do a zero-downtime upgrade. Here is where the `Deployment` object comes into the picture, as it helps roll out changes to Pods with zero downtime by keeping a predefined number of Pods active all the time before a new updated Pod is rolled out.

## Services

To expose an application that is running inside a Pod, Kubernetes offers an object called `Service`. Since Kubernetes is a very dynamic system, it is necessary to ensure that applications are talking to correct backends. Pods are short-lived processes in the Kubernetes world, as they are frequently created or destroyed. Pods are coupled with a unique IP address, which means that if you rely on just the IP address of Pods, you will most likely end up with a broken service when a Pod dies, as the Pod will get a different IP address after restart, even though you have ReplicaSets running. The `Service` object offers an abstraction by defining a logical set of Pods and a policy by which to access them. Each `Service` gets a stable IP address and a DNS name that can be used to access the Pods. You can declaratively define the services that front your Pods and use the `Label-Selector` to access the service.

## Namespaces

Since multiple teams and projects are deployed in a production-grade environment, it becomes necessary to organize the Kubernetes objects. In a simple sense, *namespaces* are virtual clusters separated by logical partitioning; that is, you can group your resources, such as deployments, Pods, and so on, based on logical partitions. Some people like to think of namespaces as directories to separate names. Every object in your cluster has a name that is unique to that particular type of resource, and similarly every object has a UID that is unique across the whole cluster. Namespaces also allow you to divide the cluster resources among multiple users by setting *resource quotas*.

## Labels and Selectors

As you start using Kubernetes and creating objects, you'll realize the need to identify or mark your Kubernetes resources in order to group them into logical entities. Kubernetes offers *labels* to identify metadata for objects, which easily allows you to group and operate the resources. Labels are key-value pairs that can be attached directly to objects like Pods, namespaces, DaemonSets, and so on. You can add labels at any time and modify them as you like. To find or identify your Kubernetes resources, you can query the labels using *label selectors*. For example, a label for a type of application tier can be:

```
"tier" : "frontend", "tier" : "backend", "tier" : "midtier"
```

## Annotations

*Annotations* are also key-value pairs, but unlike labels, which are used to identify objects, annotations are used to hold nonidentifying information about the object itself. For example, build, release, or image information such as timestamps, release IDs, the Git branch, PR numbers, image hashes, and the registry address can be recorded in an annotation.

## Ingress Controller

For your services to receive traffic from the internet, you need to expose HTTP and HTTPS endpoints from the outside to Kubernetes services running on Pods. An *ingress* allows you to expose your services running inside the cluster to the outside world by offering load balancing with Secure Sockets Layer/Transport Layer Security (SSL/TLS) terminations using name-based virtual hosting. To support an ingress, you should first choose an *ingress controller*, which is similar to a reverse proxy, to accept incoming connections for HTTP and HTTPS.

## StatefulSets

To manage and scale your stateful workloads on Kubernetes, you need to ensure that the Pods are stable (i.e., a stable network and stable storage). *StatefulSets* ensure the ordering of the Pods and maintain their uniqueness (unlike ReplicaSets). A StatefulSet is a controller that helps you deploy groups of Pods that remain resilient to restarts and reschedules. Each Pod in a StatefulSet has unique naming conventions whose ordinal value starts at 0 and has a stable network ID associated with it (unlike a ReplicaSet, in which the naming convention is random in nature).

## DaemonSets

In regular environments, we run a number of daemon services and agents on the host, including logging agents and monitoring agents. Kubernetes allows you to install such agents by running a copy of a Pod across a set of nodes in a cluster using *DaemonSets*. Just like ReplicaSets, DaemonSets are long-running processes that ensure that the desired state and observed state remain the same. Deleting a DaemonSet also deletes the Pods that it previously created.

## Jobs

Jobs in the Kubernetes world are short-lived entities, which can be small tasks such as running a standalone script, for example. Jobs eventually create Pods. Jobs are run until they are successfully terminated, which is the major difference between a Pod that controls a Job and a regular Pod that will keep getting restarted and rescheduled if terminated. If a Job Pod fails before completion, the controller will create a new Pod based on the template.

This chapter is a crash course in Kubernetes and just scratches the surface of container orchestration. Other resources are available that can help you learn more about Kubernetes. Some of the ones we recommend are:

- *Managing Kubernetes* by Brendan Burns and Craig Tracey (O'Reilly, 2018)
- *Kubernetes: Up and Running, 2nd Edition* by Brendan Burns, Joe Beda, and Kelsey Hightower (O'Reilly 2019)
- "Introduction to Kubernetes" (*https://oreil.ly/RLPL8*), a free course from LinuxFoundationX
- *Cloud Native DevOps with Kubernetes, 2nd Edition* by John Arundel and Justin Domingus (O'Reilly, 2022)

Now that we have covered some basic terminology in the Kubernetes world, let's take a look at the operational details for managing the cluster.

# Observe, Operate, and Manage Kubernetes Clusters with kubectl

One of the more common ways to interact with a container orchestrator is by using either a command-line tool or a graphical tool. In Kubernetes you can interact with the cluster in both ways, but the preferred way is the command line. Kubernetes offers *kubectl* as the CLI. kubectl is widely used to administer the cluster. You can consider kubectl to be a Swiss Army knife of various Kubernetes functions that enable you to deploy and manage applications. If you are an administrator for your Kubernetes cluster, you would be using the kubectl command extensively to manage the cluster. kubectl offers a variety of commands, including:

- Resource configuration commands, which are declarative in nature
- Debugging commands for getting information about workloads
- Debugging commands for manipulating and interacting with Pods
- General cluster management commands

In this section, we will explore Kubernetes in depth by focusing on basic cluster commands for managing Kubernetes clusters, Pods, and other objects with the help of kubectl.

## General Cluster Information and Commands

The first step to interacting with the Kubernetes cluster is to learn how to gain insights on the cluster, infrastructure, and Kubernetes components that you'll be working with. To see the worker nodes that run the workloads in your cluster, issue the following kubectl command:

```
$   ~ kubectl get nodes
NAME      STATUS   ROLES    AGE   VERSION
worker0   Ready    <none>   11d   v1.17.3
worker1   Ready    <none>   11d   v1.17.3
worker2   Ready    <none>   11d   v1.17.3
```

This will list your node resources and their status, along with version information. You can gain a bit more information by using the -o wide flag in the get nodes command as follows:

```
$  ~ kubectl get nodes -o wide
NAME      STATUS   ROLES    AGE   VERSION   INTERNAL-IP   EXTERNAL-IP   OS-IMAGE
worker0   Ready    <none>   11d   v1.17.3   10.240.0.20   <none>
worker1   Ready    <none>   11d   v1.17.3   10.240.0.21   <none>
worker2   Ready    <none>   11d   v1.17.3   10.240.0.22   <none>
```

```
KERNEL-VERSION      CONTAINER-RUNTIME
Ubuntu 16.04.7 LTS  4.15.0-1092-azure   containerd://1.3.2
Ubuntu 16.04.7 LTS  4.15.0-1092-azure   containerd://1.3.2
Ubuntu 16.04.7 LTS  4.15.0-1092-azure   containerd://1.3.2
```

To get even more details specific to a resource or worker, you can use the `describe` command as follows:

```
$ ~ kubectl describe nodes worker0
```

The `kubectl describe` command is a very useful debugging command. You could possibly use it to gain in-depth information about Pods and other resources.

The get command can be used to gain more information about Pods, services, replication controllers, and so on. For example, to get information on all Pods, you can run:

```
$ ~ kubectl get pods
NAME                     READY   STATUS             RESTARTS   AGE
busybox-56d8458597-xpjcg 0/1     ContainerCreating  0          1m
```

To get a list of all the namespaces in your cluster, you can use `get` as follows:

```
$ ~ kubectl get namespace
NAME                  STATUS   AGE
default               Active   12d
kube-node-lease       Active   12d
kube-public           Active   12d
kube-system           Active   12d
kubernetes-dashboard  Active   46h
```

By default, kubectl interacts with the `default` namespace. To use a different namespace, you can pass the `--namespace` flag to reference objects in a namespace:

```
$ ~ kubectl get pods --namespace=default
NAME                     READY   STATUS    RESTARTS   AGE
busybox-56d8458597-xpjcg 1/1     Running   0          47h

$ ~ kubectl get pods --namespace=kube-public
No resources found in kube-public namespace.

$ ~ kubectl get pods --namespace=kubernetes-dashboard
NAME                                         READY   STATUS    RESTARTS   AGE
dashboard-metrics-scraper-779f5454cb-gq82q   1/1     Running   0          2m
kubernetes-dashboard-857bb4c778-qxsnj        1/1     Running   0          46h
```

To view the overall cluster details, you can make use of `cluster-info` as follows:

```
$ ~ kubectl cluster-info
Kubernetes master is running at https://40.70.3.6:6443
CoreDNS is running at https://40.70.3.6:6443/api/v1/namespaces/kube-system/services/ \
  kube-dns:dns/proxy
```

The `cluster-info` command gets you the details of the API load balancer where the control plane is sitting, along with other components.

In Kubernetes, to maintain a connection with a specific cluster you use a *context*. A context helps group access parameters under one name. Each context contains a Kubernetes cluster, a user, and a namespace. The current context is the cluster that is currently the default for kubectl, and all the commands being issued by kubectl run against this cluster. You can view your current context as follows:

```
$ ~ kubectl config current-context
cloud-native-azure
```

To change the default namespace, you can use a context that gets registered to your environment's kubectl kubeconfig file. The kubeconfig file is the actual file that tells kubectl how to find your Kubernetes cluster and then authenticate based on the secrets that have been configured. The file is usually stored in your home directory under *.kube/*. To create and use a new context with a different namespace as its default, you can do the following:

```
$ ~ kubectl config set-context test --namespace=mystuff
Context "test" created.
$ ~ kubectl config use-context test
Switched to context "test"
```

Make sure you actually have the context (the *test* Kubernetes cluster) or else you won't be able to really use it.

Labels, as we mentioned before, are used to organize your objects. For example, if you want to label the busybox Pod with a value called production, you can do it as follows, where environment is the label name:

```
$ ~ kubectl label pods busybox-56d8458597-xpjcg environment=production
pod/busybox-56d8458597-xpjcg labeled
```

At times, you might want to find out what is wrong with your Pods and try to debug an issue. To see a log for a Pod, you can run the logs command on a Pod name:

```
$ ~ kubectl get pods
NAME                        READY   STATUS             RESTARTS   AGE
busybox-56d8458597-xpjcg    0/1     ContainerCreating  0          2d
$ ~ kubectl logs busybox-56d8458597-xpjcg
Error from server (BadRequest): container "busybox" in pod "busybox-56d8458597-xpjcg" is
waiting to start: ContainerCreating
```

Sometimes you can have multiple containers running inside a Pod. To choose containers inside it, you can pass the -c flag.

## Managing Pods

As we discussed earlier, Pods are the smallest deployable artifacts in Kubernetes. As an end user or administrator, you deal directly with Pods and not with containers. The containers are handled by Kubernetes internally, and this logic is abstracted. It is also important to remember that all the containers inside a Pod are placed on the same node. Pods also have a defined lifecycle whose states move from *Pending* to *Running* to *Succeeded* or *Failed*.

One of the ways you can create a Pod is by using the `kubectl run` command as follows:

```
$ kubectl run <name of pod> --image=<name of the image from registry>
```

The `kubectl run` command pulls a public image from a container repository and creates a Pod. For example, you can run a hazelcast image as follows, and expose the container's port too:

```
$ ~ kubectl run hazelcast --image=hazelcast/hazelcast --port=5701
deployment.apps/hazelcast created
```

 In production environments, you should never run or create Pods, because these Pods are not directly managed by Kubernetes and will not get restarted or rescheduled in case of a failure. You should use deployments as the preferred way of operating the Pods.

The `kubectl run` command is rich in feature sets, and you can control many Pod behaviors. For example, if you wish to run a Pod in the foreground (i.e., with an interactive terminal inside the Pod) and you don't wish to restart it if it crashes, you may do the following:

```
$ ~ kubectl run -i -t busybox --image=busybox --restart=Never
If you don't see a command prompt, try pressing enter.
/ #
```

This command will directly log you inside the container. And since you run the Pod in interactive mode, you can check out the status of the busybox changing from *Running* to *Completed*, such as in the following:

```
$ ~ kubectl get pods
NAME              READY   STATUS     RESTARTS   AGE
busybox           1/1     Running    0          52s

$ ~ kubectl get pods
NAME              READY   STATUS     RESTARTS   AGE
busybox           0/1     Completed  0          61s
```

Another way to create Pods in Kubernetes is by using the declarative syntax in Pod manifests. The Pod manifests, which should be treated with the same importance as your application code, can be written using either YAML or JSON. You can create a Pod manifest for running an Nginx Pod as follows:

```
apiVersion: v1
kind: pod
metadata:
  name: nginx
spec:
  containers:
```

```
    - image: nginx
      name: nginx
      ports:
        - containerPort: 80
          name: http
```

The Pod manifests information such as kind, spec, and other information that is sent to the Kubernetes API server to act on. You can save the Pod manifest with a YAML extension and use apply as follows:

```
$ kubectl apply -f nginx_pod.yaml
pod/nginx created
$ kubectl get pods
NAME                        READY    STATUS    RESTARTS   AGE
nginx                       1/1      Running   0          7s
```

When you run kubectl apply the Pod manifest is sent to the Kubernetes API server, which instantly schedules the Pod to run on a healthy node in the cluster. The Pod is monitored by the kubelet daemon process, and if the Pod crashes, it's rescheduled to run on a different healthy node.

Let's now move on and take a look at how you can implement health checks on your services in Kubernetes.

### Health checks

Kubernetes offers three types of HTTP health checks, called *probes*, for ensuring the application is actually alive and well: liveness probes, readiness probes, and startup probes.

**Liveness probe.** This probe is responsible for ensuring that the application is actually healthy and fully functioning. After deployment, your application may take a few seconds before it is ready, so you can configure this probe to check a certain endpoint in your application. For example, in the following Pod manifest, a liveness probe has been used to perform an httpGet operation against the / path on port 80. The initialDelaySeconds is set to 2, which means the endpoint / will not be hit until this period has elapsed. Additionally, we have set the timeout to be 1 second and the failure threshold to be 3 consecutive probe failures. The periodSeconds is defined as how frequently Kubernetes will be calling the Pods. In this case, it's 15 seconds.

```
apiVersion: v1
kind: Pod
metadata:
  name: mytest-pod
spec:
  containers:
  - image: test_image
    imagePullPolicy: IfNotPresent
    name: mytest-container
    command: ['sh', '-c', 'echo Container 1 is Running ; sleep 3600']
    ports:
    - name: liveness-port
```

```
      containerPort: 80
      hostPort: 8080
    livenessProbe:
      httpGet:
        path: /
        port: 80
      initialDelaySeconds: 2
      timeoutSeconds: 1
      periodSeconds: 15
      failureThreshold: 3
```

**Readiness probe.**  The readiness probe's responsibility is to identify when a container is ready to serve the user request. A readiness probe helps Kubernetes by not adding an unready Pod's endpoint to a load balancer too early. A readiness probe can be configured simultaneously with a liveness probe block in the Pod manifest as follows:

```
containers:
- name: test_image
  image: test_image
  command: ["/bin/sh"]
  args: ['sh', '-c', 'echo Container 1 is Running ; sleep 3600']
  readinessProbe:
    httpGet:
      path: /
      port: 80
    initialDelaySeconds: 5
    periodSeconds: 3
```

**Startup probe.**  Sometimes an application requires some additional startup time on its first initialization. In such cases, you can set up a startup probe with an HTTP or TCP check that has a `failureThreshold` * `periodSeconds`, which is long enough to cover the worst-case startup time:

```
startupProbe:
  httpGet:
    path: /healthapi
    port: liveness-port
  failureThreshold: 30
  periodSeconds: 10
```

## Resource limits

When you deal with Pods, you can specify the resources your application will need. Some of the most basic resource requirements for a Pod to run are CPU and memory. Although there are more types of resources that Kubernetes can handle, we will keep it simple here and discuss only CPU and memory.

You can declare two parameters in the Pod manifest: *request* and *limit*. In the request block you tell Kubernetes the minimum resource requirement for your application to operate, and in the limit block you tell Kubernetes the maximum threshold. If your application breaches the threshold in the limit block, it will be terminated or restarted and the Pod will be mostly evicted. For example, in the following Pod manifest, we are placing a max CPU limit of 500m[4] and a max memory limit of 206Mi,[5] which means if these values are crossed, the Pod will be evicted and rescheduled on some other node:

```
apiVersion: v1
kind: Pod
metadata:
  name: nginx
spec:
  containers:
    - image: nginx
      name: nginx
      ports:
        - containerPort: 80
          name: http
      resources:
            requests:
              cpu: "100m"
              memory: "108Mi"
            limits:
              cpu: "500m"
              memory: "206Mi"
```

## Volumes

Some applications require data to be stored permanently, but because Pods are short-lived entities and are frequently restarted or killed on the fly, all data associated with a Pod can be destroyed as well. *Volumes* solve this problem with an abstraction layer of storage disks in Azure. A volume is a way to store, retrieve, and persist data across Pods throughout the application lifecycle. If your application is stateful, you need to use a volume to persist your data. Azure provides *Azure Disk* and *Azure Files* to create the data volumes that provide this functionality.

**Persistent Volume Claim (PVC).** The PVC serves as an abstraction layer between the Pod and storage. In Kubernetes, the Pod mounts volumes with the help of PVCs and the PVCs talk to the underlying resources. One thing to note is that a PVC lets you consume the abstracted underlying storage resource; that is, it lets you claim a piece of preprovisioned storage. The PVC defines the disk size and disk type and then mounts the real storage to the Pod; this binding process can be static, as in a persistent volume (PV), or dynamic, as in a `Storage` class. For example, in the following manifest we are claiming a `PersistentVolumeClaim` having storage of `1Gi`:

---

4 Fractional requests are allowed. For example, one CPU can be broken into two 0.5s. The expression 0.1 is equivalent to 100m.

5 Limit and request are measured in bytes. Memory can be expressed as a plain integer or a fixed-point number using the suffixes E, P, T, G, M, K, or their power-of-two equivalents Ei, Pi, Ti, Gi, Mi, Ki.

```
apiVersion: v1
kind: PersistentVolumeClaim
metadata:
  name: persistent-volume-claim-app1
spec:
  accessModes:
    - ReadWriteMany
  resources:
    requests:
      storage: 1Gi
  storageClassName: azurefilestorage
```

**Persistent volume—static.**   A cluster administrator, usually the SRE or DevOps team, can create a predefined number of persistent volumes manually, which can then be used by the cluster users as they require. Persistent volume is the static provisioning method. For example, in the following manifest we are creating a `PersistentVolume` with a storage capacity of 2Gi:

```
apiVersion: v1
kind: PersistentVolume
metadata:
  name: static-persistent-volume-app1
  labels:
    storage: azurefile
spec:
  capacity:
    storage: 2Gi
  accessModes:
    - ReadWriteMany
  storageClassName: azurefilestorage
  azureFile:
    secretName: static-persistence-secret
    shareName: user-app1
    readOnly: false
```

**Storage class—dynamic.**   Storage classes are dynamically provisioned volumes for the PVC (i.e., they allow storage volumes to be created on demand). Storage classes basically provide the cluster administrators a way to describe the *classes* of storage that can be offered. Each storage class has a provisioner that determines which volume plug-in is used for provisioning the persistent volumes.

In Azure, two kinds of provisioners determine the kind of storage that will be used: *AzureFile* and *AzureDisk*.

AzureFile can be used with ReadWriteMany access mode:

```
apiVersion: storage.k8s.io/v1
kind: StorageClass
metadata:
  name: azurefile
provisioner: kubernetes.io/azure-file
parameters:
  skuName: Standard_LRS
```

```
  location: eastus
  storageAccount: azure_storage_account_name
```

AzureDisk can only be used with ReadWriteOnce access mode:

```
apiVersion: storage.k8s.io/v1
kind: StorageClass
metadata:
  name: slow
provisioner: kubernetes.io/azure-disk
parameters:
  storageaccounttype: Standard_LRS
  kind: Shared
```

Figure 4-3 showcases the logical relationship between the various storage objects that Kubernetes offers.

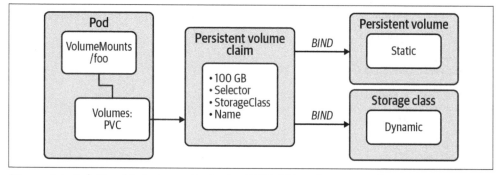

*Figure 4-3. Relationship between Pods, the PVC, PV, and* Storage *class*

Lastly, you can delete a Pod by using kubectl delete pod as follows:

```
$  ~ kubectl delete pod nginx
pod "nginx" deleted
```

You should make sure that when you delete a Pod, it's not actually controlled with a Deployment, because if it is, it will reappear. For example:

```
$  ~ kubectl get pods
NAME                          READY   STATUS    RESTARTS   AGE
hazelcast-84bb5bb976-vrk97    1/1     Running   2          2d7h
nginx-76df748b9-rdbqq         1/1     Running   2          2d7h
$  ~ kubectl delete pod hazelcast-84bb5bb976-vrk97
pod "hazelcast-84bb5bb976-vrk97" deleted
$  ~ kubectl get pods
NAME                          READY   STATUS    RESTARTS   AGE
hazelcast-84bb5bb976-rpcfh    1/1     Running   0          13s
nginx-76df748b9-rdbqq         1/1     Running   2          2d7h
```

The reason it spun off a new Pod is because Kubernetes observed that a state in the cluster was disturbed where the desired and observed states did not match, and hence the reconciliation loop kicked in to balance the Pods. This could happen because the Pod was actually deployed via a Deployment and would have ReplicaSets associated with it. So, in order to delete a Pod, you would need to delete the Deployment, which in turn would automatically delete the Pod. This is shown as follows:

```
$ ~ kubectl get deployments --all-namespaces
NAMESPACE        NAME                           READY   UP-TO-DATE   AVAILABLE   AGE
default          hazelcast                      1/1     1            1           2d21h
default          nginx                          1/1     1            1           2d21h
kube-system      coredns                        2/2     2            2           3d7h
$ ~ kubectl delete -n default deployment hazelcast
deployment.apps "hazelcast" deleted
$ ~ kubectl get pods
NAME                          READY   STATUS        RESTARTS   AGE
hazelcast-84bb5bb976-rpcfh    0/1     Terminating   0          21m
nginx-76df748b9-rdbqq         1/1     Running       2          2d7h
```

# Kubernetes in Production

Now that we have covered the basics of Pods, Kubernetes concepts, and how the Kubernetes cluster works, let's take a look at how to actually tie together the Pods and become production ready in a Kubernetes cluster. In this section, we will see how the concepts discussed in the previous section empower production workloads and how applications are deployed onto Kubernetes.

## ReplicaSets

As we discussed, ReplicaSets enable the self-healing capability of Kubernetes at the infrastructure level by maintaining a stable number of Pods. In the event of a failure at the infrastructure level (i.e., the nodes that hold the Pods), the ReplicaSet will reschedule the Pods to a different, healthy node. A ReplicaSet includes the following:

*Selector*
ReplicaSets use Pod labels to find and list the Pods running in the cluster to create replicas in case of a failure.

*Number of replicas to create*
This specifies how many Pods should be created.

*Template*
This specifies the associated data of new Pods that a ReplicaSet should create to meet the desired number of Pods.

In actual production use cases, you will need a ReplicaSet to maintain a stable set of running Pods by introducing redundancy. But you don't have to deal with the ReplicaSet directly, since it's an abstraction layer. Instead, you should use Deployments, which offer a much better way to deploy and manage Pods.

A ReplicaSet looks like this:

```
apiVersion: apps/v1
kind: ReplicaSet
metadata:
  name: myapp-cnf-replicaset
  labels:
    app: cnfbook
spec:
  replicas: 3
  selector:
    matchLabels:
      app: cnfbook
  template:
    metadata:
      labels:
        app: cnfbook
    spec:
      containers:
      - name: nginx
        image: nginx
        ports:
        - containerPort: 80
```

To create the ReplicaSet from the preceding configuration, save the manifest as *nginx_Replicaset.yaml* and apply it. This will create a ReplicaSet and three Pods, shown as follows:

```
$ kubectl apply -f nginx_Replicaset.yaml
replicaset.apps/myapp-cnf-replicaset created

$ kubectl get rs
NAME                   DESIRED   CURRENT   READY   AGE
myapp-cnf-replicaset   3         3         3       6s

$ kubectl get pods
NAME                         READY   STATUS    RESTARTS   AGE
myapp-cnf-replicaset-drwp9   1/1     Running   0          11s
myapp-cnf-replicaset-pgwj8   1/1     Running   0          11s
myapp-cnf-replicaset-wqkll   1/1     Running   0          11s
```

## Deployments

In production environments, a key thing that is constant is change. You will keep updating/changing the applications in your production environment at a very rapid pace, since the most common task you will be doing in production is rolling out new features of your application. Kubernetes offers the Deployment object as a standard for doing rolling updates, and provides a seamless experience to the cluster administrator as well as end users. This means you can push updates to your applications without taking down your applications, since Deployment ensures that only a certain number of Pods are down while they are being updated. These are known as *zero downtime deployments*. By default, Deployments ensure that at least 75% of the desired number of Pods are up. Deployments are the reliable, safe, and current way to roll out new versions of applications with zero downtime in Kubernetes.

You can create a `Deployment` as follows:

```
apiVersion: apps/v1
kind: Deployment
metadata:
  name: nginx-deployment
  labels:
    app: nginx
spec:
  replicas: 3
  selector:
    matchLabels:
      app: nginx
  template:
    metadata:
      labels:
        app: nginx
    spec:
      containers:
      - name: nginx
        image: nginx
        ports:
        - containerPort: 80
```

To apply the preceding configuration, save it in a file named *nginx_Deployment.yaml* and then use `kubectl apply` as follows:

```
$ kubectl apply -f nginx_Deployment.yaml
deployment.apps/nginx-deployment created
```

Interestingly, the Deployment handles ReplicaSets as well, since we declared that we would need three replicas for the deployment Pod. We can check this as follows:

```
$ kubectl get deployment
NAME               READY   UP-TO-DATE   AVAILABLE   AGE
nginx-deployment   3/3     3            3           18s
$ kubectl get rs
NAME                          DESIRED   CURRENT   READY   AGE
nginx-deployment-d46f5678b    3         3         3       29s
$ kubectl get pods
NAME                                READY   STATUS    RESTARTS   AGE
nginx-deployment-d46f5678b-dpc7p    1/1     Running   0          36s
nginx-deployment-d46f5678b-kdjxv    1/1     Running   0          36s
nginx-deployment-d46f5678b-kj8zz    1/1     Running   0          36s
```

So, from the manifest file, we created three replicas in the *.spec.replicas* file, and for the `Deployment` object to find the Pods being managed by `nginx-deployment`, we make use of the `spec.selector` field. The Pods are labeled using the template field via `metadata.labels`.

Now let's roll out a new version of Nginx. Say we want to pin the version of Nginx to 1.14.2. We just need to edit the deployment manifest by editing the file; that is, changing the version and then saving the manifest file, as follows:

```
$ kubectl edit deployment.v1.apps/nginx-deployment
deployment.apps/nginx-deployment edited
```

This will update the `Deployment` object, and you can check it as follows:

```
$ kubectl rollout status deployment.v1.apps/nginx-deployment
Waiting for deployment "nginx-deployment" rollout to finish: 1 out of 3 new replicas have
been updated...
Waiting for deployment "nginx-deployment" rollout to finish: 1 out of 3 new replicas have
been updated...
Waiting for deployment "nginx-deployment" rollout to finish: 2 out of 3 new replicas have
been updated...
Waiting for deployment "nginx-deployment" rollout to finish: 2 out of 3 new replicas have
been updated...
Waiting for deployment "nginx-deployment" rollout to finish: 2 out of 3 new replicas have
been updated...
Waiting for deployment "nginx-deployment" rollout to finish: 2 old replicas are pending
termination...
Waiting for deployment "nginx-deployment" rollout to finish: 1 old replicas are pending
termination...
Waiting for deployment "nginx-deployment" rollout to finish: 1 old replicas are pending
termination...
deployment "nginx-deployment" successfully rolled out
```

The `Deployment` object ensures that a certain number of Pods are always available and serving while the older Pods are updated. As we already mentioned, by default, no more than 25% of Pods are unavailable while an update is being performed. Deployment ensures a max surge percentage of 25%, which ensures that only a certain number of Pods are created over the desired number of Pods. So, from the `rollout status`, you can clearly see that at least two Pods are available at all times while rolling out a change. You can get the details for your deployment again by using `kubectl describe deployment`.

> We directly issued a deployment command using `kubectl edit`, but the preferred approach is to always update the actual manifest file and then apply `kubectl`. This also helps you keep your deployment manifests in version control. You can use the `--record` or `set` command to update as well.

## Horizontal Pod Autoscaler

Kubernetes supports dynamic scaling through the use of the Horizontal Pod Autoscaler (HPA), where the Pods are scaled horizontally; that is, you can create $n$ number of Pods based on observed metrics for your Pod if, for example, you want to increase or decrease the number of Pods dynamically based on the CPU metric being observed. The HPA works via a control loop which, at an interval of 15 seconds by default, checks the resource utilization specified against the metrics (see Figure 4-4).

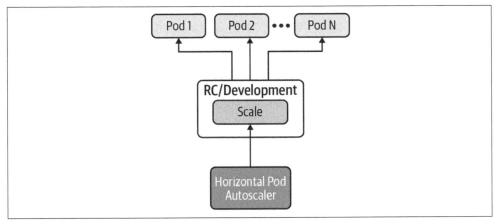

*Figure 4-4. Horizontal Pod Autoscaler at work*

It is important to note that to use the HPA, we need metrics-server (*https://oreil.ly/ x8Pp6*), which collects metrics from kubelets and exposes them in the Kubernetes API server through the metrics API for use by the HPA. We first create an autoscaler using kubectl autoscale for our deployment, as follows:

```
$  ~ kubectl autoscale deployment nginx-deployment --cpu-percent=50 --min=3 --max=10
horizontalpodautoscaler.autoscaling/nginx-deployment autoscaled
```

The preceding kubectl command will create an HPA that will ensure that no fewer than three and no more than 10 Pods are used in our nginx-deployment. The HPA will increase or decrease the number of replicas to maintain an average CPU utilization across all Pods of no more than 50%.

You can view your HPA using the following:

```
$  ~ kubectl get hpa
NAME                REFERENCE                    TARGETS  MINPODS  MAXPODS  REPLICAS  AGE
nginx-deployment    Deployment/nginx-deployment  0%/50%   3        10       3         6m59s
```

We can add the scaling factor on which we can create the autoscaler with the help of an HPA manifest YAML file that is tied to the deployment.

## Service

As we mentioned earlier, the Kubernetes environment is a very dynamic system where Pods are created, destroyed, and moved at a varying pace. This dynamic environment also opens a door to a well-known problem: finding the replica Pods where an application is residing, since multiple Pods are running for a deployment. Pods also need a way to find the other Pods in order to communicate. Kubernetes offers the Service object as an abstraction for a single point of entry to the group of Pods. The Service object has an IP address, a DNS name, and a port that never changes as long as the object exists. Formally known as service discovery, this feature basically helps other Pods/services reach other services in Kubernetes without dealing with the underlying complexity. We will discuss the cloud native service discovery approach in more detail in Chapter 6.

To use a Service, you can use the service manifest YAML. Suppose you have a simple "hello world" application already running as a Deployment. One default technique to expose this service is to specify the service `type` as `ClusterIP`. This service will be exposed on the cluster's internal IP and will only be reachable from within the cluster, as follows:

```
---
apiVersion: v1
kind: Service
metadata:
  name: hello-world-service
spec:
  type: ClusterIP
  selector:
    app: hello-world
  ports:
  - port: 8080
    targetPort: 8080
```

The `port` represents the port where the service will be available and the `targetPort` is the actual container port where the service will be forwarded. In this case, we have exposed port 8080 of the *hello-world app* on target port 8080 against the Pod IP:

```
$ kubectl get svc
NAME                  TYPE        CLUSTER-IP    EXTERNAL-IP   PORT(S)     AGE
hello-world-service   ClusterIP   10.32.0.40    <none>        8080/TCP    6s
```

The IP address shown is the cluster IP and not the actual machine IP address. If you SSH on a worker node, you can check whether the service was exposed on port 8080 by simply doing a `curl` as follows:

```
ubuntu@worker0:~$ curl http://10.32.0.40:8080
Hello World
```

If you try to reach this IP address from outside the cluster (i.e., any other node apart from workers), you won't be able to connect to it. So, you can use `NodePort`, which exposes a service on each node's IP at a defined port as follows:

```
---
apiVersion: v1
kind: Service
metadata:
  name: hello-world-node-service
spec:
  type: NodePort
  selector:
    app: hello-world
  ports:
  - port: 8080
    targetPort: 8080
    nodePort: 30767
```

In the service manifest, we have mapped Pod port 8080 to `NodePort` (i.e., physical instance port) 30767. In this way, you can expose the IP directly or place a load balancer of your choice. If you now do a `get svc`, you can see the mapping of ports as follows:

```
$ kubectl get svc
NAME                      TYPE       CLUSTER-IP    EXTERNAL-IP   PORT(S)          AGE
hello-world-node-service  NodePort   10.32.0.208   <none>        8080:30767/TCP   8s
hello-world-service       ClusterIP  10.32.0.40    <none>        8080/TCP         41m
```

Now we can access the service on the node at port 30767:

```
ubuntu@controller0:~$ curl http://10.240.0.21:30767
Hello World
```

The IP in the `curl` command is the worker node's physical IP (not the cluster IP) address, and the port that is being exposed is 30767. You can even directly hit the public IP of the node for port 30767. Figure 4-5 showcases how the cluster IP, node port, and load balancer relate to one another.

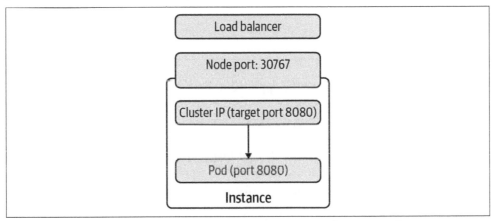

*Figure 4-5. Cluster IP, node port, and load balancer in a Kubernetes node*

Other types of services include `LoadBalancer` and `ExternalName`. `LoadBalancer` exposes the Service externally using a cloud provider's load balancer. `NodePort` and `ClusterIP` Services, to which the external load balancer routes, are automatically created, while `ExternalName` maps a service to a DNS name like `my.redisdb.inter nal.com`. In Figure 4-6, you can see how different service types are related to one another.

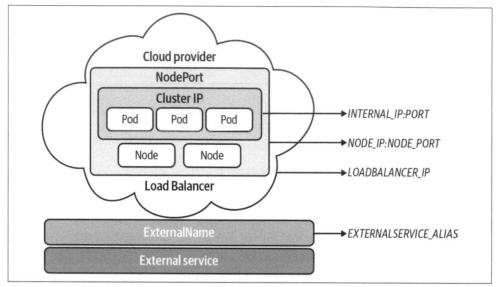

*Figure 4-6. External service and LoadBalancer in a cloud environment*

## Ingress

The Service object helps expose the application both inside and outside the cluster, but in production systems we cannot afford to keep opening new and unique ports for all the services we deploy using NodePort, nor we can create a new load balancer every time we choose the service type to be LoadBalancer. At times we need to deploy an HTTP-based service and also perform SSL offloading, and the Service object doesn't really help us in those instances. In Kubernetes, HTTP load balancing (or, formally, Layer 7 load balancing) is performed by the Ingress object.

To work with Ingress, we first need to configure an ingress controller.[6] We will configure an Azure Kubernetes Service (AKS) Application Gateway Ingress Controller to understand this better and see how it behaves, but in general, one of the easiest ways to understand it better is by looking at the following:

---

6 For the Ingress resource to work, the cluster must have an ingress controller running. Unlike other types of controllers that run as part of the kube-controller-manager binary, ingress controllers are not started automatically with a cluster. There are different types of ingress controllers; for example, Azure offers the AKS Application Gateway Ingress Controller for configuring the Azure Application Gateway.

```
apiVersion: networking.k8s.io/v1
kind: Ingress
metadata:
  name: ingress-wildcard-host
spec:
  rules:
  - host: "foo.bar.com"
    http:
      paths:
      - pathType: Prefix
        path: "/bar"
        backend:
          service:
            name: hello-world-node-service
            port:
              number: 8080
  - host: "*.foo.com"
    http:
      paths:
      - pathType: Prefix
        path: "/foo"
        backend:
          service:
            name: service2
            port:
              number: 80
```

In the ingress manifest, we have created two rules and mapped *foo.bar.com* as a host to one subdomain */bar*, which routes to our previous service `hello-world-node-service`.

Similarly, we can have multiple paths defined for a domain and route them to other services. There are various ways to configure the ingress according to your needs, which might span from a single domain routing to multiple services or multiple domains routing to multiple domains (see Figure 4-7).

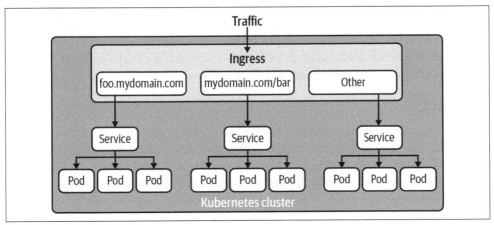

*Figure 4-7. Ingress with multiple paths for a domain*

Lastly, you can specify TLS support by creating a `Secret` object and then using that secret in your ingress spec as follows:

```
apiVersion: v1
kind: Secret
metadata:
  name: my_tls_secret
  namespace: default
data:
  tls.crt: base64 encoded cert
  tls.key: base64 encoded key
type: kubernetes.io/tls
```

You can secure the ingress by specifying just the Base64-encoded TLS certificate and the key. When you reference this secret in your ingress manifest it will appear as follows:

```
apiVersion: networking.k8s.io/v1
kind: Ingress
metadata:
  name: tls-example-ingress
spec:
  tls:
  - hosts:
      - https.mywebsite.example.come
    secretName: my_tls_secret
  rules:
  - host: https.mywebsite.example.come
    http:
      paths:
      - path: /
        pathType: Prefix
        backend:
          service:
            name: service1
            port:
              number: 80
```

Ingress controllers deal with many features and complexities, and the Azure Gateway Ingress Controller handles a lot of them; for example, leveraging Azure's native Layer 7 application gateway load balancer to expose your services to the internet. We will discuss this in more detail when we introduce AKS in Chapter 5.

## DaemonSet

DaemonSets, as we discussed earlier, are typically used to run an agent across a number of nodes in the Kubernetes cluster. The agent is run inside a container abstracted by Pods. Most of the time, SREs and DevOps engineers prefer to run a log agent or a monitoring agent on each node to gain application telemetry and events. By default, a DaemonSet creates a copy of a Pod on every node, though this can be restricted as well using a node selector. There are a lot of similarities between ReplicaSets and DaemonSets, but the key distinction between them is the requirement (with DaemonSets) of running a single agent (i.e., Pod) application across all of your nodes.

One of the ways to run a logging container is by deploying a Pod in each node using a DaemonSet. Fluentd is an open source logging solution widely used to collect logs from systems. This example shows one of the ways to deploy Fluentd using a DaemonSet:

```
apiVersion: apps/v1
kind: DaemonSet
metadata:
  name: fluentd-elasticsearch
  namespace: kube-system
  labels:
    central-log-k8s: fluentd-logging
spec:
  selector:
    matchLabels:
      name: fluentd-elasticsearch
  template:
    metadata:
      labels:
        name: fluentd-elasticsearch
    spec:
      tolerations:
      - key: node-role.kubernetes.io/master
        effect: NoSchedule
      containers:
      - name: fluentd-elasticsearch
        image: quay.io/fluentd_elasticsearch/fluentd:v2.5.2
        resources:
          limits:
            memory: 200Mi
          requests:
            cpu: 100m
            memory: 200Mi
        volumeMounts:
        - name: varlog
          mountPath: /var/log
        - name: varlibdockercontainers
          mountPath: /var/lib/docker/containers
          readOnly: true
      terminationGracePeriodSeconds: 30
      volumes:
      - name: varlog
        hostPath:
          path: /var/log
      - name: varlibdockercontainers
        hostPath:
          path: /var/lib/docker/containers
```

In the preceding DaemonSet configuration, we created a DaemonSet that will deploy the Fluentd container on each node. We have also created a *toleration*, which does not schedule the Fluentd node on the master (control plan) nodes.

Kubernetes offers scheduling features called *taints* and *tolerations*:

- Taints in Kubernetes allow a node to repel a set of Pods (i.e., if you want certain nodes not to schedule some type of Pod).

- Tolerations are applied to Pods, and allow (but do not require) the Pods to schedule onto nodes with matching taints.

Taints and tolerations work together to ensure that Pods are not scheduled onto inappropriate nodes. One or more taints are applied to a node; this indicates that the node should not accept any Pods that do not tolerate the taints.

You can check the Pods that were created automatically for each worker node as follows:

```
$ kubectl apply -f fluentd.yaml
daemonset.apps/fluentd-elasticsearch created
```

```
$ kubectl get ds --all-namespaces
NAMESPACE       NAME                    DESIRED   CURRENT   READY   UP-TO-DATE   AVAILABLE
kube-system     fluentd-elasticsearch   3         3         3       3            3
NODE SELECTOR   AGE
<none>     5m12s
```

```
$ kubectl get pods --namespace=kube-system -o wide
NAME                          READY   STATUS    RESTARTS   AGE   IP            NODE
fluentd-elasticsearch-5jxg7   1/1     Running   1          45m   10.200.1.53   worker1
fluentd-elasticsearch-c5s4c   1/1     Running   1          45m   10.200.2.32   worker2
fluentd-elasticsearch-r4pqz   1/1     Running   1          45m   10.200.0.43   worker0
NOMINATED NODE    READINESS GATES
<none>            <none>
<none>            <none>
<none>            <none>
```

## Jobs

Sometimes we need to run a small script until it can successfully terminate. Kubernetes allows you to do this with the Job object. The Job object creates and manages Pods that will run until successful completion, and unlike regular Pods, once the given task is completed, these Job-created Pods are not restarted. You can use a Job YAML to describe a simple Job as follows:

```
apiVersion: batch/v1
kind: Job
metadata:
  name: examplejob
spec:
  template:
    metadata:
      name: examplejob
    spec:
        containers:
        - name: examplejob
```

```
      image: busybox
      command: ["echo", "Cloud Native with Azure"]
    restartPolicy: Never
```

Here we created a Job to print a shell command. To create a Job, you can save the preceding YAML and apply it using kubectl apply. Once you apply the job manifest, Kubernetes will create the job and immediately run it. You can check the status of the job using kubectl describe as follows:

```
$ kubectl apply -f job.yaml
job.batch/examplejob created
$ kubectl get jobs
NAME          COMPLETIONS   DURATION   AGE
examplejob    1/1           3s         9s
$ kubectl describe job examplejob
Name:          examplejob
Namespace:     default
Selector:      controller-uid=f6887706-85ef-4752-8911-79cc7ab33886
Labels:        controller-uid=f6887706-85ef-4752-8911-79cc7ab33886
               job-name=examplejob
Annotations:   kubectl.kubernetes.io/last-applied-configuration:
                 {"apiVersion":"batch/v1","kind":"Job","metadata":
                 {"annotations":{},"name":"examplejob","namespace":"default"},
                 "spec":{"template":{"metadat...
Parallelism:   1
Completions:   1
Start Time:    Mon, 07 Sep 2020 01:08:53 +0530
Completed At:  Mon, 07 Sep 2020 01:08:56 +0530
Duration:      3s
Pods Statuses: 0 Running / 1 Succeeded / 0 Failed
Pod Template:
  Labels:  controller-uid=f6887706-85ef-4752-8911-79cc7ab33886
           job-name=examplejob
  Containers:
   examplejob:
    Image:      busybox
    Port:       <none>
    Host Port:  <none>
    Command:
      echo
      Cloud Native with Azure
    Environment:  <none>
    Mounts:       <none>
  Volumes:        <none>
Events:
  Type    Reason          Age   From            Message
  ----    ------          ----  ----            -------
  Normal  SuccessfulCreate 61s  job-controller  Created pod: examplejob-mcqzc
  Normal  Completed        58s  job-controller  Job completed
```

# Summary

Kubernetes is a powerful platform that was built from a decade of experience gained by containerizing applications at scale at Google. Kubernetes basically led to the inception of the Cloud Native Computing Foundation and was the first project to graduate under it. This led to a whole lot of streamlining of the microservices ecosystem in respect to support for and higher adoption of a cloud native environment. In this chapter, we looked at the various components and concepts that allow Kubernetes to operate at scale. This chapter also sets the stage for upcoming chapters in which we will utilize the Kubernetes platform to serve production-grade cloud native applications.

Given the underlying complexity of managing a Kubernetes cluster, in Chapter 5 we will look at how to create and use such a cluster. We will also look at the Azure Kubernetes Service, and more.

# Creating a Kubernetes Cluster in Azure

Now that you understand the basics of how a Kubernetes cluster works under the hood, it's time to put that knowledge to the test and actually build and use a Kubernetes cluster. Several tools are available for creating and running a Kubernetes cluster in a production environment with high availability. Some of the more common tools are kops, kubeadm, Kubespray, and Rancher. These tools have prewritten playbooks on building a cluster that can be run in a production environment seamlessly with a combination of technologies.

We will not use a prebuilt tool in this chapter. Instead, we will take a more hands-on approach to building a cluster that you can use in a production environment.

## Creating a Kubernetes Cluster from Scratch

In this section, we will build a Kubernetes cluster from scratch using Ansible, Terraform, and Packer. We will show you how to manually build the cluster to give you a better understanding of the cluster's various components. While this is not the preferred way to build or run a production-grade Kubernetes cluster, it will provide you with good foundational knowledge.

To get started, you'll need to clone the GitHub for this book (*https://bit.ly/3kccjZZ*) and open the Chapter5 folder. This chapter assumes you have already set up your Azure account by following the steps in Chapter 2, and that you have experimented with creating the infrastructure using the Terraform, Packer, and Ansible playbooks.

We arranged the code in the Chapter5 Git repository as follows:

```
$  Chapter5 git:(master)
.
├── AKS              - Azure Kubernetes Service Cluster
├── Ansible-Playbooks - Ansible playbooks for creating k8s cluster
├── Deployments
```

```
├── K8S_Packer_Image  - Machine images for worker and controller
├── Kubernetes_Cluster- Terraform initialization directory for k8s
├── README.md
└── terraform_modules - Terraform modules for k8s cluster
```

In this section, we will only use K8S_Packer_Image, Ansible-Playbooks, Kuber
netes_Cluster, and terraform_modules.

## Creating the Resource Group

The first step is to create a resource group for all the infrastructure components
so that we can group them together. To do this, go to the *Chapter5/Kubernetes_Clus-
ter/A-Resource_Group* directory and execute the following command:

```
$ terraform init
```

After initializing, run the following to create a resource group:

```
$terraform apply

An execution plan has been generated and is shown below.
Resource actions are indicated with the following symbols:
  + create

Terraform will perform the following actions:

  # module.CNA-Terraform-Resource-Grp.azurerm_resource_group.generic-resource-gp
  # will be created
  + resource "azurerm_resource_group" "generic-resource-gp" {
      + id       = (known after apply)
      + location = "eastus2"
      + name     = "K8Scluster"
      + tags     = {
          + "cluster"     = "k8s-experments"
          + "environment" = "dev"
        }
    }

Plan: 1 to add, 0 to change, 0 to destroy.

Do you want to perform these actions?
  Terraform will perform the actions described above.
  Only 'yes' will be accepted to approve.

  Enter a value: yes
```

To continue, enter yes. This will create a resource group named K8Scluster in the
eastus2 region of Azure.

## Creating the Machine Images for the Worker and Controller Machines

The second step is to create the Packer images of the controller and worker instance
images. In the *Chapter5/K8S_Packer_Image* directory, update both *controller.json* and
*worker.json* with the Azure credentials for client_id, client_secret, tenant_id,
and subscription_id. Now run the packer commands as follows:

---

```
$ packer build worker.json
==> Builds finished. The artifacts of successful builds are:
--> azure-arm: Azure.ResourceManagement.VMImage:

OSType: Linux
ManagedImageResourceGroupName: K8Scluster
ManagedImageName: k8s_worker
ManagedImageId: /subscriptions/b5624140-9087-4311-a94a-3b16a2e84792/resourceGroups/ \
K8Scluster/providers/Microsoft.Compute/images/k8s_worker
ManagedImageLocation: eastus2


$ packer build controller.json
==> Builds finished. The artifacts of successful builds are:
--> azure-arm: Azure.ResourceManagement.VMImage:

OSType: Linux
ManagedImageResourceGroupName: K8Scluster
ManagedImageName: k8s_controller
ManagedImageId: /subscriptions/b5624140-9087-4311-a04b-3b16a2e84792/resourceGroups/ \
K8Scluster/providers/Microsoft.Compute/images/k8s_controller
ManagedImageLocation: eastus2
```

Note the `ManagedImageId`, which we will be using later in the chapter.

## Creating a Storage Account Backend

Next, we will create the storage account to store all the infrastructure mapping to be used by Terraform. Again, we will first initialize the repo with `terraform init` in *Kubernetes_Cluster/B-Storage_Account_backend* and then apply the command as follows:

```
$ terraform apply
.

.

Apply complete! Resources: 3 added, 0 changed, 0 destroyed.

Outputs:

Blob-ID = https://cnabookprod.blob.core.windows.net/k8s-cluster-dev/test
Blob-URL = https://cnabookprod.blob.core.windows.net/k8s-cluster-dev/test
Primary-Access-Key = ymMDE1pUQgtuxh1AOJyUvlvfXnmjAeJEHl2XvMmQ38AZp108Z0Xk4Hrw4N/ \
  d8yovb8FQ5VzqtREH94gzPCzAWCA==
```

This will create a storage account with the name cnabookprod. Update your `bash_pro` `file` with a Primary-Access-Key value using the variable name ARM_ACCESS_KEY:

```
export ARM_ACCESS_KEY=ymMDE1pUQgtuxh1AOJyUvlvfXnmjAeJEHl2XvMmQ38AZp108Z0Xk4Hrw4N/ \
  d8yovb8FQ5VzqtREH94gzPCzAWCA==
```

## Creating an Azure Virtual Network

The next step is to create the virtual network where we will be hosting our Kubernetes cluster. Go to the *Chapter5/Kubernetes_Cluster/C-Virtual_Network* directory and again initialize Terraform using `terraform init`. Once initialized, apply the following configuration to create an Azure virtual network:

```
$ terraform apply
.
.
.
Apply complete! Resources: 6 added, 0 changed, 0 destroyed.
Releasing state lock. This may take a few moments...
Outputs:

subnet_id = /subscriptions/b5624140-9087-4311-a04b-3b16a2e84792/resourceGroups/ \
    K8Scluster/providers/Microsoft.Network/virtualNetworks/cna-k8s-vnet/subnets/cna-k8s-subnet
vnet_id = /subscriptions/b5624140-9087-4311-a04b-3b16a2e84792/resourceGroups/ \
    K8Scluster/providers/Microsoft.Network/virtualNetworks/cna-k8s-vnet
```

This will create a virtual network with a CIDR of 10.240.0.0/24 that is named `cna-k8s-vnet`.

## Creating Public IPs for the Load Balancer

Now we'll create public IPs for the load balancer along with all the worker and control plane nodes. Once we have created the public IPs for all the resources, we will create the load balancer for the control plane nodes to expose the API server to remote clients.

To create the public IPs, go to the *Chapter5/Kubernetes_Cluster/D-K8S_PublicIP* directory and initialize Terraform using `terraform init`. The code will be organized as follows:

```
module "K8S-API-Server-Public-IP" {
  source = "../../terraform_modules/Azure_PublicIP"
  name_of_ip = "k8s_master_lb"
  resource-grp-name = "K8Scluster"
  azure-dc = "eastus2"
  env = "dev"
  type-of-cluster = "k8s-experments"
}

module "Worker0" {
  source = "../../terraform_modules/Azure_PublicIP"
  name_of_ip = "Worker0"
  resource-grp-name = "K8Scluster"
  azure-dc = "eastus2"
  env = "dev"
  type-of-cluster = "k8s-experments"
}
module "Worker1" {
  source = "../../terraform_modules/Azure_PublicIP"
  name_of_ip = "Worker1"
```

```
      resource-grp-name = "K8Scluster"
      azure-dc = "eastus2"
      env = "dev"
      type-of-cluster = "k8s-experments"
    }
    module "Worker2" {
      source = "../../terraform_modules/Azure_PublicIP"
      name_of_ip = "Worker2"
      resource-grp-name = "K8Scluster"
      azure-dc = "eastus2"
      env = "dev"
      type-of-cluster = "k8s-experments"
    }


    module "Controller0" {
      source = "../../terraform_modules/Azure_PublicIP"
      name_of_ip = "Controller0"
      resource-grp-name = "K8Scluster"
      azure-dc = "eastus2"
      env = "dev"
      type-of-cluster = "k8s-experments"
    }
    module "Controller1" {
      source = "../../terraform_modules/Azure_PublicIP"
      name_of_ip = "Controller1"
      resource-grp-name = "K8Scluster"
      azure-dc = "eastus2"
      env = "dev"
      type-of-cluster = "k8s-experments"
    }
    module "Controller2" {
      source = "../../terraform_modules/Azure_PublicIP"
      name_of_ip = "Controller2"
      resource-grp-name = "K8Scluster"
      azure-dc = "eastus2"
      env = "dev"
      type-of-cluster = "k8s-experments"
    }
```

Once Terraform is initialized, you can apply the configuration using `terraform apply` as follows, which will create the public IPs:

```
$ terraform apply
.
.
Apply complete! Resources: 7 added, 0 changed, 0 destroyed.
Releasing state lock. This may take a few moments...
Outputs:
Controller0_IP = 52.252.6.89
Controller0_IP_ID = /subscriptions/b5624140-9087-4311-a04b-3b16a2e84792/resourceGroups/ \
  K8Scluster/providers/Microsoft.Network/publicIPAddresses/Controller0
Controller1_IP = 52.254.50.7
Controller1_IP_ID = /subscriptions/b5624140-9087-4311-a04b-3b16a2e84792/resourceGroups/ \
  K8Scluster/providers/Microsoft.Network/publicIPAddresses/Controller1
Controller2_IP = 52.251.58.212
Controller2_IP_ID = /subscriptions/b5624140-9087-4311-a04b-3b16a2e84792/resourceGroups/ \
  K8Scluster/providers/Microsoft.Network/publicIPAddresses/Controller2
PublicIP_ID = /subscriptions/b5624140-9087-4311-a04b-3b16a2e84792/resourceGroups/ \
```

```
            K8Scluster/providers/Microsoft.Network/publicIPAddresses/k8s_master_lb
Public_IP = 52.254.73.23
Worker0_IP = 52.251.59.169
Worker0_IP_ID = /subscriptions/b5624140-9087-4311-a04b-3b16a2e84792/resourceGroups/ \
            K8Scluster/providers/Microsoft.Network/publicIPAddresses/Worker0
Worker1_IP = 52.251.59.78
Worker1_IP_ID = /subscriptions/b5624140-9087-4311-a04b-3b16a2e84792/resourceGroups/ \
            K8Scluster/providers/Microsoft.Network/publicIPAddresses/Worker1
Worker2_IP = 52.254.50.15
Worker2_IP_ID = /subscriptions/b5624140-9087-4311-a04b-3b16a2e84792/resourceGroups/ \
            K8Scluster/providers/Microsoft.Network/publicIPAddresses/Worker2
```

The preceding code will create seven public IPs: six for the node instances (worker and controller) and one for the load balancer. Now we can create the load balancer and attach the load balancer IP to it by going to the *Chapter5/Kubernetes_Cluster/E-K8S-API-Public-loadbalancer* directory and initializing Terraform. Then we can again use `terraform apply` as follows:

```
$ terraform apply
.
.
.
Apply complete! Resources: 4 added, 0 changed, 0 destroyed.
Releasing state lock. This may take a few moments...

Outputs:

lb_backend_pool = /subscriptions/b5624140-9087-4311-a04b-3b16a2e84792/resourceGroups/ \
    K8Scluster/providers/Microsoft.Network/loadBalancers/k8s_master_lb/backendAddressPools/ \
    k8s-control-plane
load_balancer_frontend_id = /subscriptions/b5624140-9087-4311-a04b-3b16a2e84792/ \
    resourceGroups/K8Scluster/providers/Microsoft.Network/loadBalancers/k8s_master_lb/ \
    frontendIPConfigurations/K8S-frontend-config
load_balancer_id = /subscriptions/b5624140-9087-4311-a04b-3b16a2e84792/resourceGroups/ \
    K8Scluster/providers/Microsoft.Network/loadBalancers/k8s_master_lb
load_balancer_private_ip =
load_balancer_public_ip = /subscriptions/b5624140-9087-4311-a04b-3b16a2e84792/ \
    resourceGroups/K8Scluster/providers/Microsoft.Network/publicIPAddresses/k8s_master_lb
```

This step will create a load balancer and apply the load balancer rules that we predefined in the Terraform config file.

## Creating Worker and Controller Instances

At this point, we're ready to create the instance nodes that will constitute our Kubernetes cluster. We will be creating a six-node cluster in which three nodes will be worker nodes that will run the actual workload (Pods, etc.) and three will be part of the control plane.

Before we do this, we need to update the *main.tf* file in the */Chapter5/Kubernetes_Cluster/F-K8S-Nodes/main.tf* directory with the image ID for the worker node and controller node. Also, we need to update the path for the location of the Secure Shell (SSH) key that will be used to `ssh` onto the machines:

```
module "master" {
  source = "../../terraform_modules/Azure_VMs-Master"
  azure-dc = "eastus2"
  resource-grp-name = "K8Scluster"
  private_ip_addresses = ["10.240.0.10", "10.240.0.11", "10.240.0.12"]
  vm_prefix = "controller"
  username = "ubuntu"
  public_ip_address_id = [data.terraform_remote_state.k8s_public_ip.outputs. \
    Controller0_IP_ID,data.terraform_remote_state.k8s_public_ip.outputs. \
    Controller1_IP_ID,data.terraform_remote_state.k8s_public_ip.outputs.Controller2_IP_ID]
  vm_size = "Standard_D1_v2"
  env = "dev"
  type-of-cluster = "k8s-experments"
  vm_count = 3
  subnet_id = data.terraform_remote_state.k8s_vnet.outputs.subnet_id
  image_id = "/subscriptions/b5624140-9087-4311-a04b-3b16a2e84792/ \
  resourceGroups/K8Scluster/providers/Microsoft.Compute/images/k8s_controller"
  ssh_key = "${file("/Users/nissingh/TESTING/SSH_KEYS/id_rsa.pub")}"
  lb_backend_pool = data.terraform_remote_state.k8s_loadbalancer.outputs.lb_backend_pool
}
```

In the preceding configuration (*main.tf*), the image ID was updated for the controller (master) node along with the path to the SSH key. Now you can generate an SSH key pair using the ssh-keygen command for ssh_key. Similarly, you can update the worker config file and then initialize Terraform as before. Once the initialization is done, you can use terraform apply to create the worker and controller instances:

```
$ terraform apply
 .
 .
 .

Apply complete! Resources: 17 added, 0 changed, 0 destroyed.
Releasing state lock. This may take a few moments...

Outputs:

master_machine_id = [
  [
    "/subscriptions/b5624140-9087-4311-a04b-3b16a2e84792/resourceGroups/K8Scluster/ \
      providers/Microsoft.Compute/virtualMachines/controller0",
    "/subscriptions/b5624140-9087-4311-a04b-3b16a2e84792/resourceGroups/K8Scluster/ \
      providers/Microsoft.Compute/virtualMachines/controller1",
    "/subscriptions/b5624140-9087-4311-a04b-3b16a2e84792/resourceGroups/K8Scluster/ \
      providers/Microsoft.Compute/virtualMachines/controller2",
  ],
]
master_machine_name = [
  [
    "controller0",
    "controller1",
    "controller2",
  ],
]
master_machine_private_ips = [
  [
    "10.240.0.10",
    "10.240.0.11",
```

```
      "10.240.0.12",
    ],
  ]
  worker_machine_id = [
    [
      "/subscriptions/b5624140-9087-4311-a04b-3b16a2e84792/resourceGroups/K8Scluster/ \
        providers/Microsoft.Compute/virtualMachines/worker0",
      "/subscriptions/b5624140-9087-4311-a04b-3b16a2e84792/resourceGroups/K8Scluster/ \
        providers/Microsoft.Compute/virtualMachines/worker1",
      "/subscriptions/b5624140-9087-4311-a04b-3b16a2e84792/resourceGroups/K8Scluster/ \
        providers/Microsoft.Compute/virtualMachines/worker2",
    ],
  ]
  worker_machine_name = [
    [
      "worker0",
      "worker1",
      "worker2",
    ],
  ]
  worker_machine_private_ips = [
    [
      "10.240.0.20",
      "10.240.0.21",
      "10.240.0.22",
    ],
  ]
```

Once the `terraform apply` is complete, you will see that the nodes have been provisioned for your Kubernetes cluster (see Figure 5-1).

*Figure 5-1. Worker and controller nodes up and running*

## Using Ansible to Deploy and Configure the Kubernetes Controller Nodes

With the infrastructure running, it's time to configure the cluster, since currently we just have the bare skeleton prepared. To deploy and configure Kubernetes to work on the node, we will use Ansible playbooks.

First, update the *hosts* file in *Chapter5/Ansible-Playbooks/hosts* with the IP addresses of the worker and controller instances, along with the SSH username and the path of the SSH private key that was generated with `ssh-keygen`:

```
[controllers]
inventory_hostname=controller0 ansible_host=52.252.6.89
inventory_hostname=controller1 ansible_host=52.254.50.7
inventory_hostname=controller2 ansible_host=52.251.58.212

[workers]
inventory_hostname=worker0 ansible_host=52.251.59.169
inventory_hostname=worker1 ansible_host=52.251.59.78
inventory_hostname=worker2 ansible_host=52.254.50.15

[all:vars]
ansible_user = ubuntu
ansible_ssh_private_key_file = /Users/SSH_KEYS/id_rsa
```

Once the *hosts* file is updated, we need to update the `groupvars` (located in the *all* file in the *Chapter5/Ansible-Playbooks/group_vars* directory) with the `loadbalancer_pub lic_ip` and the encryption key. Since Kubernetes stores a variety of data, including cluster state, application configurations, and secrets, we need to encrypt this data at rest. Kubernetes supports the ability to encrypt cluster data at rest.

To create an encryption key, you can simply issue the following command on your terminal and paste the generated secret in the *group_vars/all* file as follows:

```
$ head -c 32 /dev/urandom | base64
Uvivn+4ONy9yqRf0ynRVOpsEE7WsfyvYnM7VNakiNeA=
```

You will also need to update the load balancer IP. The final `group_vars` should look like this:

```
---
#Change loadbalancer_public_ip
loadbalancer_public_ip : 52.254.73.23
controller_private_ips_list : 10.240.0.10,10.240.0.11,10.240.0.12
# Keep k8s_internal_virtual_ip as it is
k8s_internal_virtual_ip: 10.32.0.1
k8s_cluster_cidr: "10.200.0.0/16"
k8s_cluster_name: "cloud-native-azure"
# Generate your own encryption_key : "head -c 32 /dev/urandom | base64"
encryption_key: Uvivn+4ONy9yqRf0ynRVOpsEE7WsfyvYnM7VNakiNeA=
#ETC config below for systemd file, place private ip's. No need to change
controller_0_ip: 10.240.0.10
controller_1_ip: 10.240.0.11
controller_2_ip: 10.240.0.12
```

Once we are done updating the files, we need to install the client-side tools on the local system; mainly `kubectl`, `cfssl`, and `cfssljson`. CFSSL is Cloudflare's public key infrastructure/Transport Layer Security (PKI/TLS) toolkit for signing, verifying, and bundling the TLS certificates in general. We will be using this toolkit to generate the TLS certificate for the Kubernetes nodes.

You can install the `cfssl` and `cfssljson` programs on macOS as follows:

```
$ brew install cfssl
```

On Linux, you can do the following:

```
$ wget -q --show-progress --https-only --timestamping \
  https://github.com/cloudflare/cfssl/releases/download/v1.4.1/cfssl_1.4.1_linux_amd64 \
  https://github.com/cloudflare/cfssl/releases/download/v1.4.1/cfssljson_1.4.1_linux_amd64
$ chmod +x cfssl_1.4.1_linux_amd64 cfssljson_1.4.1_linux_amd64
$ sudo mv cfssl_1.4.1_linux_amd64 /usr/local/bin/cfssl
$ sudo mv cfssljson_1.4.1_linux_amd64 /usr/local/bin/cfssljson
```

Run the `cfssl version` command to make sure it installed correctly:

```
$ ~ cfssl version
Version: dev
Runtime: go1.14
```

To install the kubectl binary on OS X, we can do the following:

```
$ curl -LO "https://storage.googleapis.com/kubernetes-release/release/$(curl -s https:// \
  storage.googleapis.com/kubernetes-release/release/stable.txt)/bin/darwin/amd64/kubectl"
$ chmod +x ./kubectl
$ sudo mv ./kubectl /usr/local/bin/kubectl
```

Here is the command for installing on Linux:

```
$ curl -LO https://storage.googleapis.com/kubernetes-release/release/`curl -s https:// \
  storage.googleapis.com/kubernetes-release/release/stable.txt`/bin/linux/amd64/kubectl
$ chmod +x ./kubectl
$ sudo mv ./kubectl /usr/local/bin/kubectl
```

You can verify that the kubectl client is working correctly by running the following:

```
$ kubectl version --client
Client Version: version.Info{Major:"1", Minor:"17", GitVersion:"v1.17.3",
GitCommit:"06ad960bfd03b39c8310aaf92d1e7c12ce618213", GitTreeState:"clean",
BuildDate:"2020-02-11T18:14:22Z", GoVersion:"go1.13.6", Compiler:"gc",
Platform:"darwin/amd64"}
```

Now we are ready to build our controller nodes with Ansible. Move into the Ansible playbook directory (*Chapter5/Ansible-Playbooks*) and run the following command:

```
$ ansible-playbook -vi hosts controllers.yaml
```

This will take some time to run; upon completion, you should see the following output:

```
PLAY RECAP *******************************************************************************
inventory_hostname=controller0 : ok=43    changed=39   unreachable=0    failed=0    skipped=4
   rescued=0    ignored=0
inventory_hostname=controller1 : ok=22    changed=19   unreachable=0    failed=0    skipped=7
   rescued=0    ignored=0
inventory_hostname=controller2 : ok=22    changed=19   unreachable=0    failed=0    skipped=7
   rescued=0    ignored=0
```

This completes the setup of controller nodes. Essentially, with the *controllers.yaml* playbook we have bootstrapped the etcds and controller nodes. The Ansible playbook contains step-by-step instructions, which are self-explanatory, for bootstrapping the controller nodes for the cluster. We highly recommend that you follow the plays in the playbook for the execution path to understand the nitty-gritty details.

## Using Ansible to Deploy and Configure the Kubernetes Worker Nodes

Now that the controller nodes have been deployed, we can deploy the worker nodes using the *workers.yaml* file:

```
$ ansible-playbook -vi hosts workers.yaml
.
.
.

PLAY RECAP ***********************************************************************
inventory_hostname=worker0 : ok=31   changed=29   unreachable=0   failed=0   skipped=20
   rescued=0   ignored=0
inventory_hostname=worker1 : ok=23   changed=21   unreachable=0   failed=0   skipped=23
   rescued=0   ignored=0
inventory_hostname=worker2 : ok=23   changed=21   unreachable=0   failed=0   skipped=23
   rescued=0   ignored=0
```

This will deploy and configure the worker nodes with the necessary Kubernetes binaries.

## Setting Up Pod Networking and Routing

We still need to set up the Pod networking and routing for our cluster. To do this, we first need to set up the networking between the Pods by moving into the *Chapter5/Kubernetes_Cluster/G-K8S-PodsNetwork* directory and running `terraform init`:

```
$ terraform init
```

Once we have initialized Terraform in the directory, we can run `terraform apply`:

```
$ terraform apply
.
.
Apply complete! Resources: 2 added, 0 changed, 0 destroyed.

Outputs:

route_table_id = /subscriptions/b5624140-9087-4311-a04b-3b16a2e84792/resourceGroups/ \
   K8Scluster/providers/Microsoft.Network/routeTables/k8s-pod-router
```

This sets up the Pod route table in Azure. Now we can finally create the routes by moving into the final directory, *Chapter5/Kubernetes_Cluster/H-k8S_Route-creation*, and initializing Terraform as before. Once initialized, we can run `terraform apply`:

```
$ terraform apply
.
.
.
Plan: 3 to add, 0 to change, 0 to destroy.

Do you want to perform these actions?
  Terraform will perform the actions described above.
  Only 'yes' will be accepted to approve.

  Enter a value: yes

module.route0.azurerm_route.generic-routes: Creating...
module.route1.azurerm_route.generic-routes: Creating...
module.route0.azurerm_route.generic-routes: Creation complete after 4s [id=/subscriptions/
b5624140-9087-4311-a04b-3b16a2e84792/resourceGroups/K8Scluster/providers/Microsoft.Network/
routeTables/k8s-pod-router/routes/k8s-pod-router0]
module.route2.azurerm_route.generic-routes: Creating...
module.route1.azurerm_route.generic-routes: Creation complete after 5s [id=/subscriptions/
b5624140-9087-4311-a04b-3b16a2e84792/resourceGroups/K8Scluster/providers/Microsoft.Network/
routeTables/k8s-pod-router/routes/k8s-pod-router1]
module.route2.azurerm_route.generic-routes: Creation complete after 4s [id=/subscriptions/
b5624140-9087-4311-a04b-3b16a2e84792/resourceGroups/K8Scluster/providers/Microsoft.Network/
routeTables/k8s-pod-router/routes/k8s-pod-router2]

Apply complete! Resources: 3 added, 0 changed, 0 destroyed.
```

This completes the setup of our networking for the Kubernetes cluster.

## Generating the kubeconfig File for Remote Access and Cluster Validation

Lastly, we need to download the kubeconfig file for the cluster we just created and test whether the cluster setup was successful. Go back to the Ansible directory, *Chapter5/ Ansible-Playbooks*, and execute the following:

```
$ ansible-playbook -vi hosts remote_access_k8s.yaml
.
.
.

PLAY RECAP ***********************************************************************************
inventory_hostname=controller0 : ok=6    changed=5    unreachable=0    failed=0    skipped=0
   rescued=0    ignored=0
inventory_hostname=controller1 : ok=1    changed=0    unreachable=0    failed=0    skipped=0
   rescued=0    ignored=0
inventory_hostname=controller2 : ok=1    changed=0    unreachable=0    failed=0    skipped=0
   rescued=0    ignored=0
```

This will download the kubeconfig file and store it locally so that you can access and interact with the cluster. Check whether you can do this by issuing kubectl get nodes from your local machine as follows:

```
$ kubectl get nodes
NAME     STATUS   ROLES    AGE   VERSION
worker0  Ready    <none>   27m   v1.17.3
```

```
worker1    Ready    <none>    27m    v1.17.3
worker2    Ready    <none>    27m    v1.17.3
```

The output will list the worker nodes of your cluster. You can now use this cluster to experiment and explore the features we covered in this chapter. Of course, this is not a production-ready cluster, but it does give you an understanding of how to build, run, and maintain a Kubernetes cluster from scratch.

Now that you know how to do this the hard (semiautomated) way, let's take a look at the preferred, effortless way to run a production Kubernetes cluster in Azure.

# Azure Kubernetes Service

As you've seen, the process of managing and maintaining a Kubernetes cluster is complex. From an operational perspective, it's not just about running a cluster; it's about security, performance, logging, upgrading the cluster, applying patches, and so on. To reduce this toil, Azure offers a managed solution called *Azure Kubernetes Service* or *AKS*.

AKS makes the process of deploying and managing a Kubernetes cluster in Azure a cakewalk. An Azure-managed Kubernetes solution eliminates a big chunk of the Kubernetes management process, and all you are left with is your application to manage. AKS offers several advantages, including the following:

- Health monitoring of clusters is fully managed by Azure.
- Maintenance tasks of the underlying nodes are the responsibility of Azure.
- The control plane is managed and maintained by Azure, and you as a user only have to manage the agent nodes.
- AKS lets you integrate with Azure Active Directory and the Kubernetes RBAC API for security and access control.
- All logs for your application and cluster are stored in the Azure Log Analytics workspace.
- The Horizontal Pod Autoscaler (HPA) and Cluster Autoscaler are seamless to use in respect to setting up a Kubernetes cluster from scratch and taking care of underlying resource permissions.
- AKS offers seamless support for the storage volume.

Now that you understand the advantages of AKS, let's create an AKS cluster. There are two simple ways to do this: use the Azure portal (the manual approach) or use Terraform (the automated approach).

You can navigate through the Azure console and start deploying your AKS cluster by clicking the Add button (Figure 5-2) and then following the instructions as they appear.

*Figure 5-2. Clicking the Add button to create an AKS cluster*

Alternatively, in Terraform you can go to the AKS directory of the repo */cloud_native_azure/Chapter5/AKS* and execute the following command:

```
$ terraform apply
```

Click Apply, and in a few minutes you should have a Kubernetes cluster of three nodes up and running (Figure 5-3).

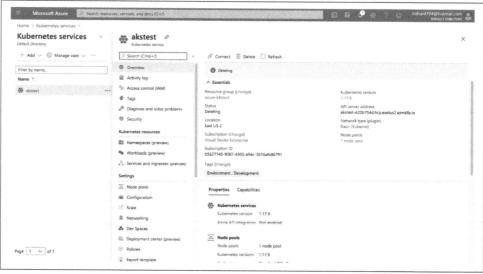

*Figure 5-3. AKS cluster created via Terraform*

To download the kubeconfig file, you can use the Azure CLI command from your local system to get access credentials for your managed Kubernetes cluster as follows:

```
az aks get-credentials --resource-group azure-k8stest  --name akstest --file config
```

Your kubeconfig will be downloaded with the name *config*; move it to the *.kube* folder. Now you can use this cluster just as you would use the cluster you created the hard way:

```
$  ~ kubectl get nodes
NAME                                STATUS   ROLES   AGE   VERSION
aks-agentpool-42554519-vmss000000   Ready    agent   29m   v1.17.9
aks-agentpool-42554519-vmss000001   Ready    agent   29m   v1.17.9
aks-agentpool-42554519-vmss000002   Ready    agent   29m   v1.17.9
```

While you can pretty much create any resource and deploy applications at this point, obviously this is not a production-grade cluster. There are plenty of resources online[1] that can guide you in creating production-grade clusters.

With this knowledge, we're ready to move on and learn about Helm, which serves primarily as a tool to streamline the installation and management of Kubernetes applications.

# Deploying Applications and Services Using Helm: A Package Manager for Kubernetes

It's likely quite clear to you by now that when it comes to Kubernetes, there are too many things to take care of. Even though you can make use of a managed service like Microsoft AKS, it's difficult to maintain Deployments and ReplicaSets as your requirements expand.

Helm is a package manager for Kubernetes that allows you to fetch, deploy, and manage applications. Basically, Helm takes care of the pain of maintaining long YAML files, which hold information on Pods, ReplicaSets, Services, RBAC settings, and so forth. Helm also offers rollbacks, release history information, and integrated testing hooks, which makes it super easy to manage the full lifecycle of your applications on a Kubernetes cluster.

In this book, we are using the stable version of Helm, v3.3.1. Older versions (i.e., v2) used to have a server-side component called the *Tiller*, which needed to be deployed on the Kubernetes cluster. Tiller possessed a potential security risk due to wider user privileges and management overhead, which initially caused less traction of Helm in the user community. With the introduction of the RBAC API, Helm now contains only client-side binaries and Tiller has been completely removed. Figure 5-4 depicts the basic workings of the Helm package manager.

---

1 See *https://kubernetes.io/docs/setup/production-environment*, *https://kubernetes.io/docs/setup/production-environment/tools*, and *https://github.com/kubernetes/kops*.

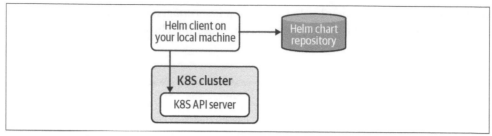

*Figure 5-4. Helm chart repository and client interaction*

## Helm Basics

The Helm client is installed as a command-line utility for the end user. The client's main responsibility is to assist in chart development and manage repositories and releases. Helm consists of the following components:

*Chart*
Charts are the Kubernetes packages that Helm manages. Charts consist of all the information required to create an application in Kubernetes, including the resource definitions required to run an application or service in a Kubernetes cluster.

*Repository*
This is the database where all the Helm charts are stored.

*Config*
This is the configuration that can be merged into a packaged chart to create a releasable object.

*Release*
Releases are a way of tracking all applications that Helm installs on the Kubernetes cluster. A single chart can be installed multiple times, and each new installation creates a new release.

## Installing and Managing Helm

You can download the latest version of the Helm client for your machine from its official repositories at *https://github.com/helm/helm/releases*.

After installing Helm, we need to add a chart repository from where the packages can be downloaded. Google offers the Kubernetes charts repository, and it can be added as follows:

```
$helm repo add stable https://kubernetes-charts.storage.googleapis.com/
```

From a rather simple perspective, Helm pulls charts or packages from a central repository and then installs/releases them on the Kubernetes cluster.

## Searching Helm repositories

You can search Helm repositories using the `helm search` command in two different ways. The first way is to search the repository that you added locally (as in the previous step, when we added a `stable` repo):

```
$ helm search repo stable
NAME                          CHART VERSION    APP VERSION
    DESCRIPTION
stable/acs-engine-autoscaler  2.2.2            2.1.1
    DEPRECATED Scales worker nodes within agent pools
stable/aerospike              0.3.3            v4.5.0.5
    A Helm chart for Aerospike in Kubernetes
stable/airflow                7.6.0            1.10.10
    Airflow is a platform to programmatically autho...
stable/ambassador             5.3.2            0.86.1         DEPRECATED A Helm chart for...
stable/anchore-engine         1.6.9            0.7.2          Anchore container analysis...
stable/apm-server             2.1.5            7.0.0          The server receives data...
stable/ark                    4.2.2            0.10.2         DEPRECATED A Helm...
.
.
.
```

This search is performed on the local data on your machine.

The other way to search Helm repositories is by searching the Helm Hub. The Helm Hub consists of multiple available public repositories, so if you do not find a chart in your local repository, you can always look for it in the Hub. In the following, we searched for all the "kafka" charts:

```
$  ~ helm search hub kafka
URL                                                CHART VERSION APP VERSION
    DESCRIPTION
https://hub.helm.sh/charts/kafkaesque/imagepuller  1.0.0         1.0
    Pull container images to your nodes so that the...
https://hub.helm.sh/charts/kafkaesque/pulsar       1.0.26        1.0
    Apache Pulsar Helm chart for Kubernetes
https://hub.helm.sh/charts/kafkaesque/pulsar-mo... 0.1.5         1.0
    A Helm chart for the Pulsar Monitor application
https://hub.helm.sh/charts/kafkaesque/teleport     1.0.0
    Teleport Community
https://hub.helm.sh/charts/bitnami/kafka           11.8.4        2.6.0
    Apache Kafka is a distributed streaming platform.
https://hub.helm.sh/charts/stable/kafka-manager    2.3.1         1.3.3.22
    A tool for managing Apache Kafka.
https://hub.helm.sh/charts/touk/hermes             0.3.1         1.5.2
    A Helm chart for Kubernetes of Hermes, a reliab...
```

## Installing a Helm chart on Kubernetes

To install a chart, you can run the `helm install` command as follows:

```
$  ~ helm install my-first-server stable/tomcat
NAME: my-first-server
LAST DEPLOYED: Thu Sep 10 00:04:17 2020
NAMESPACE: default
STATUS: deployed
```

```
REVISION: 1
TEST SUITE: None
NOTES:
1. Get the application URL by running these commands:
     NOTE: It may take a few minutes for the LoadBalancer IP to be available.
          You can watch the status of by running 'kubectl get svc -w my-first-server-tomcat'
   export SERVICE_IP=$(kubectl get svc --namespace default my-first-server-tomcat -o \
     jsonpath='{.status.loadBalancer.ingress[0].hostname}')
   echo http://$SERVICE_IP:
```

Here we tried to deploy a Tomcat server, and the release name we picked is *my-first-server*. Using kubectl, you can check the resources that were created for the Tomcat chart:

```
$ ~ kubectl get svc --namespace default my-first-server-tomcat
NAME                      TYPE           CLUSTER-IP   EXTERNAL-IP   PORT(S)        AGE
my-first-server-tomcat    LoadBalancer   10.32.0.3    <pending>     80:31495/TCP   56s
```

## Changing default chart values

At times you may want to customize a chart before you actually install it. To change a value of a default chart, first you need to view the value using `helm show values`:

```
$ helm show values stable/tomcat
# Default values for the chart.
# This is a YAML-formatted file.
# Declare variables to be passed into your templates.
replicaCount: 1

image:
  webarchive:
    repository: ananwaresystems/webarchive
    tag: "1.0"
  tomcat:
.
.
.
resources: {}
#  limits:
#    cpu: 100m
#    memory: 256Mi
#  requests:
#    cpu: 100m
#    memory: 256Mi

nodeSelector: {}

tolerations: []

affinity: {}
```

To change the value, you can use either the `--values` argument or the `--set` argument. The advantage of using the former is that you can specify a YAML file that you can pass while installing a chart. This overrides the chart values. For example, in the preceding chart, if we want to change the default values, we can create a YAML file as follows and save it as *custom_vals.yaml*:

---

```
limits:
    cpu: 200m
    memory: 256Mi
requests:
    cpu: 100m
    memory: 256Mi
```

To install the changed values, you can do the following:

```
$ helm install --values custom_vals.yaml new-v2-install stable/tomcat
```

In the next section, we'll discuss how to manage releases in Helm.

# Managing Helm Releases

In Helm terminology, a release is an instance of a chart running in a Kubernetes cluster. A chart can be installed many times in the same cluster, and every time it is installed, a new release is created. In this section, we will show how you can manage Helm releases.

### Checking a release

To find the release state, you can use `helm status`, which will give you details such as the revision number and when it was last deployed:

```
$ helm status my-first-server
NAME: my-first-server
LAST DEPLOYED: Thu Sep 10 00:04:17 2020
NAMESPACE: default
STATUS: deployed
REVISION: 1
TEST SUITE: None
NOTES:
1. Get the application URL by running these commands:
     NOTE: It may take a few minutes for the LoadBalancer IP to be available.
           You can watch the status of by running 'kubectl get svc -w my-first-server-tomcat'
   export SERVICE_IP=$(kubectl get svc --namespace default my-first-server-tomcat -o \
     jsonpath='{.status.loadBalancer.ingress[0].hostname}')
   echo http://$SERVICE_IP:
$  ~ helm show values stable/tomcat
# Default values for the chart.
# This is a YAML-formatted file.
# Declare variables to be passed into your templates.
replicaCount: 1
```

### Upgrading a release

You can use `helm upgrade` to upgrade your installed charts when a new version is released or if you have made a configuration change:

```
$ helm upgrade --values new_vals.yaml new-v2-install stable/tomcat
```

This will upgrade the `new-v2-install` with the same chart (*stable/tomcat*), but you can update new values in the *new_vals.yaml* file.

### Rolling back a release

If you need to roll back a deployed chart (release), you can simply use the `helm rollback` option as follows:

```
$  ~ helm rollback my-first-server 1
Rollback was a success! Happy Helming!
$  ~
```

Here we rolled back `my-first-server` to version 1.

### Uninstalling a release

To permanently remove a release from the cluster, you can use `helm uninstall`:

```
$  ~ helm uninstall my-first-server
release "my-first-server" uninstalled
```

## Creating Charts for Your Applications

To create a chart for your application, follow the default packaging format provided by Helm. You can make use of the charts to deploy a simple Pod or a full web application stack containing HTTP servers, databases, and so on. The charts contain a collection of files inside a directory. The structure of the directory is as follows, where the name of the top-level directory (*nginx* in this case) is the name of the chart:

```
~ nginx/
                Chart.yaml
                LICENSE
                README.md
                values.yaml
                values.schema.json
                charts/
                crds/
                templates/
```

In the directory, Helm expects the file to have the same structure and names, since Helm reserves them. Each item in the directory serves a specific purpose:

- *Chart.yaml* contains all the information about the chart in YAML format.
- *LICENSE* is an optional plain-text file that contains the license for the chart.
- *README.md* is a human-readable README file.
- *values.yaml* contains all the default configuration values for the chart.
- *values.schema.json* is an optional JSON schema file that imposes a structure on *values.yaml*.
- *charts/* includes all the dependent charts on which the current chart depends.
- *crds/* contains custom resource definitions.

- *templates/* is the directory that holds templates, which can be combined with values to generate Kubernetes manifest files.

The *Chart.yaml* file is required to create the chart, and it contains the following fields:

```
apiVersion: The chart API version (required)
name: The name of the chart (required)
version: A SemVer 2 version (required)
kubeVersion: A SemVer range of compatible Kubernetes versions (optional)
description: A single-sentence description of this project (optional)
type: The type of the chart (optional)
keywords:
  - A list of keywords about this project (optional)
home: The URL of this projects home page (optional)
sources:
  - A list of URLs to source code for this project (optional)
dependencies: # A list of the chart requirements (optional)
  - name: The name of the chart (nginx)
    version: The version of the chart ("1.2.3")
    repository: The repository URL ("https://example.com/charts") or alias ("@repo-name")
    condition: (optional) A yaml path that resolves to a boolean, used for
      enabling/disabling charts (e.g. subchart1.enabled )
    tags: # (optional)
      - Tags can be used to group charts for enabling/disabling together
    enabled: (optional) Enabled bool determines if chart should be loaded
    import-values: # (optional)
      - ImportValues holds the mapping of source values to the parent key to be imported.
        Each item can be a string or pair of child/parent sublist items.
    alias: (optional) Alias to be used for the chart. Useful when you have to add the same
      chart multiple times
maintainers: # (optional)
  - name: The maintainers name (required for each maintainer)
    email: The maintainers email (optional for each maintainer)
    url: A URL for the maintainer (optional for each maintainer)
icon: A URL to an SVG or PNG image to be used as an icon (optional).
appVersion: The version of the app that this contains (optional). This needn't be SemVer.
deprecated: Whether this chart is deprecated (optional, boolean)
annotations:
  example: A list of annotations keyed by name (optional).
```

## Using Helm to create and manage charts

You can create each file in your chart directory manually, or you can use Helm to create a blueprint for you as follows:

```
$ helm create examplechart
Creating examplechart
```

Then you can edit the files in the chart directory and package them into a chart archive:

```
$ helm package examplechart
Archived examplechart.1.-.tgz
```

Once you have packaged your chart, you can use it with `helm install` to create a release.

---

# Summary

In this chapter, you learned how to create a Kubernetes cluster, both manually from scratch with Azure and by using Azure AKS as a managed service. We also explored Helm, which serves as a Kubernetes package manager that helps you create and manage your applications with a single template.

Before we move on, we want to emphasize that Kubernetes is hard to manage single-handedly (especially in production), and it is definitely not a silver bullet to ease all the pain of managing applications in cloud native environments. Given the underlying complexity of managing a Kubernetes cluster, it is evident that an approach such as AKS is a better way of managing services running on Kubernetes clusters. With AKS, you don't have to worry about the underlying infrastructure or the moving parts of the ecosystem, since most of the critical points, like high availability and redundancy of the Kubernetes cluster, are taken care of.

Having said this, let's now move on to Chapter 6, which deals with building observability into distributed systems and helping your cloud native applications be more reliable.

# Observability: Following the Breadcrumbs

The rapid evolution of cloud native systems has introduced complexities around infrastructure provisioning, infrastructure deployment, and software management. Applications are being architected to be more resilient, and this requires a deeper understanding of the underlying infrastructure of the cloud environment, including failure modes and bottlenecks. Having visibility into the application stack becomes even more critical due to the multitude of new moving parts and design changes in today's applications.

In this chapter, we will introduce the concept of observability and explain why it's necessary in today's cloud native world. You will learn about the three pillars of observability—logs, metrics, and traces—and gain insights on how they work together to create observable systems. We will also look at various well-known cloud native tools that can be used to create an observable system, and demonstrate how observability is a superset of monitoring. Finally, we will show how you can leverage Azure as a cloud platform to gain observability in your applications, underlying infrastructure, and networking stack.

## Introduction to Observability

The first thing to understand about observability is the word itself. The term *observability* originated in the world of control theory in mathematics, which primarily deals with creating a way to control *dynamic systems* using a controller with the help of feedback from the system itself. In control theory, observability is the ability to measure a system's internal state from the knowledge of external outputs. With respect to software engineering, observability means knowing the *exact* state of an application from its outputs. By designing your application and infrastructure to be observable, you will essentially be able to track down *why* a problem is happening and *how* you can fix it. The underlying goal of making a system observable is to enable an engineer to clearly see a problem, from its cause to its effect.

Observability is even more relevant in today's cloud native infrastructure because of the fast-paced, distributed environment where software and systems could eventually fail. The rise of microservices, containers, and serverless computing has resulted in a complicated mesh of interconnected services performing huge numbers of calls to each other. When these intertwined networks of services misbehave, it's nearly impossible to find the root cause of the problem while avoiding disruption to the business. It becomes critical to have a fast way to pinpoint a problem in the underlying environment of complex services such that the business doesn't suffer. Observability tackles this by letting you ask questions about your systems and quickly get answers.

Before we discuss how observability assists in modern distributed environments, let's take a look at what constitutes an observable system, and discuss the principle behind the term and the philosophy behind the idea of building observability into systems.

## Observability: More Than Three Pillars

The fundamental idea behind observability is to gain a better understanding of an application through meaningful insights. As applications become more ephemeral and distributed, it becomes critical to define the guiding principles of an observable system. Cloud practitioners have defined *logs*, *metrics*, and *traces* as three major verticals, or pillars, that are foundational to building a modern observable system. Let's take a quick look at these pillars and see why they are important.

### Metrics

Metrics represent numerical data measured over an interval of time. Metrics are usually collected by running an agent on a host, which periodically sends the data to a central data store and later aggregates the data to be represented over dashboards. Then the metrics are used to build alerting systems, since the metrics are stored in a time series database. An example of a metric is queries per second (qps).

### Logs

Logs represent the events that occur in a system (application and infrastructure). Logs contain details of internal state and events. Generally, they are written and stored on the application system in a structured format that can be parsed easily. A good logging architecture is the most fundamental tool for gaining most of the information in a system and is often the first debugging tool used by software developers. Following is an example of simple Apache server access logs:

```
10.185.248.71 - - [09/Jan/2015:19:12:06 +0000] 808840 "GET /inventoryService/inventory/ \
    purchaseItem?userId=20253471&itemId=23434300 HTTP/1.1" 500 17 "-" \
    "Apache-HttpClient/4.2.6 (java 1.5)"
```

### Traces

Last but not least, traces are the modern solution to the problem of learning how a single event is behaving in a distributed system. Traces help you identify the amount of processing (i.e., latency) being done at each layer of the stack. In the world of microservices and distributed systems, traces provide valuable insights to events by creating a visual of correlated distributed calls between services.

Figure 6-1 showcases simple traces.

*Figure 6-1. A sample application showing traces*

Just because you have built a system to include logs, metrics, and traces doesn't necessarily mean the system is observable, however. All three pillars have their pros and cons, which we will discuss in the rest of the chapter, and individually, they are just the starting point since they enable you to look into a problem but they don't directly address the use case or business needs of your company. To take advantage of the pillars you must use all of them together, along with the factors impacting your business. If you collect metrics data separately from logs and traces, you can easily lose context and end up observing only a single underlying system in isolation. Observability with respect to a unified approach means collecting and preserving the underlying context along with all its richness and dimensionality.

## Observability: A Superset of Monitoring

Monitoring primarily focuses on the passive collection of a system's events, logs, and metrics. You generally monitor a critical service, which you think might go wrong, because either you have experienced errors with the service before or you are aware of the service's failure modes. Monitoring takes a proactive approach by assisting you with alerting and capacity planning, while observability takes a more reactive approach by enabling you to examine the application stack more closely to see what broke and learn why it broke.

Let's look at an example. Imagine that a developer in your company changes a critical code path while trying to add a new feature in a flagship application. Unfortunately, he accidentally introduces a bug, which then causes an outage. In such a situation, your monitoring systems will be able to clearly show the increased rate of error from a service but will not be able to drill down further. However, having observability embedded in your stack can help you quickly drill down to the problem—say, an issue with a Redis Cluster—and then traces can lead you straight to the root cause.

It's important to reiterate that there's nothing wrong with your monitoring systems in this scenario. They are doing what they're designed to do—tell you when something is wrong. Observability is what's helping you figure out what went wrong.

It's also important to note that observability is not an alternative to monitoring. Rather, it is a superset of monitoring because it provides both a high-level overview of services along with granular insights into various events inside a distributed system. Moreover, in a distributed cloud environment where multiple services run and interact with one another, the task of finding the fault becomes extremely painful if the system is not instrumented to expose the correct fault to bubble up. Observability handles such scenarios by pinpointing the problem chain as the request travels through the services.

## Observability-Driven Development

As we have discussed, cloud native applications are primarily distributed and microservices based, which makes them inherently complex to maintain and manage. Anyone who runs a production-grade application also realizes that when applications start to misbehave, it becomes nearly impossible to figure out which particular moving part is the root cause of the misbehavior. Sometimes failures are caught with the help of traditional logging and monitoring setups, which can point you in the right direction given the complexity of your application stack. But as your services evolve, you cannot know with certainty all of the failure modes of your application or its underlying infrastructure.

Observability-driven development is an effort toward solving the problem of finding the unknowns in production environments by encouraging the addition of observability aspects early in the software development lifecycle. Moreover, it advocates for the instrumentation of application code during the software design phase so that it becomes easier to add instrumentation in one place rather than many places at a later stage. It also aims to bridge the gap between developers and the operational folks by letting the developers own the code and debug easily in production environments. Not only are the engineering teams able to diagnose faults and failures early in production, but it also helps these teams measure and analyze both operational and business performance.

In the following sections, we will look at various ways in which modern cloud native infrastructure and applications can be made observable. We will dive into each of the three pillars and see what is the preferred way of building your systems in cloud native environments, starting with metrics.

# Monitoring Metrics with Prometheus in a Cloud Native World

As we discussed in Chapter 4, Kubernetes has immensely changed how modern applications are created and deployed. Microservices and service-oriented architectures have transformed the landscape of cloud native environments as the speed of feature additions and deployments has increased. With the shift toward these modern architectures, the traditional approach of monitoring can't keep up with the current pace of such architectures, which revolve around ephemeral infrastructure, multiple regions and availability zones, and sometimes even span across clouds. All of these added layers of complexity also open doors to new and unseen failure modes, which the traditional monitoring approach cannot really keep up with.

To step up to the problem of monitoring modern cloud native applications and infrastructure, we need to revisit one of the core pillars of observability: metrics. As we discussed, metrics are one of the key areas that provide an immense amount of information about the state of your application. When it comes to completely understanding your cloud native applications, the traditional set of metrics often doesn't meet the bar, and a custom set of metrics needs to be collected to provide a better measure of the application's overall performance and health. Such metrics are usually configured to be emitted by the application itself, and hence they provide more precise information. This is where Prometheus shines.

Prometheus is an open source monitoring and alerting system originally built by SoundCloud and later inducted as the second project after Kubernetes by the Cloud Native Computing Foundation (CNCF). It is primarily designed for modern cloud native applications specifically focused on the metrics space. With the advent of Kubernetes, Prometheus has become one of the de facto ways to monitor new cloud native applications that are exposing a wide array of custom metrics. Prometheus is also lighter than its predecessor in the monitoring space as it works in pull-based models of exporters, which basically scrape data from applications and infrastructure.

## Prometheus Components and Architecture

Prometheus was primarily built with a focus on monitoring container-based applications that are running at scale. Modern cloud native applications expose the variety of data that needs to be collected, along with the complexity of underlying moving parts, and Prometheus was built from the ground up to tackle this dynamic environment.

To support the new era of cloud native applications, the Prometheus ecosystem consists of the following five main components:

*Prometheus server*
Responsible for scraping the metrics and storing them in a time series database.

*Client libraries*
Used to instrument application code and send the extracted metrics data to the Prometheus server. Client libraries are available in different languages, including C#, Python, Java, and Ruby.

*Pushgateway*
Used to support short-lived jobs.

*Exporters*
Run alongside applications that cannot be instrumented directly, such as HAProxy and statsd, to extract metrics that can be sent to the Prometheus server in the desired format.

*Alertmanager*
Receives alerts from the Prometheus server and bubbles up the notifications efficiently. The Alertmanager does this in a number of consistent and effective ways:

- It groups alerts of a similar type so that fewer alerts are sent across during a large outage.
- It can throttle the notifications sent to the receiver system.
- It allows the suppression of notifications for selected alerts if related alerts are already firing.
- It can send alerts to a number of systems, such as OpsGenie and PagerDuty, among others.

Figure 6-2 shows what these main components look like in the Prometheus architecture.

Prometheus stores all data as a *time series*; that is, streams of timestamped values that belong to the same metric and the same set of labeled dimensions. Each time series is uniquely identified by its *metric name* and an optional key-value pair called *labels*. Moreover, the client libraries offer basic quad-core metric types: Counter, Gauge, Histogram, and Summary. We will talk about these four types later in the chapter, as well as provide instrumentation examples.

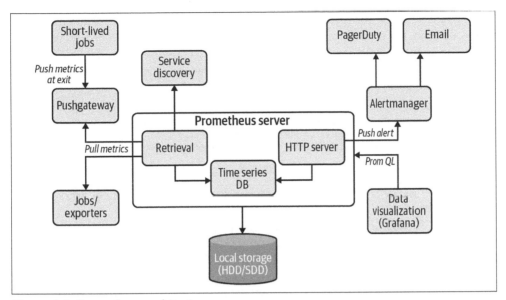

*Figure 6-2. Prometheus architecture*

### Jobs and Instances

In Prometheus terms, an endpoint you can scrape is called an *instance*, and it usually corresponds to a single process. A collection of instances with the same purpose—a process replicated for scalability or reliability, for example—is called a *job*.

Here is an example of an API server job with four replicated instances:

```
job: api-server
instance 1: 1.2.3.4:5670
instance 2: 1.2.3.4:5671
instance 3: 5.6.7.8:5670
instance 4: 5.6.7.8:5671
```

Let's install and configure Prometheus to gain an understanding of some additional key concepts around the Prometheus ecosystem.

## Installing and Configuring Prometheus

To install and run Prometheus locally, first you need to download the correct release for your platform (*https://prometheus.io/download*). At the time of this writing, the latest version of Prometheus is 2.23. Once you have downloaded the tarball, go to the directory and extract it by using the following command:

```
$ tar xvfz prometheus-2.23.0.darwin-amd64.tar.gz
$ cd prometheus-2.23.0.darwin-amd64
```

Once you are inside the Prometheus directory, you can configure Prometheus to scrape its own HTTP endpoint with the help of the *prometheus.yaml* file, which is in the Prometheus directory. The default file already contains TCP port 9090 on the localhost where the Prometheus server runs. You can run Prometheus by executing the binary using the following command:

```
$ ./prometheus
level=info ts=2020-11-29T06:51:43.519Z caller=head.go:659 component=tsdb msg="On-disk
  memory mappable chunks replay completed" duration=7.944µs
level=info ts=2020-11-29T06:51:43.519Z caller=head.go:665 component=tsdb msg="Replaying WAL,
  this may take a while"
level=info ts=2020-11-29T06:51:43.520Z caller=head.go:717 component=tsdb msg="WAL segment
  loaded" segment=0 maxSegment=0
level=info ts=2020-11-29T06:51:43.520Z caller=head.go:722 component=tsdb msg="WAL replay
  completed" checkpoint_replay_duration=93.857µs wal_replay_duration=695.77µs
  total_replay_duration=812.641µs
level=info ts=2020-11-29T06:51:43.521Z caller=main.go:742 fs_type=19
level=info ts=2020-11-29T06:51:43.521Z caller=main.go:745 msg="TSDB started"
level=info ts=2020-11-29T06:51:43.521Z caller=main.go:871 msg="Loading configuration file"
  filename=prometheus.yml
level=info ts=2020-11-29T06:51:43.712Z caller=main.go:902 msg="Completed loading of
  configuration file" filename=prometheus.yml totalDuration=190.710981ms
  remote_storage=6.638µs web_handler=591ns query_engine=807ns scrape=189.731297ms
  scrape_sd=42.312µs notify=322.934µs notify_sd=20.022µs rules=3.538µs
level=info ts=2020-11-29T06:51:43.712Z caller=main.go:694 msg="Server is ready to receive
  web requests."
```

You can access the Prometheus UI on your browser at *http://localhost:9090*, and check out the various metrics that the Prometheus server is serving about itself at *http://localhost:9090/metrics*.

You can make use of the *Expression browser* now to basically run queries or write PromQL expressions (*https://oreil.ly/svnH8*).

PromQL is Prometheus's functional query language that lets you select and aggregate time series data in real time. The data can be visualized on the Prometheus UI in table or graph format.

To use the Expression browser, use any metric being exposed from *localhost:9090/metrics*, such as `prometheus_http_requests_total` (which is a counter for all HTTP requests to the Prometheus server). Then click the Graph tab and enter the metric in the Expression console, as shown in Figure 6-3.

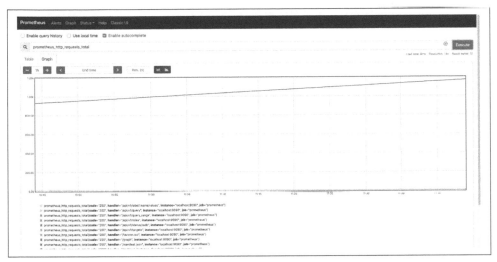

*Figure 6-3. Expression browser result for* `prometheus_http_requests_total`

The query language is very extensive and supports a number of functions and operators on the metrics. For example, if you want to count the number of returned time series for the metric `prometheus_target_interval_length_seconds`, you can issue the following command in the Expression browser.

```
count(prometheus_target_interval_length_seconds)
```

Similarly, if you want to find out how fast a metric is increasing per second, you can use `rate` in the Expression browser:

```
rate(prometheus_tsdb_head_samples_appended_total[1m])
```

## node_exporter

The `node_exporter` exposes an array of host-level metrics, such as CPU, memory, disk space, I/O, and network bandwidth, along with a variety of kernel-level metrics. You can download the `node_exporter` from *https://prometheus.io/download*. Once you have downloaded and extracted the tarball, you can run the binary directly without making any changes:

```
$ cd node_exporter-1.0.1.darwin-amd64
$ ./node_exporter
level=info ts=2020-12-01T13:20:29.510Z caller=node_exporter.go:177 msg="Starting
  node_exporter" version="(version=1.0.1, branch=HEAD,
  revision=3715be6ae899f2a9b9dbfd9c39f3e09a7bd4559f)"
level=info ts=2020-12-01T13:20:29.510Z caller=node_exporter.go:178 msg="Build context"
  build_context="(go=go1.14.4, user=root@4c8e5c628328, date=20200616-12:52:07)"
level=info ts=2020-12-01T13:20:29.511Z caller=node_exporter.go:105 msg="Enabled collectors"
level=info ts=2020-12-01T13:20:29.511Z caller=node_exporter.go:112 collector=boottime
level=info ts=2020-12-01T13:20:29.511Z caller=node_exporter.go:112 collector=cpu
level=info ts=2020-12-01T13:20:29.511Z caller=node_exporter.go:112 collector=diskstats
level=info ts=2020-12-01T13:20:29.511Z caller=node_exporter.go:112 collector=filesystem
```

```
level=info ts=2020-12-01T13:20:29.511Z caller=node_exporter.go:112 collector=loadavg
level=info ts=2020-12-01T13:20:29.511Z caller=node_exporter.go:112 collector=meminfo
level=info ts=2020-12-01T13:20:29.511Z caller=node_exporter.go:112 collector=netdev
level=info ts=2020-12-01T13:20:29.511Z caller=node_exporter.go:112 collector=textfile
level=info ts=2020-12-01T13:20:29.511Z caller=node_exporter.go:112 collector=time
level=info ts=2020-12-01T13:20:29.511Z caller=node_exporter.go:112 collector=uname
level=info ts=2020-12-01T13:20:29.511Z caller=node_exporter.go:191 msg="Listening on"
    address=:9100
level=info ts=2020-12-01T13:20:29.511Z caller=tls_config.go:170 msg="TLS is disabled and it
    cannot be enabled on the fly." http2=false
```

The `node_exporter` runs at *http://localhost:9100* by default. The *scrape_configs* file in *prometheus.yml* needs to be updated with a bit more information so that it can monitor the `node_exporter` by scraping the data from it:

```
scrape_configs:
  - job_name: node
    static_configs:
      - targets:
          - localhost:9100
```

Once you restart Prometheus to pick up the new change, Prometheus will have two endpoint targets from which to scrape the metrics data. You can check the *http://localhost:9090/targets* endpoint as well. Now, say you need to find out how many seconds each CPU spends doing different types of work (i.e., user, system, iowait, etc.); to do this, you can run the following query in the Expression browser, using the `irate` function:

```
irate(node_cpu_seconds_total{job="node"}[5m])
```

The `job="node"` is the label that was matched and which filters the metrics. Let's now take a look at how instrumentation of applications can work with Prometheus.

## Instrumentation of Applications

To monitor custom services, we need to add instrumentation, which involves adding a tracing library to the application code to allow us to implement the Prometheus metric types. In this section, we will look at how to achieve this with the help of client libraries, which you can use to instrument your application code. The client library primarily lets you define and expose internal metrics using HTTP endpoints on your application, and when Prometheus scrapes your application instance, the client library sends the current metrics state to it. We will be making use of Python as the preferred instrumentation library, though more client library implementations are available at *https://prometheus.io/docs/instrumenting/clientlibs*.

The first thing to do is install the client library on your host using `pip` as follows:

```
$ pip install prometheus_client
```

Based on the four metric types we mentioned earlier, there are primarily four different ways that you can instrument your code. We discuss them in the following sections.

## Counters

As the name suggests, counters are mainly used to count values that increase and can be reset to zero on restart when the application restarts. For example, when a GET request is sent to the Python HTTP server the following code increments the counter value by 1:

```
import http.server
from prometheus_client import Counter, start_http_server

http_requests = Counter('my_app_http_request','Description: Num of HTTP request')

class SampleServer(http.server.BaseHTTPRequestHandler):
    def do_GET(self):
        http_requests.inc()
        self.send_response(200)
        self.end_headers()
        self.wfile.write(b"Simple Counter Example")

if __name__ == "__main__":
    start_http_server(5555)
    server = http.server.HTTPServer(('localhost', 5551), SampleServer)
    server.serve_forever()
```

You can run this code block as `python counter.py` in your terminal and it will start a simple HTTP server. We are using start_http_server as an endpoint from where the metrics will be scraped. You can access metrics on *http://localhost:5555*. To ingest these metrics into Prometheus, you need to again configure the *scrape_configs* file in the *prometheus.yml* file as follows:

```
scrape_configs:
  - job_name: 'prometheus'
    static_configs:
    - targets: ['localhost:9090']
  - job_name: node
    static_configs:
    - targets:
        - localhost:9100
  - job_name: my_application
    static_configs:
    - targets:
        - localhost:5555
```

You will be able to access the metric through the Expression browser via the PromQL expression rate(my_app_http_request_total[1m]), once you restart Prometheus. The counter will increase every time you hit the application URL at *http://localhost:5551*. The graph in Figure 6-4 shows an increased rate of incoming HTTP requests.

*Figure 6-4. Counter metric for an instrumented application*

As you can see, it's quite easy to instrument code with counters. You can also use counters to count exceptions and errors in code, and even have a custom value for your counter instead of increasing it by one.

## Gauges

Gauges primarily indicate the current state of an entity and can go up or down. Gauges can be used in a couple of different scenarios: for instance, say you need to know the number of active threads or number of items in a queue, or you want to know the number of items in a cache.

Gauges use three main methods: `inc`, `dec`, and `set`. The following example showcases how you can use the three methods independently to track a metric that you are interested in:

```
from prometheus_client import Gauge
sample_gauge_1 = Gauge('my_increment_example_requests', 'Description of increment gauge')
sample_gauge_2 = Gauge('my_decrement_example_requests', 'Description of decrement gauge')
sample_gauge_3 = Gauge('my_set_example_requests', 'Description of set gauge')

sample_gauge_1.inc()      # This will increment by 1
sample_gauge_2.dec(10)    # This will decrement by given value of 10
sample_gauge_3.set(48)    # This will set to the given value of 48
```

In the preceding code, the `inc()` method will increment the value for `'my_incre ment_example_requests'` by 1, decrement the value for `'my_decrement_exam ple_requests'` by 10, and set the value for `'my_set_example_requests'` to 48.

## Summary

A summary usually tracks the request duration or response size. It is typically used to find the size and number of events. It uses an `observe` method that accepts the size of the event. For example, in the following code, we are trying to find the time it took for a request to complete:

```
import http.server
import time
from prometheus_client import Summary, start_http_server

LATENCY = Summary('latency_in_seconds','Time for a request')

class SampleServer(http.server.BaseHTTPRequestHandler):
    def do_GET(self):
        start_time = time.time()
        self.send_response(200)
        self.end_headers()
        self.wfile.write(b"My application with a Summary metric")
        LATENCY.observe(time.time() - start_time)

if __name__ == "__main__":
    start_http_server(5555)
    server = http.server.HTTPServer(('localhost', 5551), SampleServer)
    server.serve_forever()
```

To run the preceding code, you can follow the same approach we took in "Counters" on page 131. The metric endpoint at *http://localhost:5555/metrics* will have two time series: `latency_in_seconds_count` and `latency_in_seconds_sum`. The former represents the number of observe calls that were made and the latter is the sum of the values passed to `observe`. If you divide the rate of these two metrics —rate(`latency_in_seconds_count`[1m])/rate(`latency_in_seconds_sum`[1m])—you will get the average latency for the last minute.

## Histograms

Histograms help you track the size and number of events in buckets while allowing you to aggregate calculations of quantiles. Histograms can be used to measure request durations for a specific HTTP request call.

Code instrumentation for histograms also uses the `observe` method, and you can combine it with time to track latency, as in our previous example. The following code adds 10 seconds as a request latency:

```
from prometheus_client import Histogram
req_latency = Histogram('request_latency_seconds', 'Description of histogram')
req_latency.observe(10)    # Observe 10 (seconds in this case)
```

Instrumentation is usually applied at the service level or to the client libraries that are being used in the services. It's important to note that there are limits to the level of instrumentation that you can/should add, even though Prometheus is efficient in handling multiple metrics.[1]

Now that you understand how code instrumentation works and how hosts are added to Prometheus and scraped, let's see how to add hosts to Prometheus to be scraped in a production environment.

# Finding Hosts

Prometheus uses the *static_configs* file under *scrape_configs* in the *prometheus.yml* file to find host targets to scrape. Cloud environments are very dynamic in nature, and change occurs quite frequently, especially in containerized environments. In such environments, manually adding hosts to the *prometheus.yml* file will not scale very well. Prometheus offers a wide variety of ways to handle such situations by supporting many sources, including Kubernetes, Azure, and custom service discovery platforms. Service discovery is a simple way to find all the services running in a distributed cloud environment. We will talk in detail about service discovery in Chapter 7. Here, we'll take a look at a couple of ways we can find hosts in production to be scraped by Prometheus.

## Using Ansible

If the hosts are running node exporters, one of the simplest ways to find the hosts is to statically update the *prometheus.yml* file with the inventory hosts. Basically, every time you add a machine you should also have a provision to add it to the *prometheus.yml* configuration file. The following is a snippet for updating *prometheus.yml* using Ansible:

```
scrape_configs:
  - job_name: {{ hostname }}
    static_configs:
      - targets:
        - {{ hostname }}:9100
```

You can also loop over the hosts under any group in an Ansible inventory and add them directly.

## Using Files

You can also provide a list of targets that can be read straight from a YAML or JSON file without any network overhead. This is yet another static method of service discovery in which Prometheus can read hosts directly from a static file—for example, if you have an *inventory.json* file:

---

1 The Prometheus team has compiled best practices on the use of instrumentation at *https://prometheus.io/docs/practices/instrumentation/#counter-vs-gauge-summary-vs-histogram*.

```json
[
  {
    "targets": [
      "192.168.101.11:9100"
    ],
    "labels": {
      "job": "node",
      "Team": "dev"
    }
  },
  {
    "targets": [
      "192.168.101.155:9200"
    ],
    "labels": {
      "job": "node",
      "Team": "sre"
    }
  }
]
```

Now you can update *prometheus.yml* using `file_sd_configs` under `scrape_configs` as follows:

```
scrape_configs:
  - job_name: file
    file_sd_configs:
      - files:
          'inventory.json'
```

You can find the targets being scraped at *http://localhost:9090/service-discovery*.

### Using azure_sd_config

Prometheus allows out-of-the-box support to scrape Azure virtual machines. Azure service discovery (SD) configurations allow you to retrieve scrape targets from Azure virtual machines. You can use Azure service discovery by setting the Azure credentials in the *prometheus.yml* file as follows:

```
- job_name: 'azure-nodes'
    azure_sd_configs:
      - subscription_id: '$SUBSCRIPTION_ID'
        tenant_id: '$TENANT_ID'
        client_id: '$CLIENT_ID'
        client_secret: '$CLIENT_SECRET'
        port: 9100
    relabel_configs:
      - source_labels: [__meta_azure_machine_tag_cloudnative]
        regex: true.*
        action: keep
      - source_labels: [__meta_azure_machine_name]
        target_label: web_instance
      - source_labels: [__meta_azure_machine_tag_public_ip]
        regex: (.+)
        replacement: ${1}:9100
        target_label: __address__
```

In this configuration, we are also using *relabeling*, which dynamically rewrites the label set of a target before it gets scraped. Relabeling helps to manipulate the metrics to keep your storage clean and not pollute it with nonrequired data. Multiple relabelings are applied to the label set of each target in order of occurrence in the configuration file.

Let's take a closer look at key parts of the preceding *relabel_configs*:

__meta_azure_machine_tag_cloudnative
> Prometheus looks through all the Azure virtual machine instances, and if an instance has a tag called cloudnative it keeps the service. Basically, this tells Prometheus: "If any virtual machine is found in the Azure account whose tag is cloudnative: true, then scrape it; otherwise, ignore it.

__meta_azure_machine_name
> Here, Prometheus looks for machine_name and then puts it into a web_instance label.

__meta_azure_machine_tag_public_ip
> Here, Prometheus appends :9100 to the public IP. It also replaces the content of __address__ label.

Once you have some Azure virtual machines running, you can find the discovered target at *http://localhost:9090/service-discovery* along with the metadata extracted from the virtual machine.

Now that we have seen how traditional service discovery works in Prometheus, let's see how Prometheus works with Kubernetes and helps close the monitoring gap in cloud native applications.

## Prometheus on Kubernetes

Kubernetes service discovery support is built right into Prometheus out of the box, allowing retrieval of scrape targets from the Kubernetes REST API. To make use of this capability, Prometheus must already be running inside the Kubernetes cluster. You can use Helm charts to configure and deploy Prometheus easily on an AKS cluster.

Five types of roles can be configured to discover targets in Kubernetes clusters: node, service, Pod, endpoints, and ingress. Let's take a closer look at these service discovery roles.

### The node role

The *node* role discovers all the nodes in the Kubernetes cluster. Since kubelet runs on each node in a Kubernetes cluster, the node role discovers the target nodes in the

---

cluster with the address defaulting to kubelet's HTTP port. You can scrape kubelet nodes using the following Prometheus `scrape_configs` command:

```
scrape_configs:
- job_name: 'kubelet'
  kubernetes_sd_configs:
   - role: node
  scheme: https
  tls_config:
    ca_file: ca.crt
```

In the preceding *prometheus.yml* configuration, the label is provided as `kubelet` and the role is provided as `node`. We use the scheme `HTTPS` since kubelet metrics are available only over HTTPS, which requires a Transport Layer Security (TLS) certificate as well.

### The service role

The *service* role primarily helps you monitor opaque systems to check whether all the services are responding. The service role finds a target for each service port for every service. You can scrape a service object as follows:

```
scrape_configs:
- job_name: prometheus-pushgateway
  kubernetes_sd_configs:
  - role: service
```

### The Pod role

The *Pod* role is responsible for discovering all the Pods running in the cluster and exposing the containers running in them as targets. It also returns all the metadata related to the Pods. You can scrape Pods as follows:

```
scrape_configs:
- job_name: 'pods'
  kubernetes_sd_configs:
   - role: pod
```

### The endpoints role

The *endpoints* role finds the targets from the service endpoints in a Kubernetes cluster. For each endpoint address, one target is discovered per port. You can scrape endpoints as follows:

```
scrape_configs:
- job_name: 'k8apiserver'
  kubernetes_sd_configs:
   - role: endpoints
  scheme: https
  tls_config:
    ca_file: cert.crt
```

### The ingress role

Lastly, the *ingress* role discovers a target for each path of each ingress. This role is also a way to perform opaque monitoring of the ingress. You can scrape an ingress as follows:

```
scrape_configs:
- job_name: 'gateway'
  kubernetes_sd_configs:
   - role: ingress
  scheme: https
  tls_config:
    ca_file: cert.crt
```

Having covered metrics in depth, let's take a look at how logging is implemented in cloud native applications.

# Logging in the Cloud Native World

Logs are a crucial piece of information in any environment. They are primarily used by engineers while troubleshooting an issue or gaining insights into a system. But logging in general is complex. The complexity arises due to the various ways to consume logs, differences in data formats, and the need to ensure that the underlying application that is responsible for storing the logs also scales well as the number of logs grows. In cloud native distributed environments, logging becomes even more important. Not only do these environments have many moving parts, but they're also more complex, since now the systems are distributed and ephemeral, like Kubernetes Pods. This means the logs need to be shipped away and stored centrally to be viewed later.

To solve the problems of logging at scale in a cloud native environment, we need a solution that can be plugged into an environment easily and integrate seamlessly. This is where *Fluentd* comes into the picture.

## Logging with Fluentd

Fluentd is an open source project from CNCF that can collect, parse, transform, and analyze logs. Fluentd basically acts as a unified logging layer by structuring the data as JSON (see Figure 6-5). This in turn helps it collect, filter, buffer, and output the logs across multiple sources and destinations.

Fluentd is written in CRuby, which is a C implementation of the Ruby programming language that comes with a small memory footprint of 30 to 40 MB and processes approximately 13K events per second per core. Let's take a look at some of the core concepts of Fluentd and how it can be used to enable logging in cloud native environments.

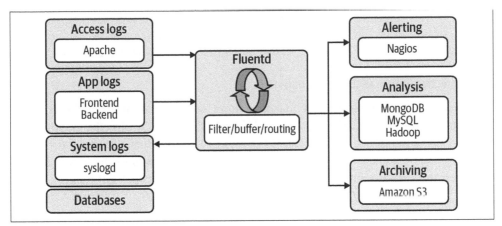

*Figure 6-5. Fluentd acting as a logging layer*

To start, install the agent, based on your operating system distribution, from the official Fluentd website (*https://docs.fluentd.org/installation*).

> The official stable Fluentd distribution package is called *td-agent*. It ensures stability and comes preconfigured with recommended settings from the original author, Treasure Data Inc.

Once you have downloaded and installed *td-agent* for your distribution, ensure that it is up and running. For example, on macOS you can do this via `launchctl`:

```
$ ~ sudo launchctl load /Library/LaunchDaemons/td-agent.plist
Password:
$
```

You can confirm that the agent is running via the logs available at the following location:

```
$ ~ tail -f /var/log/td-agent/td-agent.log
2020-12-17 22:57:46 +0530 [info]: adding match pattern="td.*.*" type="tdlog"
2020-12-17 22:57:46 +0530 [warn]: #0 [output_td] secondary type should be same with primary
   one primary="Fluent::Plugin::TreasureDataLogOutput" secondary="Fluent::Plugin::FileOutput"
2020-12-17 22:57:46 +0530 [info]: adding match pattern="debug.**" type="stdout"
2020-12-17 22:57:46 +0530 [info]: adding source type="forward"
2020-12-17 22:57:46 +0530 [info]: adding source type="http"
2020-12-17 22:57:46 +0530 [info]: adding source type="debug_agent"
2020-12-17 22:57:46 +0530 [info]: #0 starting fluentd worker pid=96320 ppid=95841 worker=0
2020-12-17 22:57:47 +0530 [info]: #0 [input_debug_agent] listening dRuby
   uri="druby://127.0.0.1:24230" object="Fluent::Engine"
2020-12-17 22:57:47 +0530 [info]: #0 [input_forward] listening port port=24224
   bind="0.0.0.0"
2020-12-17 22:57:47 +0530 [info]: #0 fluentd worker is now running worker=0
```

Fluentd is best understood with the help of its configuration file. You can find the default configuration file for Fluentd at *etc/td-agent/td-agent.conf*. The configuration file contains a number of directives, as discussed in the following subsections.

### source directive (where all the data is ingested)

The `source` directive determines the data input source that needs to be enabled (i.e., where the data needs to be ingested from). The `source` directive submits an event to the Fluentd routing system. By default, Fluentd offers two standard input plug-ins. The `http` plug-in provides an HTTP endpoint to listen for incoming HTTP messages; the `forward` plug-in provides a TCP endpoint to accept TCP packets:

```
<source>
@type forward
port 24224
</source>

<source>
@type http
port 9999
bind 0.0.0.0
</source>
```

The preceding definition specifies two sources: in the first source we are receiving events from TCP port 24224 and in the second source we have an HTTP server listening on TCP port 9999.

The event submitted by `source` to the Fluentd routing engine contains three entities: tag, time, and record. For example, in the following log output:

```
2020-12-16 15:38:27 +0900 test.root: {"action":"logout","user":3}
```

`2020-12-16 15:38:27 +0900` is the time, which is specified by input plug-ins and has to be in Unix time format; `test.root` is the tag (according to Fluentd, it is strongly recommended that the tag be in lowercase and a mix of digits and underscores); and `{"action":"logout","user":3}` is a JSON object.

The input plug-ins are responsible for retrieving the event logs from external sources. Generally, an input plug-in creates a thread, a socket, and a listening socket. Input plug-ins are not just limited to `http` and `forward`. Following are some additional plug-ins:

`in_syslog`
For retrieving log events via the Syslog protocol on UDP or TCP. Fluentd creates a socket on port 5140; then, all you need to do is set up your syslog daemon to send log events on this socket:

```
<source>
  @type syslog
  port 5140
  bind 0.0.0.0
```

```
      tag system
  </source>
```

in_tail

Allows Fluentd to read events from the tail of logfiles, just like the Unix `tail -f` command:

```
<source>
  @type tail
  path /var/log/httpd-access.log
  pos_file /var/log/td-agent/httpd-access.log.pos
  tag apache.access
  <parse>
    @type apache2
  </parse>
</source>
```

Fluentd offers additional input plug-ins, such as `in_unix` for retrieving records from the Unix domain socket, and `in_exec` for executing external programs and pulling event logs. You can even write your own custom input plug-ins.

### match directive (what to do with the input data)

The `match` directive determines the output destination by looking for the events with matching tags. The standard output plug-ins for Fluentd include `file` and `forward`. The match directive must include a match pattern and an `@type` parameter that defines the output plug-in to use. Once an event with a tag matches the pattern, it will be sent to the output destination. Here's an example use of the `match` directive:

```
<match mywebapp.access>
  @type file
  path /var/log/mywebapp/access
</match>
```

In the preceding configuration, we are matching events tagged with `mywebapp.access` and storing them in `file` at `/var/log/mywebapp/access`.

In addition to `file` and `forward`, you can have other types of output plug-ins that basically determine where you want to write the data to. For example, `out_elasticsearch` is an output plug-in that writes the records to an Elasticsearch cluster endpoint. You would first need to install the plug-in using:

```
fluent-gem install fluent-plugin-elasticsearch
```

Then you can use the following configuration to send the output data to an Elasticsearch endpoint:

```
<match my.logs>
  @type elasticsearch
  host 192.168.23.13
  port 9200
  logstash_format true
</match>
```

Similarly, you can use out_copy to copy events to multiple outputs, out_kafka2 to send records to a Kafka cluster, out_mongo to write records to a MongoDB database, and stdout to simply write events to standard output.

### filter directive (the event processing pipeline)

The filter directive acts like a rule to pass or reject an event based on a condition. filter has the same syntax as match, but filter can be chained to a processing pipeline. You can add a filter as follows:

```
<source>
  @type http
  port 9999
  bind 0.0.0.0
</source>

<filter test.session>
  @type grep
  <exclude>
    key action
    pattern ^logout_session$
  </exclude>
</filter>

<match test.session>
  @type stdout
</match>
```

In the preceding configuration, once the data is sourced, it goes through the filter section and then the match section. The filter will accept or reject the event based on its type and rule. Here we discarded the logout_session action and used the type grep inside filter to exclude any message on which the action key has the logout string.

Following are some additional filter plug-ins:

filter_record_transformer
    Used to change an incoming event stream. You can use the following configuration example for record_transformer:

```
<filter myweb.access>
  @type record_transformer
  <record>
    host_param "#{Socket.gethostname}"
  </record>
</filter>
```

    In the preceding configuration, record_transformer will add the host_param field to the log event.

filter_geoip
> Adds geographic location information to logs using the MaxMind GeoIP database.

filter_stdout
> Prints events to standard output and is used mostly for debugging purposes.

### system directive (sets system-wide configuration)

You can set a variety of system-wide configurations using the system directive. Some of the configuration options available in the system directive are:

- log_level
- suppress_repeated_stacktrace
- emit_error_log_interval
- suppress_config_dump
- without_source
- process_name

You can use the system configuration as follows:

```
<system>
  process_name my_app
  log_level error
  without_source
</system>
```

Here we are first setting the supervisor and worker process names to my_app and then setting the default log level to error. We are also instructing Fluentd to start without any input plug-in.

### label directive (for output grouping and routing)

Labels primarily solve the problem of maintaining and managing the configuration file by allowing routing sections that do not follow the top-to-bottom parsing order in the configuration file. You can think of labels as go-to statements as well. Here is a simple configuration example for using labels:

```
<source>
  @type http
  bind 0.0.0.0
  port 9999
  @label @MYCLUE
</source>

<filter test.session>
  @type grep
  <exclude>
```

```
      key action
      pattern ^login$
    </exclude>
  </filter>

  <label @MYCLUE>
    <filter test.session>
      @type grep
      <exclude>
        key action
        pattern ^logout$
      </exclude>
    </filter>

    <match test.session>
      @type stdout
    </match>
  </label>
```

In the preceding configuration, the @label parameter under source is the redirection toward the @MYCLUE label section. The control will skip the filter definition for login and move directly to the @MYCLUE label.

### @include directive (to import config files)

Using the @include directive, you can import configuration files from a separate directory. The @include directive supports regular file path, glob pattern, and HTTP URL conventions as follows:

```
# absolute path
@include /path/to/config.conf

# if using a relative path, the directive will use
# the dirname of this config file to expand the path
@include extra.conf

# glob match pattern
@include config.d/*.conf

# http
@include http://example.com/fluent.conf
```

Before moving forward, let's take a quick look at how you run the agent to see your logs. To run a simple configuration like the following:

```
<source>
  @type http
  port 9999
  bind 0.0.0.0
</source>

<filter myapp.test>
  @type grep
  <exclude>
    key action
    pattern ^logout$
  </exclude>
```

```
  </filter>

  <match myapp.test>
    @type stdout
  </match>
```

you would replace the preceding configuration at the default location */etc/td-agent/
td-agent.conf.* You can now reload the td-agent in macOS as follows:

```
$ sudo launchctl load /Library/LaunchDaemons/td-agent.plist
#check logs
$ tail -f /var/log/td-agent/td-agent.log
2020-12-21 12:21:57 +0530 [info]: parsing config file is succeeded \
  path="/etc/td-agent/td-agent.conf"
2020-12-21 12:21:58 +0530 [info]: using configuration file: <ROOT>
  <source>
    @type http
    port 9999
    bind "0.0.0.0"
  </source>
  <filter myapp.test>
    @type grep
    <exclude>
      key "action"
      pattern ^logout$
    </exclude>
  </filter>
  <match myapp.test>
    @type stdout
  </match>
</ROOT>
2020-12-21 12:21:58 +0530 [info]: starting fluentd-1.0.2 pid=43215 ruby="2.4.2"
2020-12-21 12:21:58 +0530 [info]: spawn command to main: \
  cmdline=["/opt/td-agent/embedded/bin/ruby", "-Eascii-8bit:ascii-8bit", \
  "/opt/td-agent/usr/sbin/td-agent", "--log", "/var/log/td-agent/td-agent.log", \
  "--use-v1-config", "--under-supervisor"]
2020-12-21 12:21:58 +0530 [info]: gem 'fluent-plugin-elasticsearch' version '2.4.0'
2020-12-21 12:21:58 +0530 [info]: gem 'fluent-plugin-kafka' version '0.6.5'
2020-12-21 12:21:58 +0530 [info]: gem 'fluent-plugin-rewrite-tag-filter' version '2.0.1'
2020-12-21 12:21:58 +0530 [info]: gem 'fluent-plugin-s3' version '1.1.0'
2020-12-21 12:21:58 +0530 [info]: gem 'fluent-plugin-td' version '1.0.0'
2020-12-21 12:21:58 +0530 [info]: gem 'fluent-plugin-td-monitoring' version '0.2.3'
2020-12-21 12:21:58 +0530 [info]: gem 'fluent-plugin-webhdfs' version '1.2.2'
2020-12-21 12:21:58 +0530 [info]: gem 'fluentd' version '1.0.2'
2020-12-21 12:21:58 +0530 [info]: adding filter pattern="myapp.test" type="grep"
2020-12-21 12:21:58 +0530 [info]: adding match pattern="myapp.test" type="stdout"
2020-12-21 12:21:58 +0530 [info]: adding source type="http"
2020-12-21 12:21:58 +0530 [info]: #0 starting fluentd worker pid=43221 ppid=43215 worker=0
2020-12-21 12:21:58 +0530 [info]: #0 fluentd worker is now running worker=0
```

Now you can run the following curl commands to simulate different actions:

```
$ curl -i -X POST -d 'json={"action":"login","user":2}' http://localhost:9999/myapp.test

HTTP/1.1 200 OK
Content-Type: text/plain
Connection: Keep-Alive
Content-Length: 0
```

Since we are currently passing the action as `login`, we can check the logs at the location to verify that they have been printed:

```
2020-12-21 12:31:31.529967000 +0530 myapp.test: {"action":"login","user":2}
```

If you try to post an action as a `logout` in the following `curl` command, it will get dropped based on the filter rule we specified, and you won't be able to see any logs being printed:

```
$ curl -i -X POST -d 'json={"action":"logout","user":2}' http://localhost:9999/myapp.test
HTTP/1.1 200 OK
Content-Type: text/plain
Connection: Keep-Alive
Content-Length: 0
```

Now that you understand how Fluentd works, let's examine how to integrate it in cloud native environments and deploy it over container orchestrators like Kubernetes.

## Fluentd on Kubernetes

By default, in Kubernetes the logs from containers are written to standard output and the standard error stream. This is basic I/O logging, which Kubernetes offers out of the box. The container engine redirects the streams to a logging driver configured in Kubernetes to write the logs to a file in JSON format. As a user, if you wish to see the logs you can use the `kubectl logs` command. The problem with this approach, though, is very evident: if a container crashes, or a Pod is evicted, or the node itself dies, you will no longer be able to access the application logs. Therefore, logs should have storage that is independent from containers, Pods, and nodes. This concept is formally referred to as *cluster-level logging* and it requires a separate backend to store, analyze, and query the logs. While Kubernetes doesn't natively provide a solution for cluster-level logging, we can combine Fluentd with a storage solution like Elasticsearch to construct a scalable solution.

Before moving on to the preferred way of deploying Fluentd on Kubernetes, let's take a look at the different approaches by which cluster-level logging can be implemented, along with their pros and cons. There are essentially two ways to build a cluster-level logging solution:

- Use a sidecar container in every application Pod.
- Use a node-level logging agent that runs on every node.

Let's take a closer look at each of these solutions.

### Sidecar container approach

Generally, in Kubernetes you run your applications in a Pod, as described in Chapter 5. In the sidecar approach, you can create one or more sidecar containers inside the application Pod. The sidecar container approach can be used in two different ways:

- You can use the sidecar container to stream the application logs to the container's own stdout.
- You can run a logging agent inside a sidecar container, which basically picks the logs from application containers and ships them to a logging backend.

There are some advantages to the sidecar container approach:

- You can ship application logs being produced in different log formats (structured or unstructured) by having two sidecar containers to stream a particular logfile to different log streams.
- Sidecar containers can read logs from files, sockets, or journald, and each sidecar container will print the log to the stdout and stderr streams.
- Sidecar containers can also be used to rotate the logfiles that cannot be rotated by the application itself.

There are also some disadvantages to running a sidecar container:

- Disk I/O can increase significantly in a scenario where you are writing the logs to a file and then streaming to stdout.
- Since there is more than one Pod running your application, you would also have to deploy multiple sidecar containers in each Pod.

### Node-level logging agent approach

Another way to deal with logging in Kubernetes is to deploy a logging agent on each node of the Kubernetes cluster. The agent can be run as a container to a daemon that can have access to all the logs being produced by the application Pods. This is, in fact, the preferred way of running Fluentd agents as well.

A Kubernetes DaemonSet is used to implement such a strategy where every node can run a copy of a Fluentd logging agent Pod. Fluentd officially provides a DaemonSet (*https://oreil.ly/OE3hD*) with correct rules to be deployed on Kubernetes clusters. You can grab a copy of the DaemonSet by cloning from the official Fluentd repository:

```
$ git clone https://github.com/fluent/fluentd-kubernetes-daemonset
```

Before you begin using the aforementioned DaemonSet, you need a Kubernetes cluster. If you are already running an Azure Kubernetes cluster (such as the Azure

Kubernetes Service [AKS]), you can start by deploying a logging backend for storing the logfiles. Elasticsearch is one of the logging backends that can be used to store the generated logs. You can deploy Elasticsearch using Helm on Kubernetes as follows:

```
$ helm repo add elastic https://helm.elastic.co
$ helm install elasticsearch elastic/elasticsearch
```

You can use port forwarding to check that the Elasticsearch cluster has been successfully deployed:

```
$ kubectl port-forward svc/elasticsearch-master 9200
Forwarding from 127.0.0.1:9200 -> 9200
Forwarding from [::1]:9200 -> 9200
Handling connection for 9200
Handling connection for 9200
```

Elasticsearch should be available on *http://localhost:9200*. To deploy the Fluentd DaemonSet you first need to modify the following environment variables in the *fluentd-daemonset-elasticsearch-rbac.yaml* file:

- FLUENT_ELASTICSEARCH_HOST (the Elasticsearch endpoint)
- FLUENT_ELASTICSEARCH_PORT (the Elasticsearch port, usually 9200)

Once you have updated the YAML file with Elasticsearch details, you can deploy the Fluentd DaemonSet on AKS by moving to the GitHub repository and applying the DaemonSet as follows:

```
$ kubectl apply -f fluentd-daemonset-elasticsearch-rbac.yaml
```

This will deploy the Fluentd DaemonSet on the Kubernetes cluster, and every node will now have at least one Fluentd Pod running that will forward your logs to Elasticsearch:

```
$ ~ kubectl get pods --namespace=kube-system -o wide
NAME                               READY   STATUS    RESTARTS   AGE    IP
  NODE                             NOMINATED NODE   READINESS GATES
fluentd-6pttr                      1/1     Running   2          3h37m  10.240.0.27
  aks-agentpool-25245360-vmss000000   <none>          <none>
fluentd-9fj59                      1/1     Running   1          3h37m  10.240.0.147
  aks-agentpool-25245360-vmss000001   <none>          <none>
fluentd-dh7pn                      1/1     Running   1          139m   10.240.1.84
  aks-agentpool-25245360-vmss000003   <none>          <none>
fluentd-g5cnv                      1/1     Running   2          3h37m  10.240.1.25
  aks-agentpool-25245360-vmss000002   <none>          <none>
fluentd-mzw2j                      1/1     Running   2          139m   10.240.2.0
  aks-agentpool-25245360-vmss000004   <none>          <none>
fluentd-z52r2                      1/1     Running   2          139m   10.240.2.143
  aks-agentpool-25245360-vmss000005   <none>          <none>
kube-proxy-56bv2                   1/1     Running   0          139m   10.240.2.47
  aks-agentpool-25245360-vmss000005   <none>          <none>
```

You also need to view these logs, and you can do this by using Kibana.[2] You can deploy Kibana similarly with the help of Helm and port-forward locally as follows:

```
$ helm repo add elastic https://helm.elastic.co
$ helm install kibana elastic/kibana
$ kubectl port-forward deployment/kibana-kibana 5601
Forwarding from 127.0.0.1:5601 -> 5601
Forwarding from [::1]:5601 -> 5601
```

Kibana (Figure 6-6) should now be up and ready on your *http://localhost:5601*.

*Figure 6-6. Showcasing logs with Kibana*

Another new log aggregation tool is Loki from Grafana Labs (*https://oreil.ly/vUFFW*). Loki efficiently logs specific log labels instead of an entire log stream and can easily integrate with Fluentd. We will not take a deep dive into this topic since it is beyond the scope of this book.

Now that you understand how logging works in cloud native environments, let's close the chapter with a discussion on distributed tracing.

---

2 Kibana is an open source UI that is generally used to visualize data (logs). More information is available at *https://elastic.co/kibana*.

# Distributed Tracing in the Cloud Native World

Distributed tracing is one of the critical pillars for gaining and building observability into modern cloud native applications. Distributed tracing enables you to track the flow of requests in a distributed system as they pass through multiple services and emit metadata information, such as the time spent at each service and underlying call details to other service endpoints. This metadata can be reassembled later to provide a more complete picture of the application's behavior at runtime, which can help you solve issues such as pinpointing application latency problems and locating bottlenecks.

Distributed tracing answers important questions, such as:

- What are the bottlenecks in a service?
- How much time is spent at each stage/service of a distributed system?
- What are the upstream and downstream services and what endpoints does a request touch?

To better understand the fundamentals of distributed tracing, take a look at the simple web application depicted in Figure 6-7.

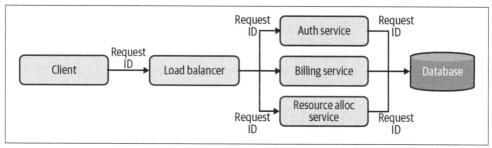

*Figure 6-7. A simple web application showcasing request propagation through various layers of services*

Referencing Figure 6-7, assume you have a sample service that provisions some resources over a cloud based on the user's plan. The normal flow of execution starts with the client making a request to the load balancer, which talks to the authentication service and the billing service, and allocates resources to the client by making a final call to the resource allocation service. In Figure 6-8, you can see the unique request IDs being propagated in the flow, which later helps to stitch together the traces.

This flow of transactions can be visualized with the help of a Gantt chart (see Figure 6-8).

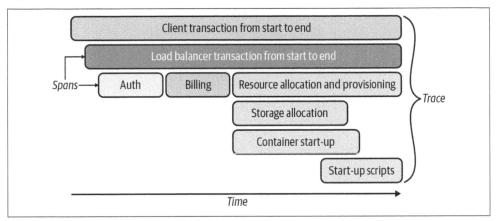

*Figure 6-8. Spans and traces in a simple web application*

## Tracing: Key Concepts

The Gantt chart in Figure 6-8 summarizes the following important key concepts of a distributed tracing system.

### Spans

A span represents a single operational call and is the primary building block of a distributed trace, which represents an individual unit of work done in a distributed system. Spans contain *references* to other spans, which allows multiple spans to be assembled into one complete trace. For example, in Figure 6-8, the span "load balancer transaction from start to end" includes other spans, like load balancer interacting with authentication service or load balancer interacting with billing service.

The spans are created in the form of a parent–child relationship in which each span has a child, except for the root and the start service (Figure 6-9).

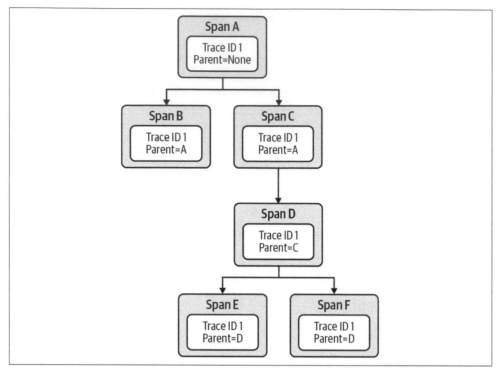

*Figure 6-9. Anatomy of a span*

## Traces

A trace represents the entire journey of a request across all the services it touches during its traversal. A single complete trace usually consists of multiple spans for the request. For example, the complete transaction of the client from start to end consists of multiple spans.

## Context propagation

With every request from a service to a downstream service, a global request execution identifier is passed along as metadata, which remains unique for each request. This global request execution identifier is used later to reconstruct the full execution of the request by grouping the records on the basis of the request identifier. The process of passing the execution identifier as request metadata is called *distributed context propagation.*

The metadata that is being propagated across the spans also includes the trace ID and span ID along with two additional details: tags and logs. *Tags* are key-value pairs that can be added to spans to provide extra information like error codes and host details. *Logs* are also key-value pairs that capture span-specific logging messages and assist in debugging.

### Sampling

Collecting all the data in memory and then sending it to a tracing backend can have a severe impact on the network, application latency, and cost. To avoid this problem, the tracing system implements sampling. Sampling is the process of collecting and storing only a subset of trace data to avoid storage costs and performance overhead. There are various types of sampling methods, primarily classified as either head-based or tail-based sampling. For example, if you want to collect $x$ number of traces per minute, you can use a type of sampling known as *rate limiting*. Similarly, if you want to sample traces when a certain type of error becomes prominent, you can use *context-sensitive sampling*.

## General Tracing System Architecture and Trace Assembly

To implement a tracing system in a cloud native environment, you can make use of the already existing open source libraries (we will discuss this further in the next section), which will help you instrument your application without reinventing the wheel. In general, most tracing systems have a simple architecture, as shown in Figure 6-10.

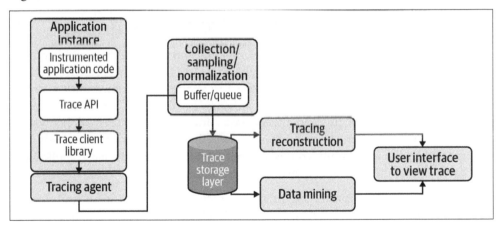

*Figure 6-10. General distributed tracing system architecture*

To use distributed tracing, you first need to instrument your application code using a client library. Client libraries are available in many languages, including Java, Go, and Python. The library sends the data to an agent, which usually is available on the same instance or host. The agent is responsible for forwarding the traces to the backend (e.g., to the storage layer via an asynchronous buffered layer). Later, the traces are reconstructed and displayed to the user interface. The traces can also be used to perform further analysis and aggregation using data mining techniques.

Traces are assembled by looking at the following in a request:

*Incoming request span*
> When a request comes into a service, the tracing system checks whether the request has a tracing header attached to it. If no tracing header is attached, a root span is created; otherwise, a child span needs to be created.

*Outgoing request span*
> If a request is going out from one service to a different service, a span is created first and the receiving service continues the trace as described in the incoming request span.

You can implement distributed tracing in cloud environments in several ways. We'll take a look at some of them in the next section.

## Tracing Standards, Tools, and Code Instrumentation

Over the years, distributed tracing has evolved and become a standard way to profile and monitor applications in the cloud native world. In 2016, *OpenTracing* became a CNCF project whose single goal was to provide vendor-agnostic specifications for distributed tracing. During this time, Google was working on an open source community project called *OpenCensus*, which was later steered by Microsoft.

OpenTracing and OpenCensus were two competing frameworks; their architectures were different, but they basically solved the same problem. The presence of two standards led to a bit of uncertainty in respect to support and contributions, which resulted in a lack of wide adoption in the industry. In May 2019, CNCF announced the merging of OpenTracing and OpenCensus into a single standard known as *OpenTelemetry*. OpenTelemetry combines the benefits of the previous standards and is supported by the community. In this section, we will look at how basic application code can be instrumented with OpenTracing and OpenTelemetry.

Today the two most popular and practical tracing tools are *Zipkin* and *Jaeger*. Zipkin was the first tracing system that was developed by Google's *Dapper tracing infrastructure* (*https://oreil.ly/DMb08*). Jaeger was developed at Uber and is supported by CNCF. Jaeger implements the OpenTracing specification, and its preferred deployment method is Kubernetes. We will keep our discussion limited to Jaeger.

Jaeger closely follows the general architecture of a tracing system in that it consists of three main components: collectors, a query service, and a UI. It deploys an agent on every host, which basically aggregates the trace data and sends it to the collector (buffering service). The trace data then can be stored in a database, preferably Elasticsearch or Cassandra.

Let's now take a look at some simple ways we can instrument code with different tracing standards and Jaeger.

For instance, we can use a Python Jaeger client:

```
$ pip install jaeger-client
```

From there, we can run all the Jaeger components in one single Docker image:

```
$ docker run -d -p6831:6831/udp -p16686:16686 jaegertracing/all-in-one:latest
```

And we can check for the Docker container using docker ps:

```
$ ~ docker ps -a
CONTAINER ID    IMAGE                               COMMAND                 CREATED
874b2a03ebaa    jaegertracing/all-in-one:latest    "/go/bin/all-in-one-…"  About a minute ago
STATUS                PORTS
Up About a minute    5775/udp, 5778/tcp, 14250/tcp, 6832/udp, 14268/tcp,
                                    0.0.0.0:6831->6831/udp, 0.0.0.0:16686->16686/tcp

NAMES
jolly_mclean
```

You can hit *http://localhost:16686* locally to access the Jaeger UI.

Now let's discuss how to instrument simple application code with the help of Open-
Tracing. In the following example, we have a movie-booking program that has a
couple of methods which are responsible for checking whether a movie is available. If
so, it books the tickets:

```
import sys
import time
import logging
import random
from jaeger_client import Config
from opentracing_instrumentation.request_context import get_current_span, span_in_context

def initialize_tracer(service):
    logging.getLogger('').handlers = []
    logging.basicConfig(format='%(message)s', level=logging.DEBUG)
    config = Config(
        config={
            'sampler': {
                'type': 'const',
                'param': 1,
            },
            'logging': True,
        },
        service_name=service,
    )
    return config.initialize_tracer()

def booking_manager(movie):
    with tracer.start_span('booking') as span:
        span.set_tag('Movie', movie)
        with span_in_context(span):
            get_cinema_details = check_movie(movie)
            get_showtime_details = check_movie_showtime(get_cinema_details)
            book_movie_now(get_showtime_details)

def check_movie(movie):
    with tracer.start_span('CheckCinema', child_of=get_current_span()) as span:
        with span_in_context(span):
```

```
            num = random.randint(1,30)
            time.sleep(num)
            cinema_details = "Cinema Details"
            flags = ['false', 'true', 'false']
            random_flag = random.choice(flags)
            span.set_tag('error', random_flag)
            span.log_kv({'event': 'CheckCinema' , 'value': cinema_details })
            return cinema_details

    def check_movie_showtime( cinema_details ):
        with tracer.start_span('CheckShowtime', child_of=get_current_span()) as span:
            with span_in_context(span):
                num = random.randint(1,30)
                time.sleep(num)
                showtime_details = "Showtime Details"
                flags = ['false', 'true', 'false']
                random_flag = random.choice(flags)
                span.set_tag('error', random_flag)
                span.log_kv({'event': 'CheckCinema' , 'value': showtime_details })
                return showtime_details

    def book_movie_now(showtime_details):
        with tracer.start_span('BookShow',  child_of=get_current_span()) as span:
            with span_in_context(span):
                num = random.randint(1,30)
                time.sleep(num)
                Ticket_details = "Ticket Details"
                flags = ['false', 'true', 'false']
                random_flag = random.choice(flags)
                span.set_tag('error', random_flag)
                span.log_kv({'event': 'CheckCinema' , 'value': showtime_details })

assert len(sys.argv) == 2
tracer = initialize_tracer('movie_booking')
movie = sys.argv[1]
booking_manager(movie)
time.sleep(2)
tracer.close()
```

In the preceding code, first we initialize the tracer using the method `initial ize_tracer`, which sets up the configuration for logging and sampling. The next thing to note in the code is how we use the tracer instance to start a new span with `start_span`, and use `child_of` to start new child spans to the root span. For example, the root span is generated in the method `booking_manager`, and the rest of the methods (e.g., `check_movie_showtime` and `check_movie`) are primarily child spans of the root span.

We are also setting tags and logs in the methods. For example:

```
-> span.set_tag('error', random_flag)
```

```
-> span.log_kv({'event': 'CheckCinema' , 'value': showtime_details })
```

You now can simply run this program in your Python console by passing a made-up movie title as the argument, as follows:

```
$ python jaeger_opentracing.py godfather
Initializing Jaeger Tracer with UDP reporter
Using sampler ConstSampler(True)
opentracing.tracer initialized to <jaeger_client.tracer.Tracer object at 0x10eeae410> \
  [app_name=movie_booking]
Reporting span f99b147babd58321:5ca566beb40e89b0:931be7dc309045fd:1 movie_booking. \
  CheckCinema
Reporting span f99b147babd58321:1ad5d00d2acbd02:931be7dc309045fd:1 movie_booking. \
  CheckShowtime
Reporting span f99b147babd58321:f36b9959f34f61dc:931be7dc309045fd:1 movie_booking.BookShow
Reporting span f99b147babd58321:931be7dc309045fd:0:1 movie_booking.booking
```

You can now access the Jaeger UI and look for `movie_booking` in the service's drop-down menu, and you can click the Find Traces button and see the traces appear, as shown in Figure 6-11.

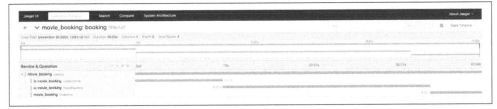

*Figure 6-11. Traces for the movie-booking service*

You can see the four spans in Figure 6-11, with `movie_booking` being the root span and the rest being the child spans. Since this is a sample program, for demonstration purposes we randomly generated some errors in the code that are being bubbled up. In production, these errors would indicate problems that are occurring in the environment (e.g., Redis timing out due to an I/O issue).

We can also instrument our code using OpenTelemetry, since OpenTracing is now being phased out. First we would need to install the OpenTelemetry API and SDK:

```
pip install opentelemetry-api
pip install opentelemetry-sdk
```

To see how OpenTelemetry works, take a look at the following Python code:

```python
from opentelemetry import trace
from opentelemetry.exporter import jaeger
from opentelemetry.sdk.trace import TracerProvider
from opentelemetry.sdk.trace.export import BatchExportSpanProcessor

trace.set_tracer_provider(TracerProvider())

jaeger_exporter = jaeger.JaegerSpanExporter(
    service_name="my-helloworld-service",
    agent_host_name="localhost",
    agent_port=6831,
)

trace.get_tracer_provider().add_span_processor(
    BatchExportSpanProcessor(jaeger_exporter)
```

```
    )

    tracer = trace.get_tracer(__name__)

    with tracer.start_as_current_span("foo"):
        with tracer.start_as_current_span("bar"):
            with tracer.start_as_current_span("tango"):
                print("Hello world from Opentelemetry! Happy Tracing")
```

The preceding code is a simple "hello world"–style Python script that uses OpenTelemetry. Note how we are using the Jaeger exporter to tell us the location of the Jaeger agent.

You need Python3 to run the preceding script:

```
$ python3 opentelemetry_simple.py
Hello world from Opentelemetry! Happy Tracing
```

You can view the spans being populated on the UI again at the same Jaeger endpoint (*http://localhost:16686*) under the my-helloworld-service service.

You can similarly instrument any code depending on your application language. For example, you can instrument a Python Flask application as follows:

```
import flask
import requests

from opentelemetry import trace
from opentelemetry.exporter import jaeger
from opentelemetry.instrumentation.flask import FlaskInstrumentor
from opentelemetry.instrumentation.requests import RequestsInstrumentor
from opentelemetry.sdk.trace import TracerProvider
from opentelemetry.sdk.trace.export import (
    ConsoleSpanExporter,
    SimpleExportSpanProcessor,
)

trace.set_tracer_provider(TracerProvider())

jaeger_exporter = jaeger.JaegerSpanExporter(
    service_name="flask_app_example",
    agent_host_name="localhost",
    agent_port=6831,
)

trace.get_tracer_provider().add_span_processor(
    SimpleExportSpanProcessor(jaeger_exporter)
)

app = flask.Flask(__name__)
FlaskInstrumentor().instrument_app(app)
RequestsInstrumentor().instrument()

@app.route("/")
def hello():
    tracer = trace.get_tracer(__name__)
    with tracer.start_as_current_span("example-request"):
        requests.get("http://www.example.com")
```

```
    return "hello"

app.run(debug=True, port=5000)
```

You can run the preceding script as follows, and hit *http://localhost:5000* to generate traces in the Jaeger UI:

```
$ python3 opentelemetry_flask.py
 * Serving Flask app "opentelemetry_flask" (lazy loading)
 * Environment: production
   WARNING: This is a development server. Do not use it in a production deployment.
   Use a production WSGI server instead.
 * Debug mode: on
 * Running on http://127.0.0.1:5000/ (Press CTRL+C to quit)
 * Restarting with stat
 * Debugger is active!
 * Debugger PIN: 156-661-048
127.0.0.1 - - [30/Dec/2020 20:54:37] "GET / HTTP/1.1" 200 -
127.0.0.1 - - [30/Dec/2020 20:54:37] "GET /favicon.ico HTTP/1.1" 404 -
```

These are a few ways you can use distributed tracing in your cloud native environments to make them observable. Apart from the approaches mentioned here, service meshes such as Istio also provide a sidecar implementation architecture to perform distributed tracing. We will introduce service meshes in Chapter 7. For more information on distributed tracing, please refer to *Mastering Distributed Tracing* by Yuki Shkuro (Packt, 2019).

Now let's discuss what Azure has to offer in the monitoring space.

# Azure Monitor

In addition to the previously mentioned tailor-made solutions for building observable systems, Microsoft Azure also offers *Azure Monitor,* an off-the-shelf solution that can help you monitor an application and infrastructure running in the cloud and in on-premises environments. Azure Monitor primarily uses metrics and logs to find out how your application is performing and proactively identifies potential issues affecting them along with any resource dependency.

Azure Monitor has various features that can help you detect a variety of issues in your application and infrastructure, as listed here and depicted in Figure 6-12:

*Application insights*
> You can detect and diagnose issues across applications and dependencies by monitoring the availability, performance, and usage of your web apps hosted in the cloud or on premises.

*Azure Monitor for containers and virtual machines*
> You can monitor the performance of your containers running on AKS as well as the virtual machine hosting them.

*Log analytics and log queries*

You can use Azure Monitor logs based on Azure Data Explorer to query logs.

*Workbooks and dashboards*

You can create flexible visualizations using workbooks and dashboards for data analysis, which will allow you to tap into multiple data resources across Azure.

*Azure Monitor metrics*

You can use Azure Monitor metrics to collect numerical data from your infrastructure and application.

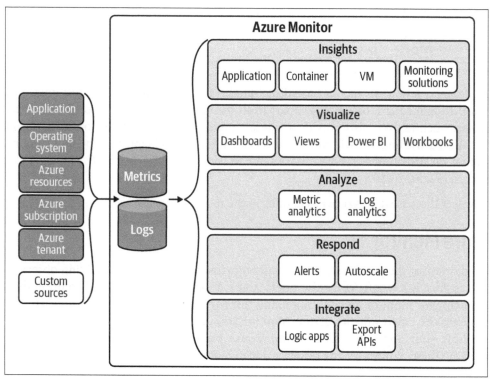

*Figure 6-12. Azure Monitor*

Azure Monitor also allows you to consume distributed trace data. There are primarily two ways to do this. The first is by using the *transaction diagnostics view*, which is similar to a call stack with a time dimension added in. The transaction diagnostics view provides visibility into one single transaction/request, and is helpful for finding the root cause of reliability issues and performance bottlenecks on a per-request basis. The second way is by using the *application map view*, which aggregates many transactions to show a topological view of how the systems interact, and what the average performance and error rates are.

Furthermore, you can integrate Azure Monitor with other systems and build a custom observability platform that uses your monitoring data.

## Summary

In this chapter, we presented observability as a growing need in the cloud native environment. We introduced observability and how it complements monitoring along with how observability-driven development is the new true north for gaining insights into your application and cloud infrastructure. We discussed the three pillars of observability and introduced the preferred ways of logging, monitoring, and tracing modern distributed systems over Azure. Lastly, we looked briefly at how Azure offers its built-in solutions to perform some similar tasks with Azure Monitor. With this knowledge under your belt, you can now confidently build observable systems in cloud native environments and build observability into your application.

In the next chapter, we will look at how service mesh and service discovery assist in cloud native environments.

# CHAPTER 7

# Service Discovery and Service Mesh: Finding New Territories and Crossing Borders

As modern applications moved to a microservices architecture, they became scalable and efficient over the cloud. Microservices favor breaking down an application into independent, decoupled components. Decoupling is usually achieved by separating the codebases into standalone applications that are connected using the network and well-defined APIs/interfaces that microservices use to communicate. Once you move your applications to a microservices architecture, a lot of opportunities open up: you can scale each individual service, decouple the release cycle for each service, choose a different language to write your individual application components, and even organize your team structure based on these independent services.

However, now that you have broken your application into smaller applications, these binaries have their own lifecycle. This lifecycle gets scheduled independently and terminated independently as needed, while it's maintaining communication over the network. Imagine if, in this scenario, you had a lot of microservices running and communicating with one another. You would likely start asking several questions, including the following:

- How do the services communicate with one another when they are dynamic in nature? (That is, since services communicate over a network, the IP address doesn't provide enough information to reach the services as they can be terminated independently and rescheduled on a different host.)

- How do I control and manage the traffic or route traffic as needed, including advanced scenarios like Canary releases, A/B testing, and circuit breaking?

- How can I ensure security between the services and encrypt the traffic between them?

To solve these problems, you could start writing and building additional infrastructure-specific logic within your application. However, this would increase the application scope beyond your business needs, and you would have to implement this logic with every microservices stack that you use.

Luckily, these problems have been solved in the cloud native environment space with the help of service discovery and service mesh technologies, which offer a much more flexible way to manage, secure, and provide far greater control over services.

*Service discovery* is a mechanism through which services discover one another so that they can communicate. Service discovery is primarily focused on finding the network location of a service in the cloud. In traditional environments, where you have to deal with physical servers, you are aware of the static IP addresses for your servers and you can use a simple configuration file to store the IPs, which can be used by your services to reach out to other services. This setup works fine in a local or physical environment setup. But for highly scalable applications in the cloud, this approach fails, since now your application is dynamic in nature, which means the application can be restarted, rescheduled, or terminated as needed. In such scenarios, one cannot hardcode the IP, since it can change. Service discovery helps by storing a mapping for each service name to the IP address in the cloud.

A *service mesh* focuses on solving the increased complexity that comes with interservice communication. A service mesh is a dedicated infrastructure that handles all service-to-service network communication within the cloud environment. It provides high visibility, resiliency, traffic management, and security control with little to no change to the existing application code.

In this chapter, we will look at CoreDNS, a prominent service discovery platform in the cloud native world that is used by the Azure Kubernetes Service (AKS) for cluster DNS management and name resolution. We will also cover Istio, a prominent service mesh that is widely used in cloud environments like Azure.

# Service Discovery

Service discovery is a fundamental component of a modern cloud native environment. It is responsible for ensuring that services can find and communicate with one another over a network. Typically, service discovery involves a *service registry* where all the services/applications in the cloud environment need to register. The service registry is the central repository that holds the location of the services. In a typical scenario, a new service first registers itself with the service registry when it enters the environment. The service registry updates the latest network location of the service, and when a consumer service requests to connect to the service, the service registry serves the consumer with a location for the service.

In this section, we will explore CoreDNS and see how it can be used as a service discovery tool in cloud environments.

## Introduction to CoreDNS

CoreDNS is an extensible DNS server that supports standard DNS, DNS over TLS, and DNS over gRPC protocols. CoreDNS was created by Miek Gieben in 2016 by utilizing a server framework developed as part of the Caddy web server (*https:// caddyserver.com*). It has a plug-in architecture that is highly configurable, flexible, and extensible. CoreDNS saw wider adoption after receiving support from the Cloud Native Computing Foundation (CNCF). In 2019, CoreDNS received the "graduated" maturity level from CNCF.[1]

CoreDNS is now the official default DNS server with Kubernetes 1.13 and later, replacing kube-dns. CoreDNS solves the reliability and security issues in the original implementation of kube-dns through several key differences:

- CoreDNS runs a single container, whereas kube-dns ran three containers: kube-dns, dnsmasq, and sidecar.
- CoreDNS is designed for use as a general-purpose DNS server that is backward compatible with Kubernetes.
- CoreDNS is primarily a Go process that enhances the functionality of kube-dns.

The CoreDNS plug-in architecture ensures that the DNS server functionality remains stable and enables further functionality to be added using plug-ins. The end user can define multiple servers by configuring zones to serve on a particular port. Each server passes the requests through a plug-in chain, which determines what type of response to send:

- If multiple servers are configured to listen on the queried port, it will check which one has the most specific zone for the query using the longest suffix match. For example, if a user makes a query for *www.health.abc.com* and there are two servers configured as *abc.com* and *health.abc.com*, the query will be routed to the latter server.

---

1 CNCF assigns different maturity levels to projects: sandbox, incubated, and graduated, which correspond to the Innovators, Early Adopters, and Early Majority tiers of the Crossing the Chasm diagram. The maturity level is a signal that CNCF assigns to a project to identify what sorts of enterprises should be adopting the project.

- Once an appropriate server has been found, it will be routed through the plug-in chain configured for the server.
- Each plug-in will inspect the query, and based on the query, the following can happen:
  — If the query is processed by the plug-in, an appropriate response will be sent back to the client. The query processing stops right here and no more plug-ins are called.
  — If the query is not processed by the plug-in, it will call the next plug-in in the chain. If the last plug-in in the chain is also not able to process the query, CoreDNS will return a SERVFAIL to the calling client.
  — If the query is processed using a fall-through method in which the other plug-ins down the chain are also called to take a look at the query, the keyword `fallthrough` is used to enable it.
  — If the query is processed by using a hint, the next plug-in in the chain will always be called. However, it will provide a hint that allows it to see the response that will be returned to the client.

Figure 7-1 showcases the steps that occur when CoreDNS processes a query.

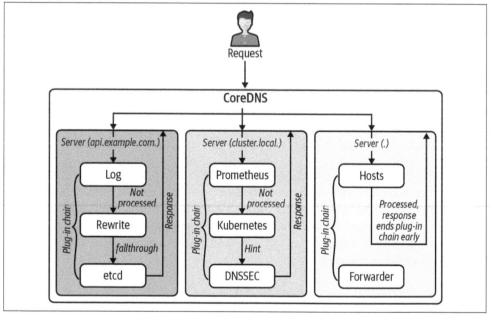

*Figure 7-1. CoreDNS query process*

Now let's see how to install CoreDNS and use the configuration file, also known as a *Corefile*, to configure it.

## Installing and Configuring CoreDNS

You can install CoreDNS by using the binary, which is available at this book's GitHub location (*https://oreil.ly/yiZNL*). Once you have grabbed the binary for your OS, you can move it to your local bin. For example, if you have downloaded the binary for macOS, *coredns_1.8.1_darwin_amd64.tgz*, you can unzip the file and move it to */usr/local/bin*. Verify that CoreDNS is working fine by issuing the following command:

```
$ coredns -version
CoreDNS-1.8.1
darwin/amd64, go1.15.7, 95622f4
```

CoreDNS offers a bunch of configuration options that are handled by a Corefile. When CoreDNS starts, it looks for a file named *Corefile* in the current directory if the -conf flag is not passed. The file primarily defines the following:

- Which server listens on which port
- For which zone each server is authoritative
- What plug-ins are loaded in a server

A Corefile normally looks like this:

```
ZONE:[PORT] {
    [PLUGIN]...
}
```

where ZONE represents the DNS zone, PORT is where the zone server runs (usually port 53), and PLUGIN defines the plug-ins the user needs to load.

Among the most common entries in a Corefile are the various *server blocks* that define a server within CoreDNS (i.e., how queries for a particular domain name are processed). Here's an example:

```
example.com {

}
```

The preceding server block will handle all the queries that end up in *example.com* unless a more specific server block, like *foo.example.com*, is present. For a more concrete example, say you have the following in your Corefile:

```
cloudnativeazure.io:53 {
    log
    errors
}


.:53 {
    forward . 8.8.8.8
    log
    errors
```

```
        cache
    }
```

In this example, we have two server blocks for the cloudnativeazure.io and root (.) server blocks. Both of them are listening on port 53. Also, several plug-ins are defined: log, to log every query that CoreDNS receives; errors, to log errors; and cache, to enable frontend cache (i.e., all records except zone transfers and metadata will be cached for up to 3600s). You can run the preceding Corefile by simply typing coredns in the same directory where Corefile is present, or do coredns -conf Corefile:

```
$ coredns -conf Corefile
.:53
cloudnativeazure.io.:53
CoreDNS-1.8.1
darwin/amd64, go1.15.7, 95622f4
```

If you do a dig for cloudnativeazure.io in another terminal, you will see the following:

```
$  ~ dig @127.0.0.1 cloudnativeazure.io:53
; <<>> DiG 9.10.6 <<>> @127.0.0.1 cloudnativeazure.io:53
; (1 server found)
;; global options: +cmd
;; Got answer:
;; ->>HEADER<<- opcode: QUERY, status: NXDOMAIN, id: 48995
;; flags: qr rd ra ad; QUERY: 1, ANSWER: 0, AUTHORITY: 1, ADDITIONAL: 1

;; OPT PSEUDOSECTION:
; EDNS: version: 0, flags:; udp: 4096
;; QUESTION SECTION:
;cloudnativeazure.io:53.      IN     A

;; AUTHORITY SECTION:
.            1800    IN     SOA    a.root-servers.net. nstld.verisign-grs.com. 2021021001 \
  1800 900 604800 86400

;; Query time: 82 msec
;; SERVER: 127.0.0.1#53(127.0.0.1)
;; WHEN: Wed Feb 10 23:45:28 IST 2021
;; MSG SIZE  rcvd: 126
```

You can see the logs on the CoreDNS terminal as follows:

```
$ coredns -conf Corefile
.:53
cloudnativeazure.io.:53
CoreDNS-1.8.1
darwin/amd64, go1.15.7, 95622f4

[INFO] 127.0.0.1:59741 - 48995 "A IN cloudnativeazure.io:53. udp 51 false 4096" NXDOMAIN \
  qr,rd,ra,ad 115 0.05160016s
```

We've only covered the fundamentals of CoreDNS here. For more information, we suggest that you read *Learning CoreDNS* by John Belamaric and Cricket Liu (O'Reilly, 2019).

Now let's discuss how CoreDNS is used in service discovery on Kubernetes.

## Kubernetes Service Discovery with CoreDNS

As we mentioned earlier, CoreDNS is the default service discovery mechanism in Kubernetes v1.13 and later, and you can start using it from the get-go. As you can see in the following code block, the Pods running in the kube-system namespace are of type core-dns:

```
$ kubectl get pods --namespace=kube-system -o wide
NAME                                        READY  STATUS    RESTARTS  AGE    IP
  NODE                                      NOMINATED NODE  READINESS GATES
coredns-748cdb7bf4-9xqqk                    1/1    Running   0         4h31m  10.244.0.3
  aks-agentpool-13363041-vmss000002         <none>          <none>
coredns-748cdb7bf4-f6glb                    1/1    Running   0         4h30m  10.244.0.5
  aks-agentpool-13363041-vmss000002         <none>          <none>
coredns-autoscaler-868b684fd4-7ck6z         1/1    Running   0         4h30m  10.244.0.4
  aks-agentpool-13363041-vmss000002         <none>          <none>


$ kubectl get deployments --namespace=kube-system
NAME                READY  UP-TO-DATE  AVAILABLE  AGE
coredns             2/2    2           2          4h31m
coredns-autoscaler  1/1    1           1          4h31m
```

The CoreDNS Kubernetes plug-in watches the Kubernetes services and endpoint resources and caches that data. When a request is made, the CoreDNS plug-in will see whether a resource corresponding to the requested name exists, and then it will return the appropriate data. The response records are built on the fly based on incoming requests by using the *watch* feature of the Kubernetes API server.

Let's take a look at how CoreDNS assists in service discovery over a Kubernetes cluster. Suppose you are running a simple Nginx Pod in a Kubernetes cluster as follows:

```
$ kubectl get pods
NAME   READY  STATUS    RESTARTS  AGE
nginx  1/1    Running   0         3m20s

$ kubectl get services
NAME        TYPE       CLUSTER-IP     EXTERNAL-IP  PORT(S)   AGE
kubernetes  ClusterIP  10.0.0.1       <none>       443/TCP   41m
nginx       ClusterIP  10.0.148.122   <none>       80/TCP    3m26s
```

To access this Nginx server, you need to run an infoblox/dnstools Pod that has some DNS utilities, such as dig and curl. To run this Pod, you can use the following command:

```
$ kubectl run --restart=Never -it --image infoblox/dnstools dnstools
If you don't see a command prompt, try pressing enter.
dnstools#
```

The preceding command will log you inside the newly spun container and leave you a command prompt.

In Kubernetes, DNS-based service discovery defines a specification, or a DNS schema, that defines the DNS name used to locate the services running in the cluster. All DNS records in a Kubernetes cluster fall under a single domain referred to as the *cluster domain*, which is usually set to `cluster.local` by default in most Kubernetes clusters. The DNS specification defines that for each IP assigned to a service (i.e., the cluster IP), an A record exists that contains the cluster IP with a name derived from the service name and namespace as `service.namespace.svc.cluster-domain`. So, to access the Nginx Pod that we created, you can issue the following command from the `infoblox/dnstools` container:

```
dnstools# curl nginx.default.svc.cluster.local
<!DOCTYPE html>
<html>
<head>
<title>Welcome to nginx!</title>
<style>
    body {
        width: 35em;
        margin: 0 auto;
        font-family: Tahoma, Verdana, Arial, sans-serif;
    }
</style>
</head>
<body>
<h1>Welcome to nginx!</h1>
<p>If you see this page, the nginx web server is successfully installed and
working. Further configuration is required.</p>

<p>For online documentation and support please refer to
<a href="http://nginx.org/">nginx.org</a>.<br/>
Commercial support is available at
<a href="http://nginx.com/">nginx.com</a>.</p>

<p><em>Thank you for using nginx.</em></p>
</body>
</html>
dnstools#
```

You can also issue a `dig` command to see the A record for the service:

```
dnstools# dig nginx.default.svc.cluster.local

; <<>> DiG 9.11.3 <<>> nginx.default.svc.cluster.local
;; global options: +cmd
;; Got answer:
;; WARNING: .local is reserved for Multicast DNS
;; You are currently testing what happens when an mDNS query is leaked to DNS
;; ->>HEADER<<- opcode: QUERY, status: NOERROR, id: 52488
;; flags: qr aa rd; QUERY: 1, ANSWER: 1, AUTHORITY: 0, ADDITIONAL: 1
;; WARNING: recursion requested but not available

;; OPT PSEUDOSECTION:
; EDNS: version: 0, flags:; udp: 4096
; COOKIE: 5086e790e261bf20 (echoed)
;; QUESTION SECTION:
;nginx.default.svc.cluster.local. IN     A
```

```
;; ANSWER SECTION:
nginx.default.svc.cluster.local. 5 IN    A       10.0.148.122

;; Query time: 1 msec
;; SERVER: 10.0.0.10#53(10.0.0.10)
;; WHEN: Sat Feb 27 07:37:10 UTC 2021
;; MSG SIZE  rcvd: 119
```

Microsoft Azure also provides DNS as a service, through a hosting service known as Azure DNS. We'll take a look at that next.

## Azure DNS

Azure DNS primarily provides Microsoft Azure infrastructure to handle name resolutions for DNS domains. You can use Azure DNS to host your DNS domain and manage your DNS records. By hosting your domains in Azure, you can manage your DNS records using the same credentials, APIs, tools, and billing as your other Azure services.

Azure DNS can be used to resolve hostnames in both public and private domains. The public DNS feature can be used to host your prepurchased domain name via Azure, while the private DNS lets you manage and resolve domain names within virtual networks.

CoreDNS also provides an Azure-specific plug-in that is used to serve zones from Azure DNS. You can enable the Azure plug-in as follows:

```
azure AZURE_RESOURCE_GROUP:ZONE... {
    tenant <TENANT_ID>
    client <CLIENT_ID>
    secret <CLIENT_SECRET>
    subscription <SUBSCRIPTION_ID>
    environment <ENVIRONMENT>
    fallthrough [ZONES...]
    access private
}
```

In the preceding code:

- `AZURE_RESOURCE_GROUP:ZONE` is the resource group to which the hosted zones belong on Azure, and `ZONE` is the zone that contains data.
- `CLIENT_ID` and `CLIENT_SECRET` are the credentials for Azure, and `tenant` specifies the `TENANT_ID` to be used. `SUBSCRIPTION_ID` is the subscription ID.
- `environment` specifies the Azure `ENVIRONMENT`.

- `fallthrough` specifies that if the zone matches and no record can be generated, the request should be passed to the next plug-in. If `ZONES` is omitted, fall-through occurs for all zones for which the plug-in is authoritative.

- `access` specifies whether the DNS zone is `public` or `private`. The default is `public`.

We've covered the role and significance of service discovery in distributed cloud native environments, so let's discuss what a service mesh brings to the table.

# The Service Mesh

A service mesh is a tool that adds observability, reliability, and security at the platform layer of cloud native applications. A service mesh is usually implemented as a scalable set of network proxies deployed as a sidecar beside the application. These proxies are primarily responsible for handling communication between the microservices and they operate at Layer 7 of the OSI stack. Along with several additional features, a service mesh also:

- Provides traffic management through load balancing, rate limiting, traffic shifting, and circuit breakers

- Helps in application release cycle management with Canary releases

- Adds some reliability checks, such as health checks, retries, and timeouts out of the box

- Assists with fault injection and debug routing

- Provides security via TLS and ACL policies

- Provides automatic metrics, logs, and traces for all the traffic within a cluster

- Secures service-to-service communication in a cluster using strong, identification-based authentication and authorization

The general architecture of a service mesh consists of two high-level components: a data plane and a control plane. Figure 7-2 depicts four services (A–D) deployed in a service mesh.

As you can see, each service instance has a sidecar proxy instance that is responsible for all the traffic flow and management. This basically means that when service A wants to talk to service C, for example, service A initiates the communication flow via its local sidecar proxy, which then reaches out to the service C sidecar proxy. This way, the service is not aware of the local network proxy and remains isolated from the larger network. So, whenever a service needs to talk to another service, the proxy intercepts the request from it and then forwards it to the receiver.

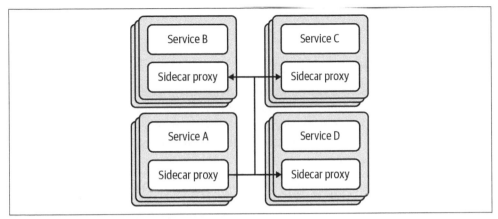

*Figure 7-2. Service mesh general architecture*

The collection of all sidecar proxies constitutes the *data plane* of the service mesh architecture. The data plane is responsible for the following:

- Request forwarding
- Service discovery
- Health checking
- Routing service requests
- Load balancing
- Authentication and authorization
- Providing observability

Hence, the data plane fundamentally touches every network request or packet in the cluster.

The control plane, on the other hand, provides the policy and configuration details for all the sidecar proxies (data planes) in the service mesh. The control plane allows you to control and configure the data planes. All the high-level configuration is sent to the control plane, which is then translated to the data-plane-specific configuration. The control plane assists the data plane by:

- Routing between services
- Populating service discovery data for data plane usage
- Specifying inputs for configurations responsible for load balancing, circuit breaking, and timeouts
- Configuring validation, authentication, and authorization settings in the cluster

In the next section we will take a look at Istio, which acts as the control plane to a service mesh in a modern cloud native environment.

## Introduction to Istio

As monolithic applications transitioned toward microservices, developers and operations teams experienced challenges with regard to how the services would talk to one another in the service mesh. As a service mesh grows in size, it becomes difficult to manage and maintain. It also becomes difficult to even understand how the different moving parts work together.

Istio is an open source service mesh that simplifies the communication between microservices in distributed cloud native applications. Istio provides rich, built-in feature sets that enforce resiliency patterns such as retries, circuit breakers, shaping traffic, routing behavior, Canary deployment, and more. Moreover, Istio allows you to easily create a network of deployed microservices using load balancing, monitoring, and authentication, with almost no application code changes.

As we discussed in the previous section, a service mesh architecture consists of a data plane and a control plane. Istio uses Envoy as its data plane and istiod as its control plane (as depicted in Figure 7-3):

*Envoy (data plane)*
Envoy is a high-performance proxy written in C++ that intercepts all inbound and outbound traffic for each application in the service mesh. It is deployed as a sidecar along with the application and provides a lot of features, including TLS termination, load balancing, circuit breaking, health checks, dynamic service discovery, fault injection, and more. This sidecar proxy model allows you to use Istio as a service mesh without any code changes.

*Istiod (control plane)*
Istiod manages and configures the proxies. Istiod consists of three subcomponents:

- Pilot, responsible for configuring the Envoy proxies at runtime
- Citadel, responsible for certificate issuance and rotation
- Galley, responsible for validating, ingesting, aggregating, transforming, and distributing the config within Istio

Istiod converts the high-level routing rules that control traffic into Envoy-specific configuration and propagates to the Envoy sidecars at runtime.

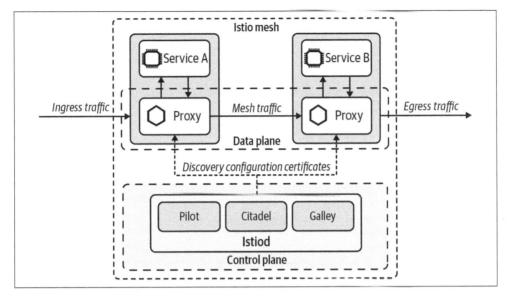

*Figure 7-3. Istio architecture*

Let's take a look at how you can use Istio and Envoy in an Azure Kubernetes environment.

# Installing Istio on Azure Kubernetes Service

You can install Istio on a Kubernetes cluster in three ways:

- Istio provides a command-line tool called *istioctl*, which can be used to provide a rich level of customization to the Istio control plane and the Envoy proxy data plane.
- You can use the Istio Kubernetes operator to manage the installation via the custom resource definitions (CRDs) of the Kubernetes API.
- You can use Helm charts to install Istio directly.

As Helm charts are also indirectly used in methods 1 and 2, we'll use them here to install Istio.

### Installing Istio using Helm

To install Istio using Helm, you need an AKS cluster already running (review Chapter 5 if you need a refresher on how to spin an AKS cluster in Azure). The following steps will install Istio on an AKS cluster:

1. Download Istio by running the following commands from your local machine:

```
$ curl -L https://istio.io/downloadIstio | ISTIO_VERSION=1.9.2 TARGET_ARCH=x86_64 sh -

$ cd istio-1.9.2
```

2. Create a new namespace for Istio components, called `istio-system`:

```
$ kubectl create namespace istio-system

namespace/istio-system created
```

3. Install the Istio base chart that contains cluster-wide resources used by the istiod control plane:

```
$ helm install istio-base manifests/charts/base -n istio-system
NAME: istio-base
LAST DEPLOYED: Sun Mar 28 15:59:16 2021
NAMESPACE: istio-system
STATUS: deployed
REVISION: 1
TEST SUITE: None
```

4. Install the Istio discovery chart that deploys the istiod service:

```
$ helm install istiod manifests/charts/istio-control/istio-discovery -n istio-system

NAME: istiod
LAST DEPLOYED: Sun Mar 28 16:02:23 2021
NAMESPACE: istio-system
STATUS: deployed
REVISION: 1
TEST SUITE: None
```

5. Verify the installation:

```
$ helm list -A
NAME            NAMESPACE       REVISION UPDATED                              STATUS
  CHART                         APP VERSION
istio-base    istio-system    1        2021-03-28 15:59:16.429126 +0530 IST   deployed
  base-1.9.2
istiod        istio-system    1        2021-03-28 16:02:23.950541 +0530 IST   deployed
  istio-discovery-1.9.2
$ kubectl get pods -n istio-system
NAME                      READY   STATUS    RESTARTS   AGE
istiod-6d68c86c8d-5nv2r   1/1     Running   0          10m
```

It's important to ensure that whenever a new Pod is being deployed in the cluster, an Istio sidecar proxy (Envoy proxy) is also injected into the same Pod so that you can take advantage of all of Istio's features. We'll discuss how to do that in the next section.

## Automatically Injecting the Sidecar Proxy (Envoy Proxy)

To take full advantage of Istio as a service mesh, Pods in the cluster must also use the Istio sidecar proxy. istio-proxy, which is basically the Envoy proxy, can be deployed in two ways: manually or automatically. The manual method allows you to modify the injection and proxy configuration. The automatic method, as the name suggests, enables an automatic proxy configuration at the time of Pod creation by using a mutating admission controller. Although the manual method is useful when you need a certain configuration, the automatic method is preferred. We'll go through how to use the automatic method next.

**Kubernetes Admission Controllers**

An admission controller is a piece of code that intercepts requests to the Kubernetes API server before the object is persisted but after the request is authenticated and authorized. Kubernetes provides a range of admission controllers that are compiled into the *kube-apiserver* library.

A MutatingAdmissionController can modify objects that it admits. That is, it calls any mutating web hook that matches the request.

To use automatic sidecar injection, use the label istio-injection on the desired namespace and set it to enabled. This allows any new Pods created in that namespace to have a proxy sidecar be deployed along with the application. To give you a better understanding of how this happens, first we'll deploy an Nginx Pod with no sidecar injection, and then we will enable sidecar injection so that with future deployments, the sidecar proxy is automatically injected.

Suppose we have deployed Nginx with one Pod:

```
$ kubectl apply -f nginx_deploy.yaml
deployment.apps/nginx-deployment created

$ kubectl get deployment -o wide
NAME              READY  UP-TO-DATE  AVAILABLE  AGE    CONTAINERS  IMAGES        SELECTOR
nginx-deployment  1/1    1           1          105s   nginx       nginx:1.14.2  app=nginx

$ kubectl get pod
NAME                                READY  STATUS   RESTARTS  AGE
nginx-deployment-6b474476c4-bqgh8   1/1    Running  0         4m5s
```

Let's label the default namespace istio-injection=enabled:

```
$ kubectl label namespace default istio-injection=enabled --overwrite
namespace/default labeled
$ kubectl get namespace -L istio-injection
NAME          STATUS  AGE  ISTIO-INJECTION
default       Active  24m  enabled
istio-system  Active  18m
```

```
kube-node-lease    Active    25m
kube-public        Active    25m
kube-system        Active    25m
```

Since injection occurs when the Pod is created, we can kill the Nginx Pod and spin a new Nginx Pod, only this time the Pod will have a sidecar injected automatically:

```
$ kubectl delete pod -l app=nginx
pod "nginx-deployment-6b474476c4-bqgh8" deleted

$ kubectl get pod -l app=nginx
NAME                                 READY   STATUS    RESTARTS   AGE
nginx-deployment-6b474476c4-pfgqv    2/2     Running   0          57s
```

Note that the deployment has spun up two containers. This is the sidecar proxy running in the Pod. You can verify this with `describe` as follows:

```
$ kubectl describe pod -l app=nginx

Events:
  Type     Reason     Age        From                     Message
  ----     ------     ----       ----                     -------
  Normal   Scheduled  <unknown>  default-scheduler        Successfully
    assigned default/nginx-deployment-6b474476c4-pfgqv to aks-agentpool-20139558-vmss000001
  Normal   Pulling    2m35s      kubelet, aks-agentpool-20139558-vmss000001  Pulling image
    "docker.io/istio/proxyv2:1.9.2"
  Normal   Created    2m34s      kubelet, aks-agentpool-20139558-vmss000001  Created
    container nginx
  Normal   Created    2m34s      kubelet, aks-agentpool-20139558-vmss000001  Created
    container istio-init
  Normal   Started    2m34s      kubelet, aks-agentpool-20139558-vmss000001  Started
    container istio-init
  Normal   Pulled     2m34s      kubelet, aks-agentpool-20139558-vmss000001  Container image
    "nginx:1.14.2" already present on machine
  Normal   Pulled     2m34s      kubelet, aks-agentpool-20139558-vmss000001  Successfully
    pulled image "docker.io/istio/proxyv2:1.9.2"
  Normal   Started    2m34s      kubelet, aks-agentpool-20139558-vmss000001  Started
    container nginx
  Normal   Pulling    2m34s      kubelet, aks-agentpool-20139558-vmss000001  Pulling image
    "docker.io/istio/proxyv2:1.9.2"
  Normal   Pulled     2m33s      kubelet, aks-agentpool-20139558-vmss000001  Successfully
    pulled image "docker.io/istio/proxyv2:1.9.2"
  Normal   Created    2m33s      kubelet, aks-agentpool-20139558-vmss000001  Created
    container istio-proxy
  Normal   Started    2m33s      kubelet, aks-agentpool-20139558-vmss000001  Started
    container istio-proxy
```

Now that you know how to deploy the sidecar proxy, you can use Istio for traffic management, security, policy enforcement, and observability. We will not go into each of these aspects as they are beyond the scope of this book.

When using a service mesh, you should be able to visualize and manage it. In the next section, we'll focus on Kiali, a management console for Istio-based service meshes.

# Managing Istio Service Meshes Using Kiali

Kiali is a management console for Istio that enables you to easily operate and configure a service mesh with added observability into your environment. Kiali provides a clear picture of the service mesh through dashboards that use traffic topology to display its structure and health. In this section, we will discuss how to install Kiali on a Kubernetes cluster to gain visibility into the Istio service mesh.

We'll start by installing the ingress and egress gateway for Istio from the *istio-1.9.2* directory that we used when we installed Istio earlier:

```
Istio-1.9.2 $ helm install istio-ingress manifests/charts/gateways/istio-ingress -n \
  istio-system
NAME: istio-ingress
LAST DEPLOYED: Mon Apr  5 15:19:01 2021
NAMESPACE: istio-system
STATUS: deployed
REVISION: 1
TEST SUITE: None

Istio-1.9.2 $ helm install istio-egress manifests/charts/gateways/istio-egress  -n \
  istio-system
NAME: istio-egress
LAST DEPLOYED: Mon Apr  5 15:19:31 2021
NAMESPACE: istio-system
STATUS: deployed
REVISION: 1
TEST SUITE: None
```

Now we can use the Helm chart to install Kiali:

```
$ kubectl create namespace kiali-operator
namespace/kiali-operator created
$ istio-1.9.2 helm install --set cr.create=true  --set cr.namespace=istio-system  \
  --namespace kiali-operator  --repo https://kiali.org/helm-charts \
  kiali-operator kiali-operator

NAME: kiali-operator
LAST DEPLOYED: Mon Apr  5 15:27:03 2021
NAMESPACE: kiali-operator
STATUS: deployed
REVISION: 1
TEST SUITE: None
NOTES:
Welcome to Kiali! For more details on Kiali, see: https://kiali.io

The Kiali Operator [v1.32.0] has been installed in namespace [kiali-operator]. It will be
ready soon.
You have elected to install a Kiali CR in the namespace [istio-system]. You should be able
to access Kiali soon.

If you ever want to uninstall the Kiali Operator, remember to delete the Kiali CR first
before uninstalling the operator to give the operator a chance to uninstall and remove all
the Kiali Server resources.

(Helm: Chart=[kiali-operator], Release=[kiali-operator], Version=[1.32.0])
```

This will install the latest Kiali operator along with the Kiali custom resource (CR), which is basically a YAML file that holds the Kiali configuration.

To access the Kiali dashboard we first need to expose it correctly to the internet. To do this, we need to get the ingress gateway address as follows:

```
$ export INGRESS_HOST=$(kubectl -n istio-system get service istio-ingressgateway -o \
  jsonpath='{.status.loadBalancer.ingress[0].ip}')
$ export INGRESS_DOMAIN=${INGRESS_HOST}.nip.io
```

Now we need to create a self-signed certificate:

```
$ CERT_DIR=/tmp/certs
$ mkdir -p ${CERT_DIR}
$ openssl req -x509 -sha256 -nodes -days 365 -newkey rsa:2048 -subj "/O=example Inc./ \
  CN=*.${INGRESS_DOMAIN}" -keyout ${CERT_DIR}/ca.key -out ${CERT_DIR}/ca.crt
$ openssl req -out ${CERT_DIR}/cert.csr -newkey rsa:2048 -nodes -keyout \
  ${CERT_DIR}/tls.key -subj "/CN=*.${INGRESS_DOMAIN}/O=example organization"
$ openssl x509 -req -days 365 -CA ${CERT_DIR}/ca.crt -CAkey ${CERT_DIR}/ca.key \
  -set_serial 0 -in ${CERT_DIR}/cert.csr -out ${CERT_DIR}/tls.crt
$ kubectl create -n istio-system secret tls telemetry-gw-cert --key=${CERT_DIR}/tls.key \
  --cert=${CERT_DIR}/tls.crt
```

At this point, we can expose Kiali using the following configurations, which will create a gateway, a virtual service, and a destination rule:

- Gateway represents a data plane that routes traffic into a Kubernetes cluster by configuring a load balancer for HTTP/TCP traffic, regardless of where it will be running.

- VirtualService defines a set of traffic routing rules to apply when a host is addressed. A routing rule can match a certain type of traffic, and when a match for a rule occurs, the traffic is sent to a named destination service.

- DestinationRule configures the set of policies to be applied while forwarding traffic to a service.

Here is the code:

```
$ cat <<EOF | kubectl apply -f -
apiVersion: networking.istio.io/v1alpha3
kind: Gateway
metadata:
  name: kiali-gateway
  namespace: istio-system
spec:
  selector:
    istio: ingressgateway
  servers:
  - port:
      number: 443
      name: https-kiali
      protocol: HTTPS
    tls:
      mode: SIMPLE
      credentialName: telemetry-gw-cert
```

```
      hosts:
      - "kiali.${INGRESS_DOMAIN}"
---
apiVersion: networking.istio.io/v1alpha3
kind: VirtualService
metadata:
  name: kiali-vs
  namespace: istio-system
spec:
  hosts:
  - "kiali.${INGRESS_DOMAIN}"
  gateways:
  - kiali-gateway
  http:
  - route:
    - destination:
        host: kiali
        port:
          number: 20001
---
apiVersion: networking.istio.io/v1alpha3
kind: DestinationRule
metadata:
  name: kiali
  namespace: istio-system
spec:
  host: kiali
  trafficPolicy:
    tls:
      mode: DISABLE
---
EOF
```

Now you can access the Kiali UI at *https://kiali.$\{INGRESS_DOMAIN\}* (in our case, it is *https://kiali.40.118.246.227.nip.io*). When you go to this URL you will be presented with the Kiali login screen, where you need to enter the token for the Kiali operator. You can get the token by doing the following:

```
$ kubectl get secrets --namespace=kiali-operator -o wide
NAME                                  TYPE                                     DATA   AGE
default-token-7ng8l                   kubernetes.io/service-account-token      3      142m
kiali-operator-token-jj88t            kubernetes.io/service-account-token      3      141m
sh.helm.release.v1.kiali-operator.v1  helm.sh/release.v1                       1      141m


$ ~ kubectl describe secret kiali-operator-token-jj88t --namespace=kiali-operator
Name:         kiali-operator-token-jj88t
Namespace:    kiali-operator
Labels:       <none>
Annotations:  kubernetes.io/service-account.name: kiali-operator
              kubernetes.io/service-account.uid: 9a30ba7a-7d21-484d-9e7a-0a38458690a4

Type:  kubernetes.io/service-account-token

Data
====
ca.crt:     1765 bytes
namespace:  14 bytes
```

token:      eyJhbGciOiJSUzI1NiIsImtpZCI6InVvQXNpV01QRG1fRjhma0RRZjVIWXBNVHRnZDhJdHhoOXI2RmQ2
eGxDZDQifQ.eyJpc3MiOiJrdWJlcm5ldGVzL3NlcnZpY2VhY2NvdW50Iiwia3ViZXJuZXRlcy5pby9zZXJ2aWNlYWNjb
3VudC9uYW1lc3BhY2UiOiJraWFsaS1vcGVyYXRvciIsImt1YmVybmV0ZXMuaW8vc2VydmljZWFjY291bnQvc2VjmV0L
m5hbWUiOiJraWFsaS1vcGVyYXRvci10b2tlbi1qajg4dCIsImt1YmVybmV0ZXMuaW8vc2VydmljZWFjY291bnQvc2Vyd
mljZS1hY2NvdW50Lm5hbWUiOiJraWFsaS1vcGVyYXRvciIsImt1YmVybmV0ZXMuaW8vc2VydmljZWFjY291bnQvc2Vyd
mljZS1hY2NvdW50LnVpZCI6IjlhMzBiYTdhLTdkMjEtNDg0ZC05ZTdhLTBhMzg0NTg2OTBhNCIsInN1Yi16InN5c3Rlb
TpzZXJ2aWNlYWNjb3VudDpraWFsaS1vcGVyYXRvcjpraWFsaS1vcGVyYXRvciJ9.uJ6056HMQGvc00QIK1O0Mj1PCSrW
MpYZL0jKiG27EBurhUcZ73ngr1S0IfzcNnRwJLuWUkMPrzzKOzVvrUUMf6biPb0MieWn001HX6mfHOzNgXRAxdP-0Ape
hmEiCyENQS4DEQL2Eg8mUuaFsExuwzpx8LAibdLRpbI7sQa4P5B7he2HuolSFzJsoySjaKcP6eJGOaIbscIz-qtDcoM3
11EXhZr6xx8G7b5O7VEYuzs-LNKNyqCJL_iDyxV73WGgaPA2KHUjM-ESpBF-qkoWZDMy6oLqbe24Kcv-Mzmji_WLTMc2
8mXttjiMgVPllUeQfFTK4wYNvpnFEQCJ6ogYC4JJoRLSUuPslSC2JX_Bi4OaiGus1BH3JtFQsxxmL3f7ZnPa-XY66Zk_
ZyKZF1rqLKnzXCa85KkZZnCA83kpKT4ksM9MnqTBGBLNMW7OV4gTDTl9zUvQm--VgaoN2lnHZ-oqHPzeNym7690YHzSA
A_C_g1un1gtc8RlkUDM8u4F-DUSDGnJTBqjUQLiwXDyJS_epCpLuuA-6xCtx9DLkWTcGy886SPX1u30LVeZUfRRlumjt
eEdId8Z884Iqx1T4V8Qo6AomdI0mLjbyFbpKoDLTfaTA98SuaEbko0oF5dzxo2xBgYXy-b1iE4KO9r_PnBZ-BLVQ0zfO
_1Bjym9JYWo

You can now copy the token and log in with it. You also need to install Prometheus with Istio to record metrics that track the health of Istio and of applications within the service mesh (refer back to Chapter 6 if you need a refresher on how to do that). Use the following manifest to install and configure Prometheus:

```
$ kubectl apply -f https://raw.githubusercontent.com/istio/istio/release-1.9/samples/ \
    addons/prometheus.yaml
```

Figure 7-4 shows the resultant Kiali dashboard. You'll notice that the Istio ingress gateway sends traffic to Kiali along with other deployments in the namespace `istio-system`. The dashboard presents a variety of Istio configurations and features that can be used directly from the UI. For example, if you check the `default` namespace in the Overview tab, you can see it already has the sidecar proxy auto-injection-enabled for all the deployments in this namespace (see Figure 7-5). You can use this feature from the UI to enable or disable automatic injection of the sidecar proxy.

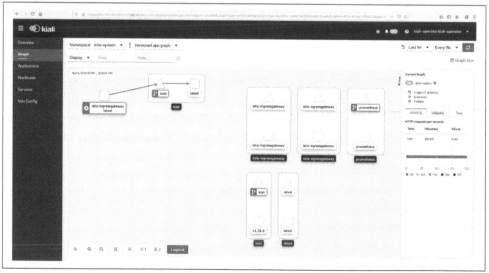

*Figure 7-4. Kiali dashboard showcasing simple inbound traffic*

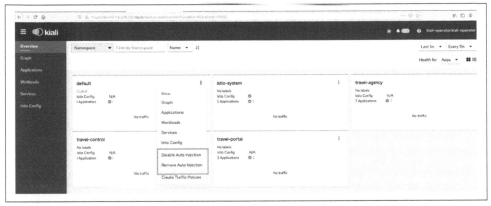

*Figure 7-5. Kiali dashboard showing the status of the auto-injection sidecar proxy in the default namespace*

### Exploring the Kiali dashboard

In this section, we'll explain how you can use the Istio features right from the Kiali dashboard. For this demonstration, we're using an example of a small travel application service. Though we will not focus much on the application, we will highlight Kiali's features and how efficiently it provides every detail about your cloud native application. We will also provide a high-level overview of the business logic of the demo application. If you want to learn more, please refer to the official Kiali documentation for the travel demo (*https://oreil.ly/vTZfc*).

This application simulates two business domains organized in different namespaces. The first namespace is called `travel-portal` and it has several travel shops, where users can search for and book flights, hotels, cars, and travel insurance. The shop applications can behave differently based on request characteristics such as channel (web or mobile) and user (new or existing). All the portals consume a service called `travels` that is deployed in the `travel-agency` namespace.

The second namespace is called `travel-agency` and it hosts a set of services created to provide quotes for travel. A main travel service will be the business entry point for the travel agency. It receives a destination city and a user as parameters and it calculates all the elements that compose a travel budget: airfare, lodging, car reservation, and travel insurance.

Each service can provide an independent quote and the travel service must then aggregate them into a single response.

There is a third namespace as well, called `travel-control`, which runs the main business dashboard with different functions.

We have deployed these three namespaces in the services as follows:

```
$ kubectl create namespace travel-agency
$ kubectl create namespace travel-portal
$ kubectl create namespace travel-control

$ kubectl apply -f <(curl -L https://raw.githubusercontent.com/kiali/demos/master/travels/ \
  travel_agency.yaml) -n travel-agency
$ kubectl apply -f <(curl -L https://raw.githubusercontent.com/kiali/demos/master/travels/ \
  travel_portal.yaml) -n travel-portal
$ kubectl apply -f <(curl -L https://raw.githubusercontent.com/kiali/demos/master/travels/ \
  travel_control.yaml) -n travel-control
```

The first thing you need to do after you have deployed the travel demo application is enable sidecar proxy support. Start by enabling auto injection for all the newly created namespaces by clicking the three dots in the highlighted box in Figure 7-6.

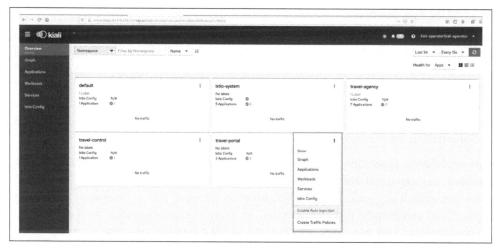

*Figure 7-6. Enabling auto injection for the `travel-portal` namespace*

You can also enable auto injection to a workload that has already been deployed (i.e., Pods) by clicking the Actions button on upper-right corner (see Figure 7-7).

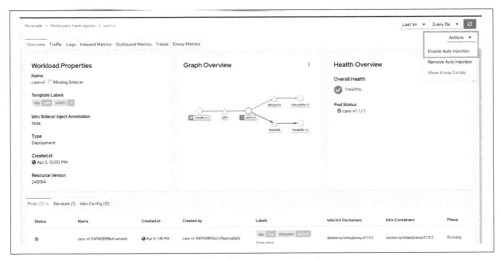

*Figure 7-7. Enabling auto injection for the cars workload*

When you enable auto injection for the workloads via the Kiali dashboard, it will redeploy the application Pod with a sidecar automatically injected, which is similar to the method we discussed previously for the Nginx Pod.

You can also use the request routing feature for a service in the Services tab, as shown in Figure 7-8, to generate a traffic rule that would create an Istio configuration for routing a desired amount of traffic to a certain gateway host, or would use circuit breakers.

*Figure 7-8. Services tab actions*

You can use the request routing feature on the control service to generate the traffic rules as well by clicking the Add Rule button, which will add a default rule where any request will be routed to the control workload. Similarly, you can add a gateway with a host to your load balancer and update the same by clicking the Update button, as shown in Figure 7-9.

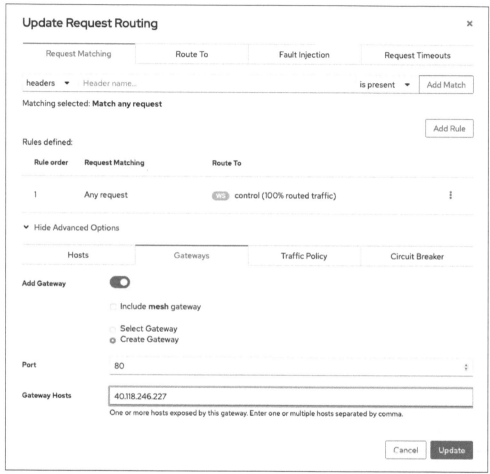

*Figure 7-9. Adding a request route for a service in an Istio configuration via Kiali*

Kiali also provides logs out of the box, metrics via Prometheus, and traces via Jaeger if you have deployed these in your environment. We highly recommend exploring the Kiali UI to see its full capabilities.

# Summary

In this chapter, we explored service discovery and service meshes, two important concepts that help you tie together your applications effectively over a cloud environment like Azure. We introduced CoreDNS as the default DNS replacing kube-dns as a service discovery mechanism in the Kubernetes environment. We also introduced the Istio service mesh, which uses Envoy as its data plane for getting useful insights regarding services and provides the full feature set of the Istio service mesh. We concluded the chapter with a section on Kiali, which provides a full management console on an Istio-based service mesh. Kiali is able to provide observability into a cloud native service by providing a single view of everything in the stack.

In the next chapter, we will talk in depth about how container networking works in Kubernetes and how you can tightly secure your infrastructure with various policy management techniques.

# CHAPTER 8

# Networking and Policy Management: Behold the Gatekeepers

In the preceding chapters, we built infrastructure in Azure and explained how to discover and monitor our applications. Now it's time to secure those applications! Although there have been numerous cloud data breaches over time because of simple misconfigurations, the reality is that securing cloud infrastructure is not difficult. Cloud networking technology has rapidly evolved, and today a number of vendors provide cloud native software that can help you enhance your network configuration as well as secure it.

Azure comes with an offering, Azure Policy, that allows you to set a policy against a tenant, management group, or subscription, which provides a layer of security by default. For example, in Azure you can set a policy that will ensure that no storage accounts are accessible publicly within a management group or subscription.

In this chapter, we will explore the power of container networking and the many ways you can use it to improve your infrastructure. We will also explain how to apply a policy to your infrastructure to keep it secure.

We will start with a discussion about container networking and the standards that multiple projects are built around, then focus on products such as Calico and Flannel, which provide networking connectivity and network policy enforcement. We'll conclude the chapter with a discussion about system policy enforcement with Open Policy Agent (OPA).

# The Container Network Interface (CNI)

As we mentioned in previous chapters, containers offer a vast array of security and portability features. One of the largest returns comes from the networking stack. The Linux cgroups and network namespace features open up a variety of network functionality that can be used to enhance security and telemetry, as well as manage performance. A good example of the flexibility and power of container network functionality is Cilium, a software tool that provides load balancing, security, telemetry, bandwidth management, and other capabilities as an add-on for Kubernetes. We'll discuss Cilium in detail later in this chapter.

In Chapter 3, we briefly mentioned how the industry has a standard specification for the container runtime and the container image. The Container Network Interface (CNI) was created in 2015 (and eventually was added to the Cloud Native Computing Foundation [CNCF] incubating project list) as a standard for configuring container network interfaces and associated network settings. The CNI specification (*https://oreil.ly/XK4A3*) allows management of the following primitives:

- Interface names and network namespace bindings
- IP addresses
- Routing
- DNS settings
- Sysctl settings

An example CNI configuration looks like this:

```
{
  "cniVersion": "1.0.0",
  "name": "dbnet",
  "plugins": [
    {
      "type": "bridge",
      "bridge": "cni0",
      "args": {
        "labels" : {
            "appVersion" : "1.0"
        }
      },
      "ipam": {
        "type": "host-local",
        "subnet": "10.1.0.0/16",
        "gateway": "10.1.0.1"
      },
      "dns": {
        "nameservers": [ "10.1.0.1" ]
      }
    },
    {
      "type": "tuning",
```

```
      "sysctl": {
        "net.core.somaxconn": "500"
      }
    }
  ]
}
```

## Why Would You Use a CNI?

You may be asking yourself why the industry needs a specification just for networking. As we alluded to in Chapter 3, the container ecosystem has a large number of networking projects that plug into container systems like Docker and Kubernetes. Multiple groups are creating publicly available networking-related plug-ins, so there is a need for a standard way to describe and control the container's network layer.

The CNI platform enables true infrastructure virtualization, meaning that you do not need to worry about managing network infrastructure—including in the cloud! Utilizing the container platform as network infrastructure greatly reduces the cost of implementing and operating a complex network infrastructure and provides the ability to scale and upgrade without having to invest in physical or dedicated virtual network devices.

## How Does CNI Work with Azure?

Azure supports CNI, but it has two special plug-ins that connect your containers to the Azure Virtual Network (VNet):

- azure-vnet, which implements the CNI network plug-in
- azure-vnet-ipam, which implements the CNI IP Address Management (IPAM) plug-in

These plug-ins ensure that the container can correctly interface with the Azure VNet control plane. You can use these plug-ins in both Azure Kubernetes Service (AKS) and standalone Azure virtual machines.

### Windows Networking

While the networking stacks for Linux and Windows are fundamentally very different, the Azure CNI plug-ins do have first-class support for Windows, which means you can run both Windows and Linux containers in the same infrastructure without having to create separate network infrastructure.

An Azure CNI configuration looks like this:

```
{
  "cniVersion": "1.0.0",
  "name": "azure",
  "plugins": [
          {
              "type":"azure-vnet",
              "mode":"bridge",
              "bridge":"azure0",
              "ipam":{
                  "type":"azure-vnet-ipam"
              }
          },
        "ipam": {
          "type": "azure-vnet-ipam",
          "Environment": "azure"
        },
        "dns": {
          "nameservers": [ "10.1.0.1" ]
        }
      },
    {
        "type": "tuning",
        "sysctl": {
          "net.core.somaxconn": "500"
        }
      }
    ]
}
```

Use of the azure-vnet and azure-vnet-ipam plug-ins moves IP configuration and management away from the host and to the Azure VNet control plane.

## Various CNI Projects

The CNI project contains a set of default CNI plug-ins split across three categories:

*Main*
> These plug-ins create interfaces (bridge, ipvlan, macvlan, ptp, host-device).

*IPAM*
> These plug-ins assign IP addresses to interfaces (dhcp, host-local, static).

*Meta*
> These are other native plug-ins that allow for actions such as:

- Sysctl tuning
- Bandwidth limiting
- Firewalls
- Flannel (which will be covered later in this chapter)

You can find more information about these native plug-ins on the CNI plug-ins page (*https://cni.dev/plugins*).

In addition to the CNI plug-ins we mentioned here, there is a vast ecosystem of third-party projects that are writing CNI-compatible plug-ins. More than 25 outside projects had taken advantage of the CNI standard at the time of this writing. These projects provide different types of functionality, including load balancing, IPAM, overlay networks, security, and network telemetry.

Some of the smaller projects include:

- Infoblox
- Juniper Contrail
- VMware NSX

While some CNI plug-ins are designed for very specific infrastructure (e.g., Cisco's ACI CNI), many work perfectly well with Azure and Azure services. In the following sections, we will explore Calico, Cilium, Flannel, and OPA, and discuss how these systems help build and secure network infrastructure.

# Calico

Calico is an open source network security and policy solution for containers, virtual machines, and bare metal installations under Windows and Linux. Calico provides network security policy enforcement as well as the ability to implement zero-trust networks. Calico supports multiple data planes, including a state-of-the-art pure Linux extended Berkeley Packet Filter (eBPF) data plane, standard Linux networking data plane, and Windows HNS data plane. Calico runs on top of the host data plane to perform network policy enforcement. It supports the standard Linux networking stack.

## Why Would You Use Calico?

Managing network connectivity and policy becomes exponentially more difficult as your infrastructure grows. Furthermore, it is exceptionally difficult to ensure that the intended policy is correct and is applied correctly, and that feedback on the policy is applied. This is where Calico shines. It allows you to define your network policy in an abstracted, scalable manner and then ensures that the policy is being applied without sacrificing network performance.

## Basic Architecture

Calico has a client/data store architecture that simplifies operation of the platform. It includes the following key components (also depicted in Figure 8-1):

*Felix*

> The network programmatic daemon that installs network access control lists (ACLs), routing information, and interface management and state reporting

*BIRD*

> Gets routing information from Felix and redistributes the routes over Border Gateway Protocol (BGP)

*confd*

> Listens for routing changes from the Calico data store and passes them on to BIRD

*Calico CNI plug-in*

> The interface to the container's network interfaces

*Data store*

> Contains operational information about policies, workloads, and IPAM allocations

*Typha*

> A caching proxy for the data store that is used to scale the number of nodes connecting to the data store

*calicoctl*

> CLI for creating, reading, updating, and deleting Calico objects

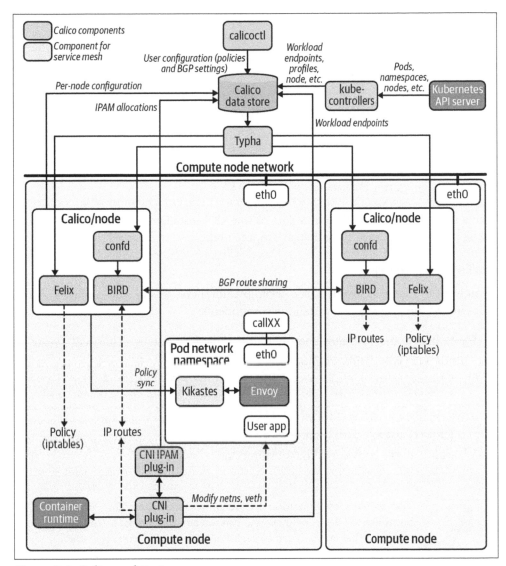

*Figure 8-1. Calico architecture*

## Deploying Calico

There are two options for deploying Calico: install it as part of the network policy engine in an AKS installation or deploy it manually on Kubernetes.

### Deploying Calico via AKS installation

Azure has introduced first-class support for Calico as a network *policy* engine; it can be installed as part of the creation of an AKS instance in the networking configuration step, as shown in Figure 8-2.

*Figure 8-2. Configuring the network policy for AKS*

In this step, if you click Calico as a part of the AKS installation, a Calico Typha Pod will be installed onto each Kubernetes compute node.

### Installing Calico manually

If you want to manually install Calico on your Kubernetes cluster, you can use kubectl to download the operator and install the components:

1. First, install the operator and then the Calico resources. This will create a `tigera-operator` namespace:

   ```
   $ kubectl create -f https://docs.projectcalico.org/manifests/tigera-operator.yaml
   $ kubectl create -f https://docs.projectcalico.org/manifests/custom-resources.yaml
   ```

2. Validate that all Calico nodes are now running:

   ```
   $ kubectl get pods -n calico-system
   ```

3. Wait until all the Pods are in the Running state.

> The `ipPools` configuration in *custom-resources.yaml* file cannot be modified after deployment. This means the `ipPools` (the IP addresses that are assigned to each Pod) are set after you apply the *custom-resources.yaml* file.

### Installing calicoctl

To control Calico, you will need to have access to its CLI utility. There are a few ways to access the utility, as described in the Calico installation documentation (*https://oreil.ly/xcqco*). For this example, we are going to simply download the CLI onto our machine and run it as a kubectl plug-in:

---

1. Log in to a host and navigate to *usr/local/bin*:

    ```
    $ cd /usr/local/bin
    ```

2. Download the binary:

    ```
    $ curl -o kubectl-calico -O -L "https://github.com/projectcalico/calicoctl/releases/ \
        download/v3.21.0/calicoctl-linux-ppc64le"
    ```

3. Set the binary to be executable:

    ```
    $ chmod +x kubectl-calico
    ```

4. Verify that the plug-in works:

    ```
    $ kubectl calico -h
    ```

# A Calico Deep Dive

We've discussed at a high level the benefits of using Calico and some basics about how it works and how to install it. Now we will look at how to use it. For the rest of this section, we will use eBPF as the data plane instead of the standard Linux network stack.

Azure does not allow unknown IPs in its data plane, so you can only use a VXLAN-based overlay network between nodes. This is only possible if you are building a self-managed cluster (Figure 8-3) and not AKS. On AKS you must use Azure as the network provider, as shown in Figure 8-4.

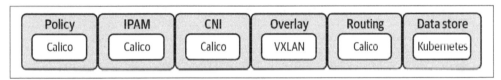

*Figure 8-3. Self-managed setup (with VXLAN)*

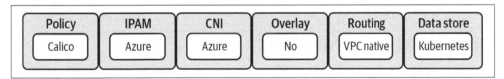

*Figure 8-4. AKS network setup*

## Enabling eBPF

The next step for setting up our Calico infrastructure is to enable the eBPF data plane. Enabling eBPF allows you to take advantage of new kernel features and remove the use of kube-proxy for load balancing. When eBPF is enabled, the use of kube-proxy will be disabled. You can find out more about Calico's implementation of eBPF in this blog post (*https://oreil.ly/uwP4Z*).

To enable eBPF, follow these steps:

1. Find the API server by running:

```
$ kubectl get configmap -n kube-system kube-proxy -o jsonpath='{.data.kubeconfig}' \
  | grep server`
    server: https://d881b853ae312e00302a84f1e346a77.hcp.us-east-1.azmk8s.io
```

2. Update your `tigera-operator` namespace:

```
kind: ConfigMap
apiVersion: v1
metadata:
  name: kubernetes-services-endpoint
  namespace: tigera-operator
data:
  KUBERNETES_SERVICE_HOST: "<API server host>"
  KUBERNETES_SERVICE_PORT: "<API server port>"
```

3. Restart the operator to pick up the change:

```
$ kubectl delete pod -n tigera-operator -l k8s-app=tigera-operator
```

4. Disable the deployment of kube-proxy (to save resources):

```
$ kubectl patch networks.operator.openshift.io cluster --type merge -p \
  '{"spec":{"deployKubeProxy": false}}'
```

5. Using calicoctl, enable eBPF:

```
$ calicoctl patch felixconfiguration default --patch='{"spec": {"bpfEnabled": true}}'
```

If you have issues running eBPF, Calico provides a troubleshooting guide (*https://oreil.ly/YvY3k*).

If you are using eBPF and have a kernel version later than 4.16, Calico will automatically attempt to use XDP to process packets, which will provide performance improvements. This is useful for high-throughput services or services that are being DOSed.

## Implementing Calico Security Policy

Now that we have our network configured, we are ready to apply some security policy. The Calico network policy has a larger set of capabilities than Kubernetes, including:

- Policy ordering
- Deny rules
- Greater flexibility on match rules

Calico network policy supports securing applications using OSI Layers 5 through 7 criteria, as well as cryptographic identity. You will find examples on the Calico network policy configuration page (*https://oreil.ly/QJCSu*).

Network policy can be enforced in a number of ways:

- Globally (applies to all Pods in all namespaces), known as GlobalNetworkPolicy
- Per network or host, known as HostEndpoint
- Per namespace, known as NetworkPolicy

### GlobalNetworkPolicy: Allowing ICMP traffic

The first policy we will create is a global network policy that allows ICMP traffic for ping and traceroute from all hosts within the cluster. Create the file *global-policy.yaml* as follows:

```
apiVersion: projectcalico.org/v3
kind: GlobalNetworkPolicy
metadata:
  name: allow-ping-in-cluster
spec:
  selector: all()
  types:
    Ingress
  ingress:
  - action: Allow
    protocol: ICMP
    source:
      selector: all()
    icmp:
      type: 8 # Ping request
  - action: Allow
    protocol: ICMPv6
    source:
      selector: all()
    icmp:
      type: 128 # Ping request
```

Apply the policy by running:

```
$ calicoctl create global-policy.yaml
```

### NetworkPolicy: Allowing traffic within a namespace between two labels

In this example, we will allow traffic from the production namespace with selector green to a Pod in the same namespace with selector blue on port TCP/1234. Create a new file called *network-policy.yaml*:

```
apiVersion: projectcalico.org/v3
kind: NetworkPolicy
metadata:
  name: allow-tcp-1234
  namespace: production
```

```
spec:
  selector: color == 'blue'
  ingress:
  - action: Allow
    protocol: TCP
    source:
      selector: color == 'green'
    destination:
      ports:
        - 1234
```

Apply the policy by running:

```
$ calicoctl create network-policy.yaml
```

Once this policy is applied, traffic will be able to flow to port TCP 1234 to any green Pod.

# Cilium

One of the most innovative networking tools to be introduced over the past five years is the Cilium project, which heavily utilizes eBPF to provide a suite of networking, observability, and security features that are oriented toward cloud native infrastructure.

Cilium utilizes the eBPF Linux kernel technology that enables low-overhead, high-powered visibility, and control logic for the kernel and the applications running on top of it. The use of eBPF makes Cilium a popular choice for infrastructure architects, as the platform provides features around three key pillars:

*Networking*
Cilium implements its own CNI that utilizes Linux eBPF. This makes Cilium highly performant and allows it to perform load balancing instead of relying on kube-proxy. It also allows for multicluster connectivity, which is important for larger installations.

*Observability*
Cilium's use of eBPF makes it a unique piece of observability software. Cilium can perform deep-packet inspection on all layers of network connectivity and data.

*Security*
One of the best features of Cilium is that it can perform transparent encryption between hosts via IPSec. This means you get end-to-end encryption via a highly efficient mechanism without having to make changes to your application. While Cilium provides its own label+CIDR matching security policy, it also does (OSI) Layer 7 filtering (e.g., filter outbound DNS queries or filter incoming HTTP requests).

---

Finally, Cilium allows you to perform Layer 7 introspection for policy-making decisions (see this blog post (*https://oreil.ly/6J9Di*) for more information).

Cilium's use of eBPF as its core enables the software to deeply introspect and manipulate (where needed) all network traffic without affecting system performance.

The Cilium agent (cilium-agent) runs on every node (see Figure 8-5) and accepts the configuration via the Kubernetes API. The agent will turn that configuration into an eBPF program that runs against the container's network interface, the host's network, or one of the host's network cards.

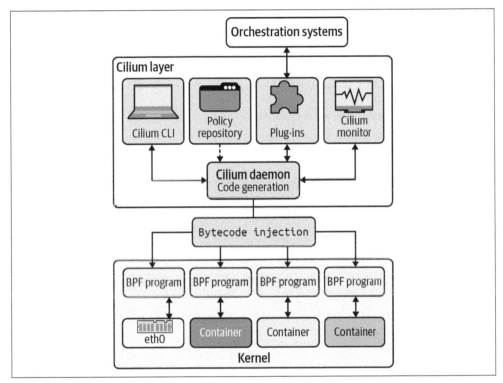

*Figure 8-5. The Cilium architecture*

## Deploying Cilium

Cilium can be installed on a self-managed Kubernetes cluster or on a managed AKS cluster. In both cases, Cilium can be deployed via Helm, which makes installation easy. Furthermore, Cilium provides a container to perform connectivity checks to verify that network traffic can flow freely between Pods on your cluster.

For more information, see the specialized documentation for deploying Cilium on Azure (*https://oreil.ly/UjGVr*).

### Self-managed Cilium installation

We will install Cilium using its quick-install file:

```
$ kubectl apply -f https://raw.githubusercontent.com/cilium/cilium/v1.9/install/ \
  kubernetes/quick-install.yaml
```

The following code will install the connectivity check between hosts:

```
$ kubectl apply -f https://raw.githubusercontent.com/cilium/cilium/v1.9/examples/ \
  kubernetes/connectivity-check/connectivity-check.yaml
```

This will deploy a series of Pods that will use various network paths to connect to one another in order to verify connectivity. Connectivity paths include with and without service load balancing and various network policy combinations.

### AKS Cilium installation

To set up Cilium on AKS, we will use a Helm chart:

1. First we will create a new AKS cluster:

   ```
   $ export RESOURCE_GROUP_NAME=aks-test
   $ export CLUSTER_NAME=aks-test
   $ export LOCATION=westus

   $ az group create --name $RESOURCE_GROUP_NAME --location $LOCATION
   $ az aks create \
       --resource-group $RESOURCE_GROUP_NAME \
       --name $CLUSTER_NAME \
       --location $LOCATION \
       --node-count 2 \
       --network-plugin azure
   ```

2. Now we will create a service principal to interact with the Azure APIs and populate environment variables to pass to Helm:

   ```
   $ az ad sp create-for-rbac --name cilium-operator > azure-sp.json

   $ AZURE_SUBSCRIPTION_ID="$(az account show | jq -r .id)"
   $ AZURE_CLIENT_ID="$(jq -r .appId < azure-sp.json)"
   $ AZURE_CLIENT_SECRET="$(jq -r .password < azure-sp.json)"
   $ AZURE_TENANT_ID="$(jq -r .tenant < azure-sp.json)"
   $ AZURE_NODE_RESOURCE_GROUP="$(az aks show --resource-group $RESOURCE_GROUP_NAME \
       --name $CLUSTER_NAME | jq -r .nodeResourceGroup)"
   ```

3. We will install the Cilium repository locally and then install Cilium on our Kubernetes cluster:

   ```
   $ helm repo add cilium https://helm.cilium.io/
   $ helm install cilium cilium/cilium --version 1.9.9 \
     --namespace kube-system \
     --set azure.enabled=true \
     --set azure.resourceGroup=$AZURE_NODE_RESOURCE_GROUP \
     --set azure.subscriptionID=$AZURE_SUBSCRIPTION_ID \
     --set azure.tenantID=$AZURE_TENANT_ID \
     --set azure.clientID=$AZURE_CLIENT_ID \
     --set azure.clientSecret=$AZURE_CLIENT_SECRET \
   ```

```
      --set tunneldisabled \
      --set ipam.mode=azure \
      --set masquerade=false \
      --set nodeinit.enabled=true
--set kubeProxyReplacement=strict \
--set hostFirewall=true \
--set loadBalancer.algorithm=maglev \
--set k8sServiceHost=REPLACE_WITH_API_SERVER_IP \
--set k8sServicePort=REPLACE_WITH_API_SERVER_PORT
```

4. We can verify the installation by checking that the four initial Pods have been created and that both a `cilium` and a `cilium-operator` Pod are running:

```
$ kubectl -n kube-system get pods --watch
cilium-operator-ad4375ds5-2x2q3        1/1     Running    0        4m18s
cilium-s5x8xk                          1/1     Running    0        4m19s
```

### Installing Hubble

You will also want to install Hubble (*https://oreil.ly/jsisf*), a UI that allows you to see a service map that depicts dependencies between services and statistics on network usage and performance. Hubble's live-updating, graph-like interface (see Figure 8-6) allows you to present a lot of information about the layout and flow of data between containers. Furthermore, it provides an interface to model Cilium policy.

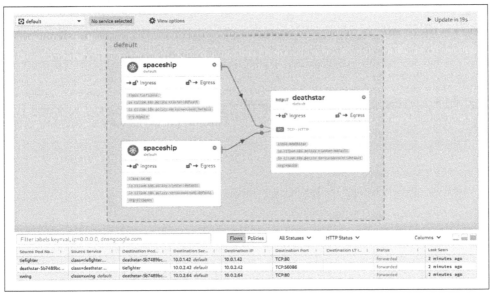

*Figure 8-6. A screenshot of the Hubble UI displaying a simple architecture*

You can install Hubble using kubectl:

```
kubectl apply -f https://raw.githubusercontent.com/cilium/cilium/v1.9/install/kubernetes/ \
    quick-hubble-install.yaml
```

# Integrating Cilium with Your Cloud

As we already mentioned, Cilium has a rich feature set that you can take advantage of. In this section, we will use Cilium as a network provider and as a policy enforcer (firewall). We will then look at observability with Cilium.

## Host firewall

Similar to our deep dive into Calico, here we will implement a set of network policies. The advantage of Cilium is that it can enforce policy on L3, L4, or L7. Network policy enforcement has three modes, as shown in Table 8-1.

*Table 8-1. Network policy enforcement modes*

| Mode | Description |
| --- | --- |
| Default | If a rule selects endpoints and the rule has an ingress or egress section, the endpoint will deny as per the policy. |
| Always | Policy enforcement is enabled on all endpoints, even if no rules select specific endpoints. |
| Never | Policy enforcement is disabled on all endpoints, and all traffic is allowed. |

To configure policy enforcement mode at runtime for all endpoints managed by a Cilium agent, use the following command and pick a mode of default, always, or never:

```
$ cilium config PolicyEnforcement={default,always,never}
```

Policy is written against an allow list model in which traffic will be blocked if there is no explicit allow rule.

L3 and L4 rules can be specified using the following methods:

*Labels (https://oreil.ly/0X1q1)*
    Use a selector to group Pods.

*Services (https://oreil.ly/3opXd)*
    Define a policy using a Kubernetes service.

*Entities (https://oreil.ly/74D8C)*
    Special predefined scopes that are managed by Cilium.

*IP/CIDR (https://oreil.ly/61Xbc)*
    An IP or IP range (CIDR).

*DNS names (https://oreil.ly/9Ztcc)*
    A DNS name.

For example, if you want to allow traffic between two labeled Pods, you can create the following policy:

```
apiVersion: cilium.io/v2
kind: CiliumNetworkPolicy
metadata:
  name: "l3-rule"
spec:
  endpointSelector:
    matchLabels:
      role: backend
  ingress:
  - fromEndpoints:
    - matchLabels:
        role: frontend
```

You can apply this policy by running:

```
$ cilium policy import l3-rule-example-1.yaml
```

Furthermore, if you want to create an L4 example where you want to limit outbound egress DNS to the Google public DNS servers, you can write the rule shown in the following example:

```
apiVersion: "cilium.io/v2"
kind: CiliumNetworkPolicy
metadata:
  name: "allow-to-google-dns"
spec:
  endpointSelector:
    {}
  egress:
  - toCIDR:
    - 8.8.8.8/32
    - 8.8.8.4/32
    toPorts:
    - ports:
      - port: '53'
        protocol: UDP
    - ports:
      - port: '53'
        Protocol: TCP
```

You can apply the rule by running:

```
$ cilium policy import l4-rule-example-1.yaml
```

Finally, Cilium also allows L7 visibility for HTTP(s), Kafka, and DNS traffic. In the next example, we are allowing traffic to the /admin endpoint on port 80 to all Pods:

```
apiVersion: "cilium.io/v2"
kind: CiliumNetworkPolicy
metadata:
  name: "rule1"
spec:
  description: "Allow HTTP GET /admin
  endpointSelector:
    {}
  ingress:
```

```
- fromEndpoints:
  toPorts:
  - ports:
    - port: "80"
      protocol: TCP
    rules:
      http:
      - method: "GET"
        path: "/admin"
```

You can find more specific details about L7 policy rules in the Layer 7 policy Cilium documentation (*https://oreil.ly/autkh*).

 Cilium provides an interactive tool to model network policies and visualize them. You can try it out on the Cilium Editor page (*https://oreil.ly/LOlAW*).

## Observability

As we briefly mentioned earlier, Hubble is where Cilium operators can observe what is happening in their infrastructure. Once you install Hubble and the connectivity test (from the installation steps), you will be able to observe network flows within the namespace. In this section, we will go one step further and utilize a new Cilium feature that provides Layer 3 and Layer 4 protocol visibility, which will give you more specific details about the traffic on each port. You will need to implement Layer 7 policies to get Layer 7 observability features.

To enable Layer 3 and Layer 4 visibility, you will need to enable annotations on your Pods. Here's an example:

```
$ kubectl annotate pods --all io.cilium.proxy-visibility="<Egress/53/UDP/DNS>, \
    <Ingress/80/TCP/HTTP>"
```

This will enable metrics on outbound (egress) DNS traffic as well as inbound (ingress) HTTP traffic to the Pod.

Visibility information is represented by a comma-separated list of tuples in the annotation:

```
<{Traffic Direction}/{L4 Port}/{L4 Protocol}/{L7 Protocol}>
```

When enabled, Hubble will display protocol-specific information. See Figure 8-7 as an example of DNS visibility.

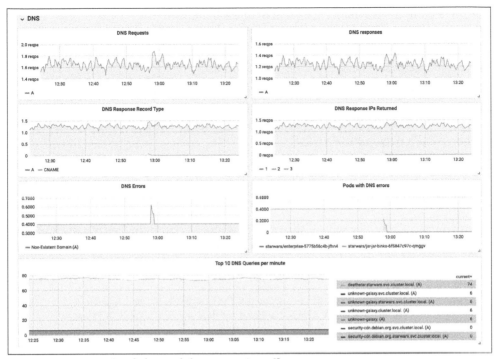

*Figure 8-7. Example of observability in DNS traffic*

If you would like to learn how to inspect Transport Layer Security (TLS) encrypted connections, please visit the Inspecting TLS Encrypted Connections with Cilium page (*https://oreil.ly/2GH2B*).

# Flannel

Flannel (*https://oreil.ly/kgo3k*) is an (OSI) Layer 3 network fabric system for Kubernetes that was originally part of Red Hat's CoreOS project. It is one of the simplest CNIs for Kubernetes. It relies on one binary agent, named flanneld, to run on each host to configure an overlay Pod network and then store the configuration in the Kubernetes data store. Flannel only provides network connectivity. It doesn't support any kind of network policy enforcement.

## Deploying Flannel

Flannel can be quickly installed when you're setting up your cluster by running:

```
$ kubectl apply -f https://raw.githubusercontent.com/coreos/flannel/master/ \
    Documentation/kube-flannel.yml
```

The application of *kube-flannel.yml* will define the following:

- A `ClusterRole` and `ClusterRoleBinding` for role-based access control (RBAC).
- A Kubernetes service account for Flannel to use.
- A `ConfigMap` containing both a CNI configuration and a Flannel configuration. The network in the Flannel configuration should match the Pod network's Classless Inter-Domain Routing (CIDR) scheme. The choice of backend is also made here, and it defaults to VXLAN.
- A DaemonSet for every architecture to deploy the Flannel Pod on each node. The Pod has two containers: the Flannel daemon itself, and an `initContainer` for deploying the CNI configuration to a location that the kubelet can read.

When you run Pods, they will be allocated IP addresses from the Pod network CIDR. No matter which node those Pods end up on, they will be able to communicate with one another.

 This manifest will configure the Pod network to be 10.244.0.0/16 and to use the VXLAN backend by default. A 10.244.X.0/24 mask will be given to each node in the Pod.

You can reconfigure your backend to use a different address space, a smaller mask, or different backend settings by modifying the data that's written into *net-conf.json* in the *fkube-flannel.yaml* file. You can find more information on backend configuration from the Flannel backend documentation (*https://oreil.ly/gi1ht*) and Flannel configuration (*https://oreil.ly/VUqtK*) pages.

Now Kubernetes worker nodes will have IP addresses from your Azure VNet, but any deployed Pod will have IP addresses from the configured Pod Network IP range. If you want to have multiple Pod Networks (for network traffic separation), you will have to run a separate `flanneld` process.

# A Flannel Deep Dive

Flannel is a simpler Kubernetes CNI and requires minimal configuration. It has pluggable backends that create overlay networks between machines on a network (see Figure 8-8). Supported transport backends include:

- VXLAN
- Host-gw
- User Datagram Protocol (UDP)

- Alivpc
- Alloc
- Amazon Virtual Private Cloud (VPC)
- Google Compute Engine (GCE)
- IPIP
- IPsec

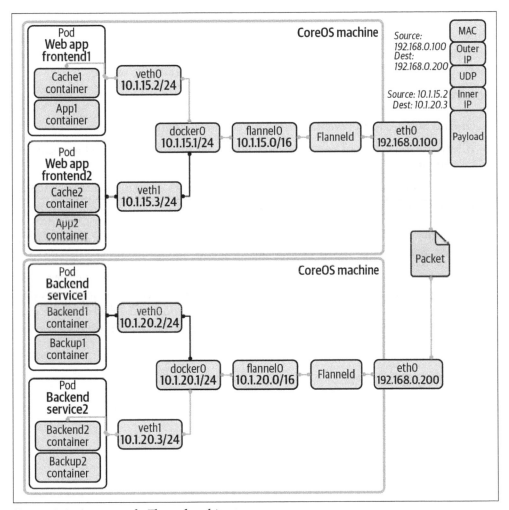

*Figure 8-8. An example Flannel architecture*

The Flannel project team recommends VXLAN or host-gw as backends for communication. If you need to encrypt traffic, IPsec is also an option. You can find more information about the supported backends in the Flannel documentation (*https://oreil.ly/gi1ht*).

Flannel does not allow you to run multiple networks from the one daemon; you will need to run separate daemons with different configuration files.

# Azure Policy

While it is undoubtedly useful to actively run software that protects your cloud-based infrastructure, Azure Policy allows you to set a comprehensive policy against many aspects of your cloud infrastructure, particularly around resource security.

Azure Policy performs three key functions:

- Creates policies that prevent or enforce a certain configuration
- Allows for reporting of compliance against your own policy as well as industry benchmarks
- Brings your resources to compliance through bulk remediation for existing resources and automatic remediation for new resources

Potential use cases for Azure Policy include implementing governance for resource consistency, regulatory compliance, security, cost, and management.

Azure Policy definitions are defined in a JSON format (*https://oreil.ly/TtvcM*) and applied in a hierarchical manner; this means that one policy could be applied to one management group (and all the subscriptions/resources in it) and a more lenient policy could be set to a separate management group (and all the subscriptions/resources in it).

## Azure Policy Quickstart

Azure contains some built-in policies by default. You can view them by running this command in your terminal:

```
$ az policy definition list
```

Or you can view them in the Portal (*https://oreil.ly/13q1f*) (Figure 8-9).

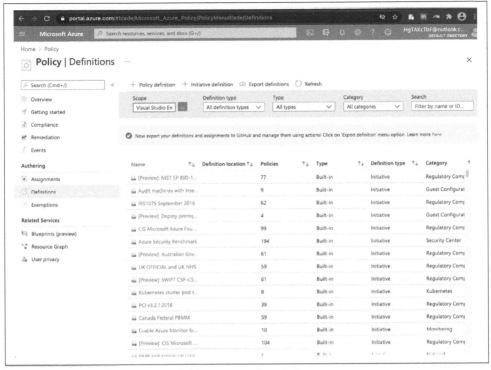

*Figure 8-9. An overview of available Azure Policy definitions*

Azure Policy also includes *initiatives*, which are collections of policies that align with an industry standard (e.g., PCI v3.2.1:2018).

At this point, the policies have been created but they have no assigned scope. You can apply a policy on a subscription (and all the resources within the subscription), or you can apply it to a management group that will cover all child management groups and subscriptions.

Either way, you will need to have the `Microsoft.PolicyInsights` resource provider registered for your subscription(s). You can enable it by running:

```
$ az provider register --namespace 'Microsoft.PolicyInsights'
```

Azure Policy has various policy enforcement modes, also known as *effects*. There are currently seven types of Azure Policy effects:

- Append
- Audit
- AuditIfNotExists
- Deny

- DeployIfNotExists
- Disabled
- Modify

You can read about their usage in the article "Understand Azure Policy effects" (*https://oreil.ly/9Nj2D*).

## Creating Your Own Azure Policy

Creating your own Azure policy is easy. In the following example, we are creating a policy that only allows the deployment of resources in Azure regions within the United States. If a user attempts to create a resource in a non-US region, it will be denied:

```
{
    "properties": {
        "displayName": "Allowed locations",
        "description": "This policy enables you to restrict the locations your organization
                        can specify when deploying resources.",
        "mode": "Indexed",
        "metadata": {
            "version": "1.0.0",
            "category": "Locations"
        },
        "parameters": {
            "allowedLocations": {
                "type": "array",
                "metadata": {
                    "description": "The list of locations that can be specified
                                    when deploying resources",
                    "strongType": "location",
                    "displayName": "Allowed locations"
                },
                "defaultValue": [ "westus2", "eastus", "eastus2", "southcentralus",
                  "centralus", "northcentralus", "westus", "westcentralus", "westus3" ]
            }
        },
        "policyRule": {
            "if": {
                "not": {
                    "field": "location",
                    "in": "[parameters('allowedLocations')]"
                }
            },
            "then": {
                "effect": "deny"
            }
        }
    }
}
```

We will create the policy by running:

```
$ az policy definition create --name 'allowed-regions' --display-name 'Deny non-US regions' \
    --description 'This policy ensures that resources are only created in US regions.' \
    --rules 'region-rule.json' --params 'region-params.json'---mode All
```

In the response, we will see the path for the new policy in the id field; for example:

```
"id": "/subscriptions/<subscription-ID>/providers/Microsoft.Authorization/ \
    policyDefinitions/allowed-regions"
```

We will assign our policy to our subscription by running:

```
$ az policy assignment create --name 'allowed-regions'  --scope ' \
    /subscriptions/<subscription-id>' --policy '/subscriptions/<subscription-ID>/ \
    providers/Microsoft.Authorization/policyDefinitions/allowed-regions"
```

The policy will now be applied. If we were to try to create a resource in a non-US region, we would receive an error similar to the one in Figure 8-10.

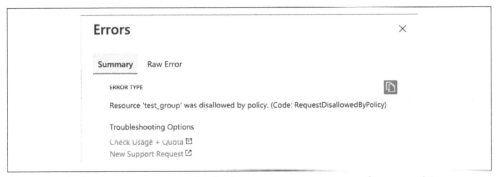

*Figure 8-10. An error message on deploying a new resource group because of Azure Policy*

**Azure Policy Limits**

Azure Policy has limits in terms of the number of policies, exceptions, parameters, and conditionals that can be applied. These limits may change depending on the scope of the policy. Read the documentation (*https://oreil.ly/Fazfu*) for more details.

## Azure Policy for Kubernetes

Azure Policy also supports Kubernetes, allowing you to gain policy insights into your Kubernetes deployment and create Kubernetes-related policies. You can find more information about how to do this by reading "Understand Azure Policy for Kubernetes clusters" (*https://oreil.ly/123qR*) and "Secure your cluster with Azure Policy" (*https://oreil.ly/3kBOZ*), which walk you through how to apply Azure Policy to Kubernetes.

# Open Policy Agent

Open Policy Agent (OPA) is an open source, general-purpose policy engine that allows you to perform authorization policy actions against your software (Figure 8-11). OPA allows you to specify policy as code and provides simple APIs for software to integrate with.

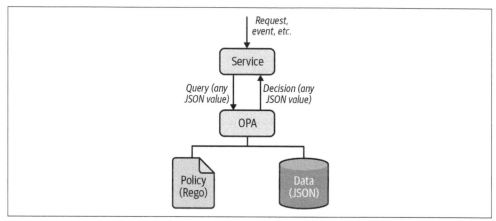

*Figure 8-11. How OPA works*

OPA policies are codified in a declarative language called Rego (see the policy language documentation (*https://oreil.ly/7wBtm*)). The policies are then deployed to the OPA service on the host. Unlike a number of the systems that we've discussed in this chapter, OPA does not perform any enforcement; rather, it performs policy decision-making. OPA evaluates policies and data to produce query results that are sent back to the client. Policies are written in a high-level declarative language and can be loaded dynamically into OPA, remotely via APIs, or through the local filesystem.

OPA provides a REST API that third-party services/systems like Kubernetes, SSH, Sudo, and Envoy can utilize to answer questions such as the following:

- Which users can access which resources
- Which subnets' egress traffic is allowed
- Which clusters a workload must be deployed to
- Which registries' binaries can be downloaded
- Which OS capabilities a container can execute with
- Which times of day the system be accessed

You can find more details on the OPA REST API documentation page (*https://oreil.ly/3blq5*). The key APIs that OPA serves are as follows:

```
GET /v1/policies
```
Gets all the policies

```
GET /v1/policies/<name>
```
Returns a specific policy

```
PUT /v1/policies/<name>
```
Creates or updates a policy

```
DELETE /v1/policies/<name>
```
Deletes a policy

```
GET/POST /v1/data/<name>
```
Allows you to return or create a document

OPA allows you to centralize multiple security policies across multiple pieces of infrastructure into one system. You can find a full list of OPA integrations on the OPA Ecosystem page (*https://oreil.ly/qirGh*). Without OPA, you would need to implement policy management for your software from scratch. Required components such as the policy language (syntax and semantics) and the evaluation engine need to be carefully designed, implemented, tested, documented, and then maintained to ensure correct behavior and a positive user experience for your customers.

## Deploying OPA on Kubernetes

Deploying OPA on Kubernetes is straightforward:

1. Create the deployment definition file (*deployment-opa.yaml*):

```
apiVersion: apps/v1
kind: Deployment
metadata:
  name: opa
  labels:
    app: opa
spec:
  replicas: 1
  selector:
    matchLabels:
      app: opa
  template:
    metadata:
      labels:
        app: opa
      name: opa
    spec:
      containers:
      - name: opa
        image: openpolicyagent/opa:edge
        ports:
        - name: http
          containerPort: 8181
```

```
      args:
      - "run"
      - "--ignore=.*"  # exclude hidden dirs created by Kubernetes
      - "--server"
      - "/policies"
      volumeMounts:
      - readOnly: true
        mountPath: /policies
        name: policy
    volumes:
    - name: policy
      configMap:
        name:  policy
```

2. Create the service definition file (*servica-opa.yaml*):

```
kind: Service
apiVersion: v1
metadata:
  name: opa
  labels:
    app: opa
spec:
  type: NodePort
  selector:
    app: opa
  ports:
    - name: http
      protocol: TCP
      port: 8181
      targetPort: 8181
```

3. Apply both files:

```
$ kubectl create -f deployment-opa.yaml
$ kubectl create -f service-opa.yaml
```

## Deploying Policy with OPA

As stated earlier, OPA is a generalized policy engine and is pluggable with a number of software ecosystems (*https://oreil.ly/qirGh*). In this example, we will provision SSH access to machines using OPA.

For this example, we'll have three groups:

*sre*
> These are the administrators for all applications.

*foo-frontend*
> These are the contributors to the foo-frontend application.

*bar-backend*
> These are the contributors to the bar-backend application.

We will implement the following policy:

---

- The group sre can SSH into any host and run sudo commands.
- Other users in groups associated with the development of the application can log in to the host, but cannot run sudo commands.

The following examples will create a policy that allows SSH authorization for the sre group and the group associated with the application:

```
package sshd.authz

import input.pull_responses
import input.sysinfo

import data.hosts

# By default, users are not authorized.
default allow = false

# Allow access to any user that has the "admin" role.
allow {
    data.roles["sre"][_] == input.sysinfo.pam_username
}

# Allow access to any user who contributed to the code running on the host.
#
# This rule gets the "host_id" value from the file "/etc/host_identity.json."
# It is available in the input under "pull_responses" because we
# asked for it in our pull policy above.
#
# It then compares all the contributors for that host against the username
# that is asking for authorization.
allow {
    hosts[pull_responses.files["/etc/host_identity.json"].host_id].contributors[_] == \
        sysinfo.pam_username
}

# If the user is not authorized, then include an error message in the response.
errors["Request denied by administrative policy"] {
    not allow
}
```

We'll create a second policy that only allows sudo access for the sre group:

```
package sudo.authz

# By default, users are not authorized.
default allow = false

# Allow access to any user that has the "admin" role.
allow {
    data.roles["sre"][_] == input.sysinfo.pam_username
}

# If the user is not authorized, then include an error message in the response.
errors["Request denied by administrative policy"] {
    not allow
}
```

Now we can register both of these policies in OPA:

```
curl -X PUT --data-binary @sshd_authz.rego localhost:8181/v1/policies/sshd/authz
curl -X PUT --data-binary @sudo_authz.rego localhost:8181/v1/policies/sudo/authz
```

After we successfully execute these commands, our policy will be applied and only users in the sre group will have SSH and sudo access to all machines. Meanwhile, the relevant service group will only have SSH access to the machine on which the service is deployed.

## Summary

Although operating cloud native infrastructure brings immense benefits to the operator, it does present significant risk to your business if the infrastructure is not well secured. In this chapter, we reviewed a means to secure and audit your infrastructure. First we reviewed the CNI standard and how it's the foundation for other platforms like Flannel and Cilium. We examined how those systems can be used to provide connectivity and network security to your cloud infrastructure. Then we looked at non–network policy mechanisms for managing your cloud infrastructure via Azure Policy as well as policy for applications via Open Policy Agent. Building your cloud infrastructure with a secure network setup as well as a well-defined policy will help ensure that your infrastructure scales in a secure manner. Now that you understand the basics of container and cloud networking, we will pivot the discussion to understanding how to store and serve data in the cloud.

# CHAPTER 9

# Distributed Databases and Storage: The Central Bank

One of the largest hurdles to overcome when building a cloud native infrastructure is operating reliable and scalable storage for both online and offline use. While earlier sentiment around storage services being run in the cloud was frowned upon, a number of cloud native storage projects have succeeded, the most prominent being Vitess. Cloud services, including Azure, have also significantly invested in managed disks (*https://oreil.ly//Jrlz*) for virtual machines and virtual machine scale sets, as well as advanced storage accounts (such as Gen2) and managed database services (such as MySQL, SQL Server, and Redis). All of this has made storage a first-class concept in Azure's cloud. In this chapter, we will look at why you should run storage solutions at scale in Azure and how you can orchestrate them in a way that is easy to manage.

## The Need for Distributed Databases in Cloud Native Architecture

Although Azure provides a number of managed data (both SQL and NoSQL) solutions, sometimes you may need to run larger and more specialized setups while operating in the cloud. The ecosystem of self-operated Cloud Native Computing Foundation (CNCF) database projects (*https://oreil.ly/VfsnY*) will allow you to scale to a larger size than Azure platform as a service (PaaS) services provide, and will give you more features and performance options.

As this chapter will further discuss, the CNCF landscape lays out a set of storage solutions that are primarily designed for cloud operations. The benefit of these systems is that server management overhead is minimized, while you still have complete control over the system.

In this chapter, we will examine some of the mature data stores that are part of the CNCF landscape. Vitess, Rook, TiKV, and etcd are all mature cloud data stores that are able to scale to a tremendous size and are being run as first-class data systems across Azure. These systems represent the foundational building blocks of a data ecosystem that's operated in a cloud infrastructure.

 **Running Stateful Workloads on AKS**

At the time of this writing, Azure Kubernetes Service (AKS) supports multiple availability zones (i.e., multiple data centers within a region); however, it does not support multiple fault domains. This means that if your AKS cluster is in only one availability zone, it is theoretically possible to have downtime because multiple nodes in your cluster are unavailable. We recommend that you split your AKS cluster over multiple availability zones until AKS supports fault domains.

## Azure Storage and Database Options

Before you start building your cloud data stores, you should thoroughly evaluate your use case, particularly the storage, performance, and cost of what you are trying to build. You may find that Azure's PaaS services might be a better fit for a particular use case, rather than using a CNCF product. For example, Azure's Hadoop Distributed File System (HDFS) storage offering, Gen2 storage accounts, is an extremely economical solution for storing large volumes of data.

At the time of this writing, Azure provides the following storage and database PaaS services:

- Azure Cosmos DB
- Azure Cache for Redis
- Azure Database for:
  - MySQL
  - PostgreSQL
  - MariaDB
- Storage accounts (providing blob, Network File System [NFS], and hierarchical storage)
- Azure Storage Explorer

We recommend that you evaluate the performance of these Azure offerings, specifically considering the performance, availability, and cost of a PaaS service, to ensure that you're using the correct system for your use case. Azure provides a pricing calculator tool (*https://oreil.ly/EPxmK*) that is extremely useful for modeling costs.

If you believe that an Azure PaaS service does not fit your requirements, continue reading this chapter to learn about other potential data storage solutions.

# Introduction to Vitess: Distributed and Sharded MySQL

Vitess (*https://vitess.io*) is a database cluster system for horizontal scaling of MySQL and MariaDB. It was created by YouTube engineers in 2010 as a means to protect and scale their databases. It provides a number of features that aid in performance, security, and monitoring, but most importantly, it offers powerful tools to manage database topologies and provide first-class support for vertical and horizontal sharding and resharding. In many aspects, it allows you to operate SQL databases in a NoSQL manner, while still getting all the benefits of running a relational database.

## Why Run Vitess?

You may be asking yourself: "Why should I run Vitess, instead of using Azure Cosmos DB?" Although Cosmos DB is an attractive option for globally distributed writes and replicas, the current cost model makes it prohibitively expensive to run at scale (thousands of queries per second), making a system like Vitess an attractive offering for those who need a high-throughput relational database with a more customizable setup.

Vitess provides the following benefits:

*Scalability*
    You can scale individual schemas up and down.

*Manageability*
    A centralized control plane manages all database-related operations.

*Protection*
    You can rewrite queries, build query deny lists, and add table-level access control lists (ACLs).

*Shard management*
    You can easily create and manage database shards.

*Performance*
    A lot of the internals are built for performance, including client connection pooling and query deduping.

Vitess helps you manage the operational and scaling overhead of relational databases and the health of your cluster. Furthermore, Vitess offers a wider range of configurables than traditional cloud database offerings (including Cosmos DB), which will help you meet your scaling and replication requirements.

## The Vitess Architecture

Vitess provides sharding as a service by creating a middleware-style system while still utilizing MySQL to store data. The client application connects to a daemon known as VTGate (see in Figure 9-1). VTGate is a cluster-aware router that routes queries to the appropriate VTTablet instances, which manage each instance of MySQL. The Topology service stores the topology of the infrastructure, including where the data is stored and the ability of each VTTablet instance to serve the data.

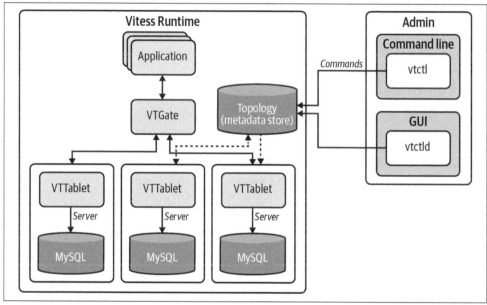

*Figure 9-1. The Vitess architecture*

Vitess also provides two administrative interfaces: vtctl, a CLI; and vtctld, a web interface.

VTGate is a query router (or proxy) for routing queries from the client to the databases. The client doesn't need to know about anything except where the VTGate instance is located, which means the client-to-server architecture is straightforward.

# Deploying Vitess on Kubernetes

Vitess has first-class support for Kubernetes, and it is very straightforward to get started with it. In this walkthrough, we'll create a cluster and a schema and then expand the cluster:

1. First, clone the *vitess* repository and move to the *vitess/examples/operator* folder:

   ```
   $ git clone git@github.com:vitessio/vitess.git
   $ cd vitess/examples/operator
   ```

2. Now, install the Kubernetes operator by running:

   ```
   $ kubectl apply -f operator.yaml
   ```

3. Next, create an initial Vitess cluster by running:

   ```
   $ kubectl apply -f 101_initial_cluster.yaml
   ```

4. You'll be able to verify that the initial cluster install was successful as follows:

   ```
   $ kubectl get pods
   NAME                                              READY  STATUS   RESTARTS  AGE
   example-etcd-faf13de3-1                           1/1    Running  0         78s
   example-etcd-faf13de3-2                           1/1    Running  0         78s
   example-etcd-faf13de3-3                           1/1    Running  0         78s
   example-vttablet-zone1-2469782763-bfadd780        3/3    Running  1         78s
   example-vttablet-zone1-2548885007-46a852d0        3/3    Running  1         78s
   example-zone1-vtctld-1d4dcad0-59d8498459-kwz6b    1/1    Running  2         78s
   example-zone1-vtgate-bc6cde92-6bd99c6888-vwcj5    1/1    Running  2         18s
   vitess-operator-8454d86687-4wfnc                  1/1    Running  0         2m29s
   ```

You now have a small, single-zone Vitess cluster running with two replicas.

You can find more database operation examples in the Vitess Kubernetes Operations example page (*https://oreil.ly/2313O*).

One of the more common use cases you will encounter is the need to add or remove replicas of the database. You can easily do this by running the following:

```
$ kubectl edit planetscale.com example

# To add or remove replicas, change the replicas field of the appropriate resource
# to the desired value. E.g.

  keyspaces:
  - name: commerce
    turndownPolicy: Immediate
    partitionings:
    - equal:
          parts: 1
          shardTemplate:
            databaseInitScriptSecret:
              name: example-cluster-config
              key: init_db.sql
            replication:
              enforceSemiSync: false
            tabletPools:
```

```
- cell: zone1
    type: replica
    replicas: 2 # Change this value
```

 One consideration of building distributed data storage is determining the size of your failure domain. Vitess recommends that you store a maximum of 250 GB of data per server. While there are some MySQL performance reasons for this, other regular operational tasks become more difficult with a larger shard size/failure domain. You can read more about why Vitess recommends 250 GB per server on the Vitess blog (*https://oreil.ly/VSi3J*).

# Introduction to Rook: Storage Orchestrator for Kubernetes

So far, we've covered relational SQL database storage and high-performance serving, but there are other types of storage that need to be served and operated in the cloud. These are known as *blob filesystems*. Blob stores are great for storing images, videos, and other files that aren't suitable for a relational database. Blob storage comes with extra challenges around storing and replicating large amounts of data efficiently.

Rook (*https://rook.io*) is a cloud native file, block, and object open source storage orchestrator that provides software-defined blob storage. Rook graduated as a CNCF project in 2018 and is specifically designed around running storage on Kubernetes. Similar to Vitess, Rook manages a lot of the daily operations of a cluster, including self-scaling and self-healing, and it automates other tasks such as disaster recovery, monitoring, and upgrades.

## The Rook Architecture

Rook is a Kubernetes orchestrator, not an actual storage solution. Rook supports the following storage systems:

- Ceph, a highly scalable distributed storage solution for block storage, object storage, and shared filesystems with years of production deployments

- Cassandra, a highly available NoSQL database featuring lightning-fast performance, tunable consistency, and massive scalability

- NFS, which allows remote hosts to mount filesystems over a network and interact with those filesystems as though they are mounted locally

Rook can orchestrate a number of storage providers on a Kubernetes cluster. Each has its own operator for deploying and managing the resources.

# Deploying Rook on Kubernetes

In this example, we will deploy a Cassandra cluster using the Rook (Cassandra) Kubernetes operator. If you're deploying a Ceph cluster via Rook, you can also use a Helm chart (*https://oreil.ly/NCQxr*) to deploy:

1. Clone the Rook operator:

   ```
   $ git clone --single-branch --branch master https://github.com/rook/rook.git
   ```

2. Install the operator:

   ```
   $ cd rook/cluster/examples/kubernetes/cassandra
   $ kubectl apply -f operator.yaml
   ```

3. You can verify that the operator is installed by running:

   ```
   $ kubectl -n rook-cassandra-system get pod
   ```

4. Now, go to the *cassandra* folder and create the cluster:

   ```
   $ cd rook/cluster/examples/kubernetes/cassandra
   $ kubectl create -f cluster.yaml
   ```

5. To verify that all the desired nodes are running, issue the following command:

   ```
   $ kubectl -n rook-cassandra get pod -l app=rook-cassandra
   ```

It is exceptionally easy to scale your Cassandra cluster up and down using the Kubernetes kubectl edit command. You can simply change the value of Spec.Members up or down to scale the cluster accordingly:

```
$ kubectl edit clusters.cassandra.rook.io rook-cassandra
# To scale up a rack, change the Spec.Members field of the rack to the desired value.
# To scale down a rack, change the Spec.Members field of the rack to the desired value
# After editing and saving the yaml, check your cluster's Status and Events for information
# on what's happening:

apiVersion: cassandra.rook.io/v1alpha1
kind: Cluster
metadata:
  name: rook-cassandra
  namespace: rook-cassandra
spec:
  version: 3.11.6
  repository: my-private-repo.io/cassandra
  mode: cassandra
  annotations:
  datacenter:
    name: us-east2
    racks:
      - name: us-east2
        members: 3 # Change this number up or down


$ kubectl -n rook-cassandra describe clusters.cassandra.rook.io rook-cassandra
```

You can find more details on Cassandra configurables in the Cassandra CRD documentation (*https://oreil.ly/jBH6b*).

Similarly, Ceph (*https://oreil.ly/tY2ZZ*) and NFS (*https://oreil.ly/eAoSJ*) clusters can be easily deployed using the Rook operator.

# Introduction to TiKV

TiKV (*https://tikv.org*) (Titanium Key-Value), created by PingCAP, Inc., is an open source, distributed, and transactional key-value store. Contrary to many key-value and NoSQL systems, TiKV provides simple (raw) APIs as well as transactional APIs that provide atomicity, consistency, isolation, and durability (ACID) compliance.

## Why Use TiKV?

TiKV provides the following features:

- Geo-replication
- Horizontal scalability
- Consistent distributed transactions
- Coprocessor support
- Automatic sharding

TiKV is an attractive option due its auto-sharding and geo-replication features, as well as its ability to scale to store more than 100 TB of data. It also provides strong consensus guarantees with its use of the Raft protocol for replication.

## The TiKV Architecture

As previously mentioned, TiKV has two APIs that can be used for different use cases: raw and transactional. Table 9-1 outlines the differences between these two APIs.

*Table 9-1. TiKV APIs: Raw versus transactional*

|  | Raw | Transactional |
| --- | --- | --- |
| Description | A lower-level key-value API for interacting directly with individual key-value pairs | A higher-level key-value API that provides ACID semantics |
| Atomicity | Single key | Multiple keys |
| Use when… | Your application doesn't require distributed transactions or multiversion concurrency control (MVCC) | Your application requires distributed transactions and/or MVCC |

TiKV utilizes RocksDB as a storage container in each node, and utilizes Raft groups to provide distributed transactions, as shown in Figure 9-2. The placement driver acts as a cluster manager and ensures that all shards have had their replication constraints met and that the data has been load-balanced over the pool. Finally, clients connect to TiKV nodes using the Google Remote Procedure Call (gRPC) protocol, which is optimized for performance.

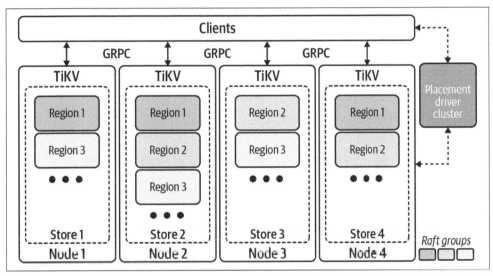

*Figure 9-2. The TiKV architecture*

Within a TiKV node (pictured in Figure 9-3), RocksDB provides the underlying storage mechanisms and Raft provides consensus for transactions. The TiKV API provides an interface for clients to interact with, and the coprocessor handles SQL-like queries and assembles the result from the underlying storage.

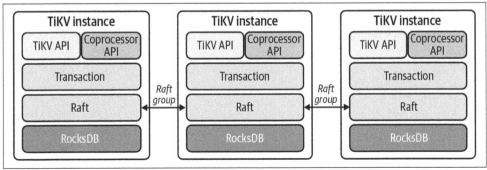

*Figure 9-3. TiKV instance architecture*

# Deploying TiKV on Kubernetes

TiKV can be deployed via multiple automation methods, including Ansible, Docker, and Kubernetes. In the following example, we will deploy a basic cluster with Kubernetes and Helm:

1. Install the TiKV custom resource definition:

    ```
    $ kubectl apply -f https://raw.githubusercontent.com/tikv/tikv-operator/master/ \
        manifests/crd.v1beta1.yaml
    ```

2. We will need to explore the Helm operator. First, add the PingCap repository:

    ```
    $ helm repo add pingcap https://charts.pingcap.org/
    ```

3. Now create a namespace for the `tikv-operator`:

    ```
    $ kubectl create ns tikv-operator
    ```

4. Install the operator:

    ```
    $ helm install --namespace tikv-operator tikv-operator pingcap/tikv-operator \
        --version v0.1.0
    ```

5. Deploy the cluster:

    ```
    $ kubectl apply -f https://raw.githubusercontent.com/tikv/tikv-operator/master/ \
        examples/basic/tikv-cluster.yaml
    ```

6. You can check the status of the deployment by running:

    ```
    $ kubectl wait --for=condition=Ready --timeout 10m tikvcluster/basic
    ```

This will create a single-host storage cluster with 1 GB of storage and a placement driver (PD) instance.

You can modify the `replicas` and `storage` parameters in the cluster definition to match your requirements. We recommend that you run your storage with at least three replicas for redundancy purposes. For example, if you run `kubectl edit ikv.org TikvCluster` and modify `replicas` to 4 and `storage` to `500Gi`:

```
apiVersion: tikv.org/v1alpha1
kind: TikvCluster
metadata:
  name: basic
spec:
  version: v4.0.0
  pd:
    baseImage: pingcap/pd
    replicas: 4
    # if storageClassName is not set, the default Storage Class of the Kubernetes cluster
    # will be used
    # storageClassName: local-storage
    requests:
      storage: "1Gi"
    config: {}
  tikv:
    baseImage: pingcap/tikv
```

```
replicas: 4
# if storageClassName is not set, the default Storage Class of the Kubernetes cluster
# will be used
# storageClassName: local-storage
requests:
  storage: "500Gi"
config: {}
```

you will get four replicas of a 500 GB storage partition.

# More on etcd

We've utilized etcd (stealthily) throughout this book. Here we will spend some time talking about it in detail.

etcd is a strongly consistent (Raft-consensus (*https://raft.github.io*)), distributed key-value store that is intended for use in distributed systems. It is designed to gracefully handle leader elections and faults such as network interruptions and unexpected node downtime. etcd has a simple API (Figure 9-4), so you will find a number of the systems we've discussed in this book (e.g., Kubernetes, TiKV, Calico, and Istio) leveraging it behind the scenes.

Often, etcd is used to store configuration values, feature flags, and service discovery information in a key-value format. etcd allows clients to watch these items for changes and reconfigures itself when they change. etcd also is suitable for leadership elections and locking uses. etcd is used as the service discovery backend in Kubernetes as well as for orchestration in Rook.

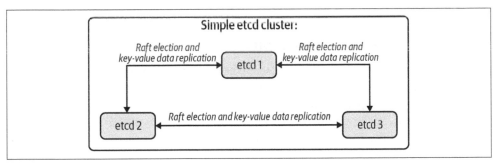

*Figure 9-4. etcd operational architecture*

If you are utilizing etcd for your core infrastructure, you will quickly understand how important it is for this infrastructure to run reliably. As an etcd cluster is a critical piece of your infrastructure, we recommend the following to ensure a stable etcd cluster in Azure.

## Hardware Platform

Consistent key-value store performance relies heavily on the performance of the underlying hardware. A poorly performing consistent key-value cluster can severely impact the performance of your distributed system. The same applies for etcd. If you are doing hundreds of transactions per second, you should utilize a managed solid state drive (SSD) with your virtual machine (we recommend a premium or ultra SSD) to prevent performance degradation. You will need at least four cores for etcd to run, and the throughput will scale with an increase in CPU cores. You can find more information on capacity planning and hardware configurations for the cloud on the general hardware page (*https://oreil.ly/Tisu4*) and the AWS guide (*https://oreil.ly/TTpZA*) (etcd doesn't currently publish an Azure-specific guide).

We recommend running etcd on the following Azure SKUs:

- Standard_D8ds_v4 (eight-core CPU)
- Standard_D16ds_v4 (16-core CPU)

These SKUs explicitly allow you to attach premium or ultra SSDs, which will increase the performance of the cluster.

 As with any production use case that we've discussed in this book, we strongly recommend that you enable accelerated networking on all Azure compute instances.

## Autoscaling and Auto-remediation

We would be remiss if we did not discuss how autoscaling and auto-remediation work with etcd. Autoscaling is not recommended for etcd as it could have unintended consequences if capacity additions or subtractions adversely affect cluster performance. That said, enabling auto-remediation (auto-healing) of bad etcd instances is considered to be OK. You can disable autoscaling for etcd by running the following command on your Kubernetes cluster:

```
$ kubectl delete hpa etcd
```

This will disable the Horizontal Pod Autoscaler (HPA), which is used in Kubernetes to automatically scale clusters up and down. You can find more information about the HPA in the Kubernetes documentation (*https://oreil.ly/bI14A*).

**Azure Autoscaling**

Azure provides autoscaling as a feature in a number of its products, including virtual machine scale sets and Azure functions. The autoscaling features allow you to efficiently scale your resources up and down when appropriate. With virtual machine scale sets, there can be up to a 10-minute delay for the new virtual machines to be available when scaling out.

## Availability and Security

etcd is a control plane service, so it is important that it is highly available and that the communications to it are secure. We recommend that you run at least three etcd nodes in a cluster to ensure availability of the cluster. Cluster throughput will be dependent on storage performance. We strongly recommend against using static discovery mechanisms for your cluster nodes, and instead to use DNS SRV records per the etcd clustering guide (*https://oreil.ly/ASLjZ*).

### etcd TLS

etcd supports client-to-server and peer (server-to-server) Transport Layer Security (TLS) encryption. We strongly recommend that you enable this as etcd is a control plane system. We won't go into implementation details here (as they are highly dependent on your infrastructure). You can find configuration options in the etcd security documentation (*https://oreil.ly/U4OeV*).

### Role-based access control

Since etcd v2.1, role-based access control (RBAC) has been a feature of the etcd API. Using RBACs, you can create access patterns that only allow certain users (or applications) access to a subset of the etcd data. Traditionally, this is done by providing HTTP basic authentication when making HTTP requests to etcd. As of etcd v3.2, if you're using the `--client-cert-auth=true` configuration option, the Common Name (CN) of the client TLS certificate will be used as the user (instead of a username/password combination).

You can find examples of how to apply RBACs to your etcd data space in the documentation (*https://oreil.ly/TMMOU*).

## Summary

Despite common misconceptions, it is possible to run large-scale data systems natively in Azure. In this chapter, we reviewed why it is advantageous to use cloud native data systems in Azure's cloud. We covered four systems: Vitess (relational), Rook (blob), TiKV (key-value), and etcd (key-value configuration/service discovery).

These systems are the bedrock of a cloud native architecture that stores and serves online data and offers a large upside over utilizing PaaS components. By now, you should understand what software makes sense for you to manage yourself as well as which PaaS services to use and how to deploy them in your infrastructure.

The cloud, and in particular, Kubernetes, has become a much friendlier place to run your stateful infrastructure. While Azure Gen2 storage accounts are a great resource for blob storage, cloud native software can really help you build long-lasting, large-scale, stateful infrastructure.

Now that you understand how you can store and serve data in a cloud environment, let's look at how to move data between systems using real-time messaging.

# CHAPTER 10

# Getting the Message

In this chapter, we will discuss the benefits of messaging in cloud native architectures and provide a brief history of messaging patterns so that you can understand their origin and evolution of interprocess communication to cloud native distributed systems.

By the end of this chapter, you will be able to deploy the most common messaging implementations used in cloud native applications and microservices today. We will compare the capabilities of mature messaging solutions such as RabbitMQ and Kafka that have been in production for years, and we will implement common messaging patterns in NATS. Given the book's focus on Azure, you will be able to manage Azure messaging offerings using Terraform. We will also provide small code samples in Python showing how easy it is to produce and consume messages and to validate proper deployment of the messaging infrastructure for both Azure and NATS.

## The Need for Messaging

The need for application and system components to pass messages in near real-time and exchange data is not unique to the cloud, or new to container-based microservices or even networked client/server applications. Anyone who has piped together commands at a shell prompt has used *interprocess communication*, which is a basic form of messaging.

Even the most primitive operating systems provide the ability to pass messages and share data. This problem space (and various solutions) dates back to the 1970s and continued to evolve in the 2000s, especially in the financial services industry, where there was a need to communicate stock information to customers, exchange data between service providers and other institutions, and process orders. Unlike client/server interactions we most commonly encounter on the internet or in enterprise applications, messaging relies on an intermediary (called a *broker*) to sit between the sender and the receiver that generally does not follow the request-response paradigm so that communication becomes asynchronous. We'll discuss why this is important shortly.

As the cloud matured in the 2010s, the use of messaging managed services, such as Amazon SQS and RabbitMQ servers running on virtual machines, played a role in increasing the reliability and scalability of websites. By the mid-2010s, Kafka became a popular solution for messaging use cases, including log aggregation, clickstream analytics, and data pipelines. NATS is another lightweight and high-performance messaging implementation that has become popular for edge analytics and Internet of Things (IoT) use cases, due to its ability to scale down to smaller-footprint devices and its ease of operability.

Queues and messaging publish/subscribe (affectionately known as "pub/sub") patterns were among the early managed services offered by cloud providers, and Azure has multiple messaging services, including Azure Event Grid, Azure Event Hubs, and Azure Service Bus, which provide standards-based protocols and implementations that are compatible with Java, .NET, Python, and other SDKs. These services allow migration of existing workloads and/or development of new cloud native applications.

Before we dive deeper into the history of messaging, the following are reasons why and when you would need to implement messaging either within your infrastructure or to be used by applications:

*Improves performance and throughput*
Using messaging patterns (whether simple queues or more complex publish/subscribe patterns) allows horizontal scalability and parallelization of workloads. Scaling producers, consumers, and brokers based on load is possible through virtual machine autoscaling approaches such as Azure virtual machine scale sets, through Kubernetes, or by the cloud service.

*Increases resiliency*
The ability to have multiple senders (producers) and receivers (consumers) that exchange messages provides better resiliency. Furthermore, the fact that messages can accumulate in a queue (the senders keep sending) while your consumers are not processing ensures that messages are not lost and that you can perform maintenance on your workers. Depending on the queuing pattern, the system can survive connectivity failures between components as well as application failures in producers or consumers.

*Ensures asynchronous operation*

Although the dreaded 502 gateway timeout errors on Apache and Nginx occur less frequently today, when we see them we are reminded of how early websites hit scalability problems when a large number of requests overwhelmed the ability of web servers to respond. The same principle applies when a database client connects to a backend database and the database runs out of threads or exhausts. When workers autoscale based on queue depth, the result is high rates of message processing responding to demand. Message queues also enable smaller-scoped service boundaries and are common in microservices application architectures. Lastly, because applications are not directly communicating (as in the case of RPC or even REST APIs), they can focus on the data that is being exchanged, assuming they are implementing a standard messaging protocol.

# A Sample Messaging Use Case: Log Ingestion and Analytics

To illustrate some of the real improvements that introduce message queues into an architecture, we will describe a log analytics software as a service (SaaS) solution that we can build and run. Log and event processing is a common use case for implementing messaging and streaming services.

The product will collect system and security logs from on-premises devices and parse and ingest them into a full-text search engine that allows security analysts to detect and find attacks on their network. We've dramatically oversimplified the description of this platform, but the following examples show the benefits of introducing message queues that we listed earlier.

Let's walk through three generations of this product's architecture and explore how the use of messaging evolved.

## Generation 1: Without Queues

The first generation of the solution was a real-time collection of events from an on-premises appliance that was posted to a load balancer that distributed logs to multiple ingest and search nodes (log collectors), as shown in Figure 10-1. This was a tightly coupled architecture in which large numbers of events being collected (based on customer usage patterns) could cause slowdowns in ingestion, which could, in turn, cause challenges in searching the UI.

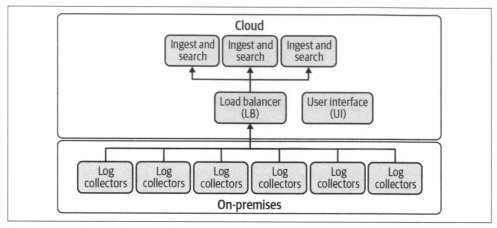

*Figure 10-1. Generation 1, without queues*

## Generation 2: With Cloud Queues and Object Storage

The second iteration of this solution used cloud provider object storage and message queues to ingest message bundles, instead of directly sending to an ingest API. On each index/search node, there was a lightweight worker process that pulled messages off the queue. The worker process contained the path to the log bundle in the object storage, as shown in Figure 10-2.

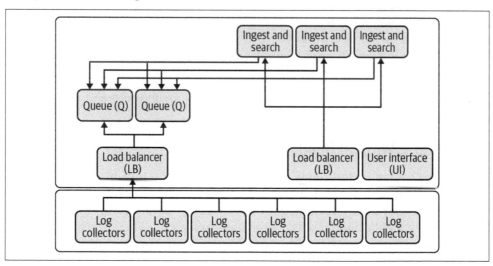

*Figure 10-2. Generation 2, with cloud queues and object storage*

Both of these solutions had a monolithic application architecture, which was addressed in the third generation of the platform. This generation also moved the parsing logic to the cloud and reduced the operational overhead for the on-premises customer teams.

## Generation 3: With Memory-Based Pub/Sub Queuing

The third generation of the platform implemented a microservices architecture and high-performance memory-based queues that allowed individual services to process messages to provide advanced analytics using a document database instead of the previous RDBMS-backed search engine. This separated the failure and performance domains and allowed for horizontal scaling of the system, as depicted in Figure 10-3.

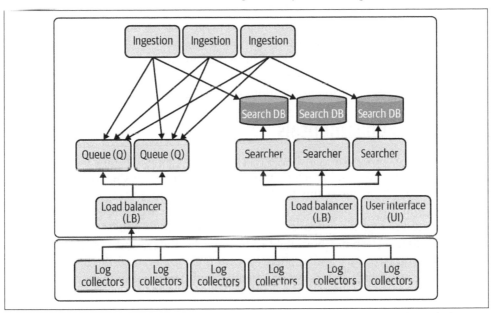

*Figure 10-3. Generation 3, with microservices architecture and horizontally scaled queues*

The adoption of messaging systems can be a key component in helping to scale a product. In the preceding example, the messaging system was used for scaling event processing. However, messaging systems can be used for other purposes, such as transporting analytics, logs, or any other formatted data that does not have to be acted upon in real time.

# The Basics of Messaging Platforms

The need for software components (whether client/server applications or individual programs running on a single computer) predates the cloud and even the internet. All but the most primitive general-purpose and embedded operating systems provide capabilities for programs to send and receive data to other programs.

## Messaging Versus Streaming

The Cloud Native Computing Foundation (CNCF) Landscape (shown in Figure 10-4) names the messaging  category *Streaming & Messaging*, but in this chapter we will focus primarily on messaging. Kafka, NATS, and RabbitMQ provide streaming capabilities, but unlike streaming analytics platforms such as Spark and Flink, they are not enabled by default and were not the initial use cases for any of these messaging platforms. We will discuss messaging concepts in detail in the next section, but it's important to note here that a key consideration for streaming systems is that operations occur on multiple messages, often with a time or ordered event window within memory operations for aggregations or filtering.

# Messaging Fundamentals

Understanding the similarities and differences between contemporary messaging solutions can help you determine which tool is best for the job or the problem at hand. As we have seen throughout this book, there is always more than one way to build something, and it is not always an easy decision to pick the right path until advertised capabilities of the tool are tested and validated with your specific infrastructure and use case. Before we explore how RabbitMQ, Apache Kafka, and NATS fit into the cloud native infrastructure and applications, we must understand the basic concepts and common capabilities in messaging, queuing, and streaming systems.

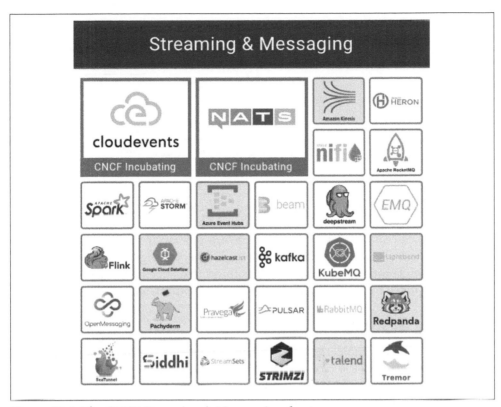

*Figure 10-4. The CNCF Streaming & Message Landscape*

## Producers and Consumers

Just as when you are communicating with another human, a message always has a sender and a receiver, but the message may or may not be sent directly and you may or may not get a response. When you send an email, there are multiple intermediate parties (see Figure 10-5). These parties include your email client, your email provider's servers (message transfer agents [MTAs], which play a broker role), the receiver's server (another MTA), and a receiving email client. In this example, there are a number of consumers and producers; the email client queues messages to send/produce to the ISP's mail servers, and the MTA then queues the sent messages and sends/produces them to the receiver's MTA. The receiver's email client will then receive/consume the messages from their ISP's MTA.

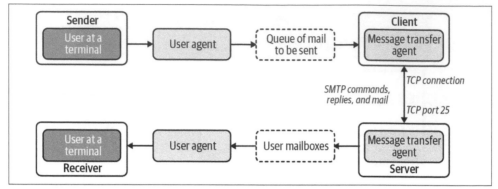

*Figure 10-5. The SMTP mail protocol, an example of a queueing system*

Just as in the case of networking where there are unicast, multicast, and broadcast delivery patterns, in messaging there may be cases where a single consumer processes data from a single producer or multiple consumers (like an email). Messages may be pushed to or pulled by consumers depending on the platform and configuration.

## Brokers and Clustering

In our earlier email example, the intermediate components, the MTAs, act as brokers between the sender and the receiver. In many cases, the MTA software can be clustered. One or more brokers in a cluster allow senders and receivers to be decoupled from one another. RabbitMQ, Kafka, and NATS, the messaging implementations discussed in this chapter, require at least one broker, and following the principle of most distributed system protocols, they often require a minimum of three brokers and generally should be odd-numbered counts (for consistency algorithms). Considerations for clustering include state replication, leader election, node membership behavior, and cluster partitioning in the event of network failure (and the dreaded split-brain problem).

Other considerations for clusters (which can quickly become a bottleneck) are how they can be scaled without downtime. The operational overhead of maintaining high-throughput and low-latency messaging clusters is why teams opt for the cloud provider to manage the infrastructure so that developers can focus on developing and optimizing producer and consumer applications.

# Durability and Persistence

Anyone who has ever sent an email to a nonexistent address has received error messages from a mail server indicating that after a certain period of time the message has expired. The implication is that your message is stored on an external system after it leaves your mail client.

Depending on the messaging use case and the type of data being stored and processed, it may have more or less criticality, have higher or lower perishability, and be more or less critical that every message (or transaction) be stored before processing. Just as in the case of Transmission Control Protocol (TCP) and User Datagram Protocol (UDP) client/server applications, the amount of error handling and retry logic implemented at the application layer versus the underlying transport layer is important to consider when building a production system. Messaging systems distribute intelligence to the producers, consumers, and brokers in different ways.

Furthermore, the mechanisms used to store the messages vary from system to system. Some systems have purely memory-based storage, which makes them less durable, particularly in cloud environments, and others have disk-backed solutions which, while having challenges in cloud environments, provide a more durable and reliable experience.

# Message Delivery

In addition to the source and destination, there are three important patterns you should be aware of for message-oriented platforms, which we will be covering in this chapter:

*At least once*
> Implies that there could be duplicates; in particular, if a consumer crashed and did not notify the broker that the message had been received, or that a message may be delivered to multiple consumers

*At most once*
> Assumes a message might be sent but not actually be received or acknowledged by a consumer, putting the burden of redelivery on the client

*Exactly once*
> A very limited situation in which transactions are required and messages must be delivered exactly one time

The messaging architecture may support one or more of these patterns. These also may be configurable on the broker itself or in the consumer and producer client libraries.

## Security

The sensitivity of the data contained in your message topic may vary, so it is necessary to have flexible controls on who can produce and consume to and from these topics. A message system should verify the identity of both the producer and consumer and then apply read/write permissions to the topic. Furthermore, the data that a system retains should be encrypted at rest.

Now that you understand some of the fundamentals of messaging, let's look at some common messaging patterns that you may come across.

# Common Messaging Patterns

We're going to look at three common messaging architectures that you will see in modern infrastructure.

## Simple Queue

Producers (P) publish to a queue (B), and as consumers (C) read off the queue, messages are deleted and no other consumers will process the message.

## Publish and Subscribe

As shown in Figure 10-6, a Producer (P) sends messages, and all listening (subscribed) consumers (C) receive the messages. There may or may not be acknowledgment, but if consumers are not online, they will miss the message.

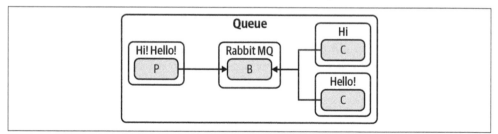

*Figure 10-6. A simple pub/sub message system*

## Durable Queue

As shown in Figure 10-7, a Producer (P) sends messages to the broker (B) and (C) consumes independently processing messages in an ordered list based on a pointer, but may rewind to a known point in the list, such as the first message within a given window.

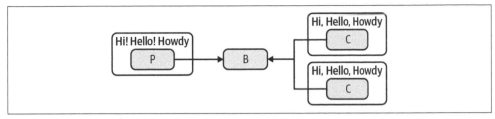

*Figure 10-7. A durable ordered message queue*

So far we've covered a lot of theory around messaging basics and architecture. We'll now dive into the various cloud native messaging platforms.

# An Overview of Popular Cloud Native Messaging Platforms

In this section, we will review a number of popular cloud native messaging platforms that have become commonplace in modern infrastructure.

## RabbitMQ

Although RabbitMQ is more than 15 years old and obviously predates widespread public adoption of the cloud and microservices, it is a proven messaging system that has powered critical workloads and has continued to be relevant in the world of containers and Kubernetes clusters. One of the reasons for this is that RabbitMQ was developed in Erlang/OTP, a functional programming language that is designed for scalability, concurrency, and reliability and is therefore ideal for building distributed systems that process millions to hundreds of millions of messages per day with very low downtime.

## Apache Kafka

In 2010, engineers at LinkedIn found that RabbitMQ could not scale to the complex nature and size of their ecosystem. Kafka was created to allow messaging to become the core of LinkedIn's technology stack and has successfully scaled to trillions of messages a day across the site.

Later in this chapter we will discuss Azure Event Hubs, a service that is compatible with Apache Kafka and allows applications to simply update the consumer/producer connection string, but may not make all of Kafka's features available. Managed Kafka is also part of HDInsight (*https://oreil.ly/lug99*), a broad suite of analytics services in the cloud on Azure. HDInsight is beyond the scope of this book.

## CNCF CloudEvents

Cloud Events (*https://cloudevents.io*) was first started in 2017 within the CNCF Serverless Working Group. In CNCF's own words: "CloudEvents is a specification for describing event data in common formats to provide interoperability across services, platforms and systems." While this project does have large potential (and is supported by Azure Event Grids), we won't cover it in further detail in this book.

# Cloud Messaging Deep Dive with NATS

NATS (*https://nats.io*) is another open source messaging implementation that has been accepted by CNCF. NATS was first released in 2011 and was initially implemented in Ruby as the messaging and service discovery layer for Cloud Foundry. It was later rewritten in Golang and is under very active development today. Although not as popular as RabbitMQ or Kafka, NATS provides multiple easily deployable options due to its single binary server available on multiple operating systems, processor architecture, and official Docker repositories. Client libraries are available for all popular programming languages. Simplicity, operability, performance, and security are cited as the advantages of NATS over other messaging implementations, as is the ability to easily use a bare minimum feature set with a preference for "at most once" delivery.

Since the base pub/sub protocol does not implement message persistence, consumers must be active to receive the message, making NATS optimal for exchanging data that is highly perishable, and data that is frequently updated such as sensor data. By default, messages will be routed to all listening subscribers to that topic, similar to multicast networking.

Given its low memory footprint and extremely high performance, NATS is also ideal for edge and IoT analytics use cases. For such a lightweight messaging implementation that focuses on simplicity, NATS has relatively sophisticated authentication and authorization capabilities and supports multitenancy by default through accounts. NATS Streams and NATS JetStream support both memory and disk-based persistence. NATS pub/sub and streaming have supported high availability and horizontal scalability from the start, and JetStream has been implementing them since early 2021.

## NATS Protocol Architecture

Like RabbitMQ, NATS offers multiple messaging patterns, and its capabilities have continued to evolve from the initial pub/sub implementation, to NATS streaming (shown in Figure 10-8), to its newest storage subsystem, JetStream. Released in 2020, JetStream is now available in NATS 2.2.x. NATS now also includes native MQTT protocol support.

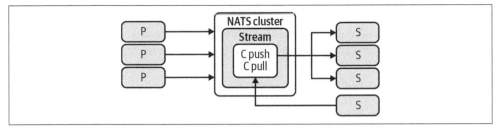

*Figure 10-8. Basic NATS architecture*

Because the foundational architecture is publish/subscribe, NATS producers are called publishers and its consumers are called subscribers. NATS JetStream uses the internal consumer abstraction.

The simplest possible exchange between a publisher and subscriber using the NATS CLI is the best way to see how simple the protocol is.

Let's look at an example. In the following code, a producer sends the message "arf" with the subject dog.food:

```
$ echo "arf" | nats pub dog.food
16:10:43 Reading payload from STDIN
16:10:43 Published 4 bytes to "dog.food"
```

In the following code, a consumer subscribes to the service for all messages that start with dog.:

```
$ nats sub dog.*
16:09:49 Subscribing on dog.*
[#1] Received on "dog.food"
```

## Clustering multiple NATS servers

NATS allows multiple servers to be clustered together to provide high availability and load balancing.

The simplest cluster can be started by doing the following:

- Configuring a cluster URL with the -cluster argument when starting the server
- Specifying routes in the additional server nodes

Assuming we have two different Linux servers on 192.168.2.238 and 192.168.2.247, we can configure a cluster with the following commands:

```
nats-server -DV -cluster nats://192.168.2.238:4248
nats-server -DV -cluster nats://192.168.2.247:4248 -routes nats://192.168.2.238:4248
```

## Using the Docker NATS server

In addition to RPM and debs, Synadia distributes and maintains Docker images that are probably the easiest way to run a NATS server, as shown in Example 10-1.

*Example 10-1. Running NATS Using Docker*

```
$ docker run -p 4222:4222 -p 8222:8222 -v ~/tmp/jetstream:/tmp/jetstream nats -js -m 8222
[1] 2021/06/26 21:23:21.572029 [INF] Starting nats-server
[1] 2021/06/26 21:23:21.572258 [INF]   Version:  2.3.0
[1] 2021/06/26 21:23:21.572289 [INF]   Git:      [56a144a]
[1] 2021/06/26 21:23:21.572311 [INF]   Name:     NDTRIDIRUYTNR5TKQCEKWFSVEKVPRPA2LICRPESRDOAFEDC
UPUSDKGX5
[1] 2021/06/26 21:23:21.572378 [INF]   Node:     N3Qm3ud7
[1] 2021/06/26 21:23:21.572399 [INF]   ID:       NDTRIDIRUYTNR5TKQCEKWFSVEKVPRPA2LICRPESRDOAFEDC
UPUSDKGX5
[1] 2021/06/26 21:23:21.574923 [INF] Starting JetStream
[1] 2021/06/26 21:23:21.576592 [INF]     _ ___ ____ _____ ___ ____ _____ ___ _ __ __
[1] 2021/06/26 21:23:21.576622 [INF]   _ | | __|_   _/ __|_ _ \ _| /\ | \/ |
[1] 2021/06/26 21:23:21.576631 [INF]  | || | _| | | \__ \ | | / _| / _ \| |V| |
[1] 2021/06/26 21:23:21.576639 [INF]   \_/|___| |_| |___/ |_| |_|\__/_/ \_\_| |_|
[1] 2021/06/26 21:23:21.576647 [INF]
[1] 2021/06/26 21:23:21.576656 [INF]          https://docs.nats.io/jetstream
[1] 2021/06/26 21:23:21.576664 [INF]
[1] 2021/06/26 21:23:21.576672 [INF] --------------- JETSTREAM ---------------
[1] 2021/06/26 21:23:21.576697 [INF]   Max Memory:    2.06 GB
[1] 2021/06/26 21:23:21.576711 [INF]   Max Storage:   4.64 GB
[1] 2021/06/26 21:23:21.576779 [INF]   Store Directory: "/tmp/nats/jetstream"
[1] 2021/06/26 21:23:21.576800 [INF] -----------------------------------------
[1] 2021/06/26 21:23:21.579799 [INF] Starting http monitor on 0.0.0.0:8222
[1] 2021/06/26 21:23:21.580581 [INF] Listening for client connections on 0.0.0.0:4222
[1] 2021/06/26 21:23:21.581147 [INF] Server is ready
```

We can pass the full command-line arguments. In this case, we are specifying a volume to be mounted in our *~/tmp* directory to be used for JetStream persistence.

## Monitoring NATS servers

NATS exposes a monitoring endpoint that can be viewed through the browser, the command line, or a web browser, as shown in Figure 10-9.

Figure 10-9. The NATS monitoring endpoint

The following is an example of the output of the NATS monitoring endpoint:

```
$ curl http://100.119.182.45:8222/varz
{
  "server_id": "ND6FZROVHED32BDLBTMCPXEN4LIKB2ROR3HO3GZ6DLDB64Z54SLG5GOD",
  "server_name": "ND6FZROVHED32BDLBTMCPXEN4LIKB2ROR3HO3GZ6DLDB64Z54SLG5GOD",
  "version": "2.2.2",
  "proto": 1,
  "git_commit": "a5f3aab",
  "go": "go1.16.3",
  "host": "0.0.0.0",
  "port": 4222,
  "connect_urls": [
    "192.168.2.247:4222",
    "192.168.122.1:4222",
    "172.17.0.1:4222",
    "100.119.182.45:4222",
    "[fd7a:115c:a1e0:ab12:4843:cd96:6277:b62d]:4222",
    "192.168.122.1:4222",
    "172.17.0.1:4222",
    "100.119.135.53:4222",
    "[fd7a:115c:a1e0:ab12:4843:cd96:6277:8735]:4222",
    "192.168.2.238:4222"
  ],
  "max_connections": 65536,
  "ping_interval": 120000000000,
  "ping_max": 2,
  "http_host": "0.0.0.0",
  "http_port": 8222,
  "http_base_path": "",
  "https_port": 0,
  "auth_timeout": 2,
```

```
"max_control_line": 4096,
"max_payload": 1048576,
"max_pending": 67108864,
"cluster": {
  "name": "xCQWcOMbOGCpM7ESUUctIc",
  "addr": "192.168.2.247",
  "cluster_port": 4248,
  "auth_timeout": 2,
  "urls": [
    "192.168.2.238:4248"
  ],
  "tls_timeout": 2
},
"gateway": {},
"leaf": {},
"jetstream": {},
"tls_timeout": 2,
"write_deadline": 10000000000,
"start": "2021-05-03T15:13:05.512147331Z",
"now": "2021-05-03T15:41:53.509877951Z",
"uptime": "28m47s",
"mem": 12353536,
"cores": 6,
"gomaxprocs": 6,
"cpu": 0,
"connections": 1,
"total_connections": 1,
"routes": 1,
"remotes": 1,
"leafnodes": 0,
"in_msgs": 117,
"out_msgs": 115,
"in_bytes": 67297,
"out_bytes": 66346,
"slow_consumers": 0,
"subscriptions": 144,
"http_req_stats": {
  "/": 3,
  "/accountz": 1,
  "/connz": 1,
  "/gatewayz": 0,
  "/leafz": 1,
  "/routez": 0,
  "/subsz": 1,
  "/varz": 2
},
"config_load_time": "2021-05-03T15:13:05.512147331Z",
"system_account": "$SYS"
}
```

You can use a tool such as Telegraf to scrape these HTTP endpoints and send them to an upstream metrics backend or the Prometheus exporter (*https://oreil.ly/KBMRh*).

# NATS Persistence with JetStream

Although NATS introduced a persistence implementation called NATS Streaming in 2019, it will be deprecated in June 2023. The second-generation implementation, called JetStream, has been under development since 2020 and will be the preferred option for use cases going forward. Although JetStream has a separate GitHub repository, it is now integrated into NATS Server 2.2.x and supported by the NATS CLI, which we will discuss shortly. NATS pub/sub only provided "at most once" delivery; JetStream allows "exactly once" delivery and more closely resembles the behavior of RabbitMQ queues and Kafka topics (see Figure 10-10).

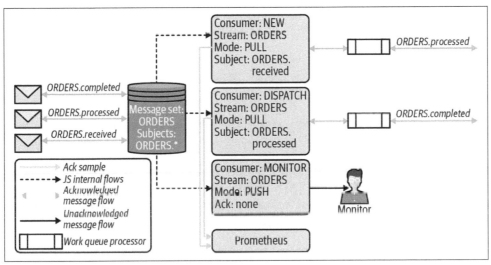

*Figure 10-10. The JetStream processing architecture*

# NATS Security

An entire chapter could easily be written on how to configure the range of authentication, authorization, and encryption capabilities of NATS 2.3.x. In this section, we will cover the basic steps necessary to raise the bar from the insecure defaults we've been using in most of our examples so far, which are inappropriate for production deployments. A strong identity and secrets management infrastructure is the foundation of secure cloud systems, but is beyond the scope of this book. NATS provides a robust permissions subsystem that allows granular control to be defined on a topic basis (*https://oreil.ly/nRsNI*) and uses distributed identity stores.

### Nkey-based authentication

Although NATS still supports token and username/password authentication, Nkey authentication is recommended going forward. It uses asymmetric cryptography and does not require a shared key to be stored on the server in plain-text or hashed format. Key management is extremely straightforward.

To generate the key pairs, use the nk (*https://oreil.ly/KqI6d*) utility found within the nkeys repository:

```
$ nk -gen user -pubout
SUAGWCAMMXKR43EDIXVC5FEA5G3767ALGQR75N27NGPK37KZUURS7F32FE
UBFHQJERKEBE323BXQEVT6257CIRJ4CIC5LGT6R2LJ524GQTUQHXCUK3
```

The public key (which begins with a "U") is configured on the server:

```
$ cat server.conf
net: 0.0.0.0
port: 4242

authorization {
  users: [
      { nkey: UBFHQJERKEBE323BXQEVT6257CIRJ4CIC5LGT6R2LJ524GQTUQHXCUK3  }
  ]
}
```

The private (or seed; that is what the "S" prefix means) key is stored on disk and passed as an argument to the NATS client or as a variable in code. As with any sensitive material, it is best if these keys are stored in an external secrets store such as Azure Key Vault or as a Kubernetes secret:

```
$ cat client.nkey
SUAGWCAMMXKR43EDIXVC5FEA5G3767ALGQR75N27NGPK37KZUURS7F32FE

$ nats -s nats://127.0.0.1:4242 --nkey client.nkey pub "foo"
12:57:17 Published 4 bytes to "foo"
```

### TLS authentication

Although we have secure authentication (and possibly authorization, depending on how we have configured subject permissions), using Nkey alone is not adequate for network security, since NATS is, by default, an ASCII plain-text protocol.

Like most cloud native protocols, NATS supports mutual TLS encryption. In general, the greatest challenge with TLS is certificate and key management, which is beyond the scope of this book. For demonstration purposes, mkcert (*https://oreil.ly/x9CZf*) provides an easier path than OpenSSL to generate the certificate authority (CA), client, and server key pairs needed for end-to-end encryption.

First, we set up the CA and create client and server certificates within the *~/nats* directory:

```
$ mkdir ~/nats && cd ~/nats

# Create the CA
$ mkcert -install

# Create the server
$ mkcert -cert-file server-cert.pem -key-file server-key.pem localhost 127.0.0.1 ::1

# Generate a certificate for client authentication.
$ mkcert -client -cert-file client-cert.pem -key-file client-key.pem localhost \
  ::1 127.0.0.1 email@localhost
$ cp -av `mkcert -CAROOT`/* ~/nats
```

Then we start the server (within the *~/nats* directory) and add the TLS certificate parameters:

```
$ nats-server -DV --tls --tlscert=server-cert.pem --tlskey=server-key.pem -ms 8222
```

Finally, we connect with the client:

```
$ nats --tlscert=client-cert.pem --tlskey=client-key.pem account info
```

On the server, we should see a successful TLS connection:

```
[10108] 2021/06/28 14:46:40.126469 [DBG] 127.0.0.1:50192 - cid:11 - Client connection
created
[10108] 2021/06/28 14:46:40.126573 [DBG] 127.0.0.1:50192 - cid:11 - Starting TLS client
connection handshake
[10108] 2021/06/28 14:46:40.157446 [DBG] 127.0.0.1:50192 - cid:11 - TLS handshake complete
[10108] 2021/06/28 14:46:40.157468 [DBG] 127.0.0.1:50192 - cid:11 - TLS version 1.3, cipher
suite TLS_AES_128_GCM_SHA256
[10108] 2021/06/28 14:46:40.157584 [TRC] 127.0.0.1:50192 - cid:11 - <<- [CONNECT
{"verbose":false,"pedantic":false,"tls_required":true,"name":"NATS CLI Version 0.0.23",
"lang":"go","version":"1.11.0","protocol":1,"echo":true,"headers":true,"no_responders":true}]
```

# Deploying NATS on Kubernetes

NATS can be installed quickly using a Helm chart. The Helm chart also will install a Prometheus operator and certificate manager that enable you to make full use of the metrics and TLS support that come with NATS:

1. Start by adding the Helm repository:

   ```
   $ helm repo add nats https://nats-io.github.io/k8s/helm/charts/
   $ helm repo update
   ```

2. Then install the NATS server:

   ```
   $ helm install my-nats nats/nats
   ```

3. Install the NATS streaming server (known as stan):

   ```
   $ helm install my-stan nats/stan --set stan.nats.url=nats://my-nats:4222
   ```

4. After these steps, there will be a Grafana Surveyor that you can view by port-forwarding to the Pod:

```
kubectl port-forward deployments/nats-surveyor-grafana 3000:3000
```

5. You will be able to view Grafana in your browser at *http://127.0.0.1:3000/d/nats/nats-surveyor?refresh=5s&orgId=1*.

Your Help deployment offers a number of Helm configurables. You can read about it more on the NATS Helm deployment configuration page (*https://oreil.ly/M6e3j*).

You can code against NATS in a very straightforward manner in Python using the `nats-py` package. In the following example, we code a basic producer and consumer in Python. NATS provides a public server for you to test against. If you want to test in your own environment, replace `nc = await nats.connect("nats://demo.nats.io:4222")` with the address of your NATS instance:

```python
import time

import asyncio
import nats
from nats.aio.errors import ErrConnectionClosed, ErrTimeout, ErrNoServers

async def run():
    # The Nats project provides a public demo server `nats://demo.nats.io:4222`.
    # You can add your own Nats server on the next line
    nc = await nats.connect("nats://demo.nats.io:4222")

    async def message_handler(msg):
        subject = msg.subject
        reply = msg.reply
        data = msg.data.decode()
        print("Received a message on '{subject} {reply}': {data}".format(
            subject=subject, reply=reply, data=data))

    # Simple publisher and async subscriber via coroutine.
    sub = await nc.subscribe("foo", cb=message_handler)

    await nc.publish("foo", b'Message1')
    await nc.publish("foo", b'Message2')

    time.sleep(5)
    # Remove interest in subscription.
    await sub.unsubscribe()

    # Terminate connection to NATS.
    await nc.drain()

if __name__ == '__main__':
    loop = asyncio.get_event_loop()
    loop.run_until_complete(run())
    loop.close()
```

# Azure Messaging Services

When commercial public cloud offerings first became available in the mid-2000s, storage and messaging services (like AWS S3 and AWS SQS) were among the first to be available to customers. Microsoft Azure provides multiple managed messaging services to support cloud-specific implementations, as well as standards-based messaging protocols such as AMQP (*https://oreil.ly/yOJj4*) and JMS (*https://oreil.ly/3V3KH*) and patterns like the worker queue and pub/sub that we already explored in this chapter. All Azure options provide "at least once" delivery.

When selecting between Azure Service Bus, Azure Event Hubs, and Azure Event Grid, you should consider the following criteria:

- Compatibility with on-premises messaging wire protocols and platforms (ActiveMQ, RabbitMQ) and tooling
- Level of integration required with other Azure managed services
- Need for ordered messaging and transactions
- Ability to handle event streaming
- Use of big data pipelines
- Maximum ingestion rate (events per second)
- Available asynchronous event patterns
- Pricing

One of the major benefits of using Azure messaging services is the ability to take advantage of Azure IAM capabilities and secrets management. Let's now look in detail at the Azure offerings.

## Azure Service Bus

Azure Service Bus is a managed queuing service that provides enterprise-level features comparable to those in ActiveMQ and RabbitMQ, but without the overhead of managing multiple brokers on virtual machines or deployments on top of Kubernetes. Azure Service Bus can span multiple availability zones with Azure Service Bus Premium (*https://oreil.ly/qJKFS*), and is designed to support migration from on-premises JMS 2.0 implementations.

Service Bus supports the simple message queue and publish/subscribe patterns we discussed at the beginning of the chapter. The most common pattern is the "pull model," in which consumers poll the service endpoint for new messages. Just as with RabbitMQ and Kafka, multiple consumers can process messages as fast as possible when messages are available, allowing work to be distributed across multiple worker nodes. Azure Service Bus implements AMQP 1.0 (*https://oreil.ly/AUSLy*) and has well-documented SDKs and code samples for .NET, Java, Python, Go, and more.

### Service Bus concepts

Azure Service Bus abstractions (see Figures 10-11 and 10-12 for reference architectures) provide similar capabilities to those available in NATS.

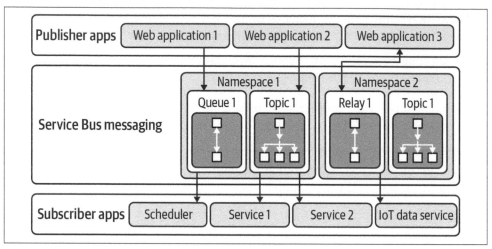

*Figure 10-11. A reference Service Bus architecture*

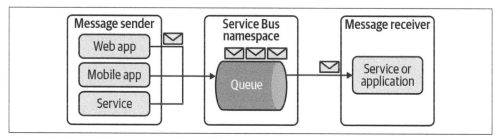

*Figure 10-12. A simple messaging architecture*

**Namespaces.**  Namespaces allow segmentation of topics, queues, and services as a container for messaging components, just like a virtual network serves a boundary for networking components such as virtual machines and load balancers. Kafka does not provide a comparable abstraction, but RabbitMQ virtual hosts and NATS accounts do.

**Queues, topics, and subscriptions.**  Azure Service Bus queues provide an ordered set of FIFO messages that are pulled similar to Kafka and RabbitMQ consumers or NATS pull-based consumers, while topics are primarily for pub/sub patterns and onc-to-many communication for messaging with large numbers of consumers. Sub-scriptions allow consumers to receive messages based on filtering rules. Just as with NATS JetStream, messages are retrieved from the subscription (similar to JetStream's consumer) and not the topic itself (comparable to the NATS JetStream stream).

## Managing Azure Service Bus with Terraform

Although Microsoft provides a Python SDK for Service Bus management, we will stick to Terraform for the creation of Service Bus namespaces, queues, and topics. The following code example deploys a new servicebus, namespace, queue, and topic:

```
provider "azurerm" {
  features {}
}

resource "azurerm_resource_group" "example" {
  name     = "terraform-servicebus"
  location = "Central US"
}

resource "azurerm_servicebus_namespace" "example" {
  name                = "mdfranz-servicebus-namespace"
  location            = azurerm_resource_group.example.location
  resource_group_name = azurerm_resource_group.example.name
  sku                 = "Standard"

  tags = {
    source = "terraform"
  }
}

resource "azurerm_servicebus_queue" "example" {
  name                = "mdfranz-servicebus-queue"
  resource_group_name = azurerm_resource_group.example.name
  namespace_name      = azurerm_servicebus_namespace.example.name
  enable_partitioning = true
}

resource "azurerm_servicebus_topic" "example" {
  name                = "mdfranz-servicebus-topic"
  resource_group_name = azurerm_resource_group.example.name
  namespace_name      = azurerm_servicebus_namespace.example.name
  enable_partitioning = true
}
```

Using the azure-cli, we can see the resources that were created:

```
$ az servicebus queue list --namespace-name mdfranz-servicebus-namespace -g \
  terraform-servicebus
[
  {
    "accessedAt": "0001-01-01T00:00:00+00:00",
    "autoDeleteOnIdle": "10675199 days, 2:48:05.477581",
    "countDetails": {
      "activeMessageCount": 0,
```

```
        "deadLetterMessageCount": 0,
        "scheduledMessageCount": 0,
        "transferDeadLetterMessageCount": 0,
        "transferMessageCount": 0
    },
    "createdAt": "2021-04-14T02:24:28.260000+00:00",
    "deadLetteringOnMessageExpiration": false,
    "defaultMessageTimeToLive": "10675199 days, 2:48:05.477581",
    "duplicateDetectionHistoryTimeWindow": "0:10:00",
    "enableBatchedOperations": true,
    "enableExpress": false,
    "enablePartitioning": true,
    "forwardDeadLetteredMessagesTo": null,
    "forwardTo": null,
    "id": "/subscriptions/1bf91ee3-5b21-4996-bd72-ae38e8f26ce9/resourceGroups/ \
      terraform-servicebus/providers/Microsoft.ServiceBus/namespaces/ \
      mdfranz-servicebus-namespace/queues/mdfranz-servicebus-queue",
    "location": "Central US",
    "lockDuration": "0:01:00",
    "maxDeliveryCount": 10,
    "maxSizeInMegabytes": 81920,
    "messageCount": 0,
    "name": "mdfranz-servicebus-queue",
    "requiresDuplicateDetection": false,
    "requiresSession": false,
    "resourceGroup": "terraform-servicebus",
    "sizeInBytes": 0,
    "status": "Active",
    "type": "Microsoft.ServiceBus/Namespaces/Queues",
    "updatedAt": "2021-04-14T02:24:28.887000+00:00"
  }
]

$ az servicebus topic list --namespace-name mdfranz-servicebus-namespace -g \
  terraform-servicebus
[
  {
    "accessedAt": "0001-01-01T00:00:00+00:00",
    "autoDeleteOnIdle": "10675199 days, 2:48:05.477581",
    "countDetails": {
      "activeMessageCount": 0,
      "deadLetterMessageCount": 0,
      "scheduledMessageCount": 0,
      "transferDeadLetterMessageCount": 0,
      "transferMessageCount": 0
    },
    "createdAt": "2021-04-14T12:32:46.243000+00:00",
    "defaultMessageTimeToLive": "10675199 days, 2:48:05.477581",
    "duplicateDetectionHistoryTimeWindow": "0:10:00",
    "enableBatchedOperations": false,
    "enableExpress": false,
    "enablePartitioning": true,
    "id": "/subscriptions/SUBSCRIPTION/resourceGroups/terraform-servicebus/providers/ \
      Microsoft.ServiceBus/namespaces/mdfranz-servicebus-namespace/topics/ \
      mdfranz-servicebus-topic",
    "location": "Central US",
    "maxSizeInMegabytes": 81920,
    "name": "mdfranz-servicebus-topic",
    "requiresDuplicateDetection": false,
```

```
        "resourceGroup": "terraform-servicebus",
        "sizeInBytes": 0,
        "status": "Active",
        "subscriptionCount": 0,
        "supportOrdering": false,
        "type": "Microsoft.ServiceBus/Namespaces/Topics",
        "updatedAt": "2021-04-14T12:32:46.487000+00:00"
    }
]
```

We can see the resources within the Azure console as well, as shown in Figure 10-13.

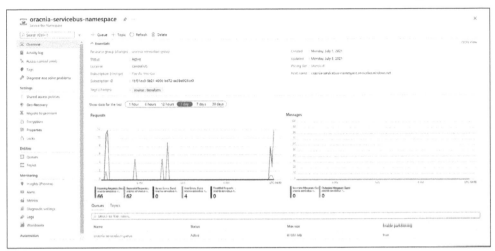

*Figure 10-13. Azure portal display of Service Bus deployment*

We can also see the overall metrics in the namespaces as well as click on a specific queue that provides more details on the storage and message size (see Figure 10-14).

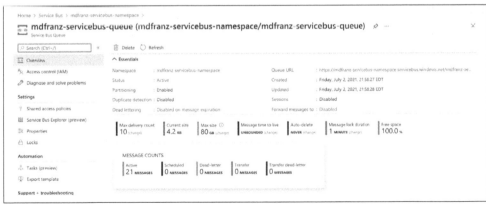

*Figure 10-14. Azure portal display of Service Bus queue*

### Sending and receiving messages to a Service Bus queue in Python

Assuming we successfully created the infrastructure in the preceding steps, we can retrieve a connection string that we can use by running an Azure CLI command:

```
$ az servicebus namespace authorization-rule keys list --resource-group $RES_GROUP \
  --namespace-name
$NAMESPACE_NAME --name RootManageSharedAccessKey --query primaryConnectionString wBY=
```

Azure provides open source libraries to send and receive messages to the Azure service in all popular programming languages. The following example builds a simple producer and consumer in Python:

```
from azure.servicebus import ServiceBusClient, ServiceBusMessage

import os
connstr = os.environ['SERVICE_BUS_CONN_STR']
queue_name = os.environ['SERVICE_BUS_QUEUE_NAME']

messages = ["Testing 1","Testing 2", "Testing 3"]

with ServiceBusClient.from_connection_string(connstr) as client:
  s = client.get_queue_sender(queue_name)
  r = client.get_queue_receiver(queue_name)

  print(s,r)

  for m in messages:
    s.send_messages(ServiceBusMessage(m))

  while True:
    print(r.receive_messages(max_message_count=1,max_wait_time=10))
```

In addition to RabbitMQ, readers familiar with AWS SNS and SQS will find Service Bus straightforward and able to meet similar use cases.

## Azure Event Hubs

Azure Event Hubs is designed to provide some of the capabilities of Apache Kafka to meet use cases for partitioning and consumer groups, but in a managed cloud service (see Figure 10-15). Although you lose the visibility into the backend infrastructure that you would have when running Kafka on virtual machines or Kubernetes, you gain tighter integration with additional data services such as Azure Blob Storage, Azure Data Lakes, and Azure Stream Analytics, to name a few. Azure also supports both AMQP 1.0 and Kafka 1.0 protocols to maintain compatibility with client libraries.

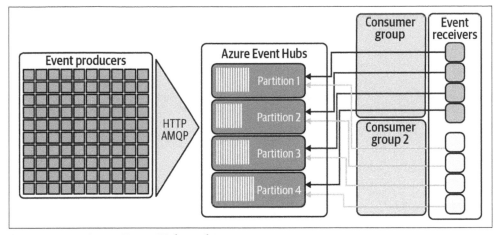

*Figure 10-15. Azure Event Hubs architecture*

Azure Event Hubs has some concepts that transfer over from Azure Service Bus. We will quickly review them here:

*Producers*
> These are the clients that send messages to Azure Event Hubs.

*Partitions*
> Messages are sharded across partitions to enable replicas of the message to be stored.

*Consumer groups*
> These are clients that work in unison to consume messages produced in a coordinated manner.

## Managing Azure Event Hubs with Terraform

The Terraform code necessary to provision the required resources to send messages to Azure Event Hubs closely resembles what we previously used to configure a queue and topic within Azure Service Bus. We must declare a resource group and a namespace that our Event Hubs instance will be part of:

```
provider "azurerm" {
  features {}
}

resource "azurerm_resource_group" "example" {
  name     = "mdfranz-eventbus-group"
  location = "East US"
}

resource "azurerm_eventhub_namespace" "example" {
  name            = "mdfranz-eventhub-namespace"
  location        = "East US"
```

```
    resource_group_name = azurerm_resource_group.example.name
    sku                 = "Standard"
    capacity            = 1
}

resource "azurerm_eventhub" "example" {
    name                = "mdfranz-eventhub"
    namespace_name      = azurerm_eventhub_namespace.example.name
    resource_group_name = azurerm_resource_group.example.name
    partition_count     = 1
    message_retention   = 1
}

resource "azurerm_eventhub_consumer_group" "example" {
    name                = "mdfranz-consumergroup"
    resource_group_name = azurerm_resource_group.example.name
    namespace_name      = azurerm_eventhub_namespace.example.name
    eventhub_name       = azurerm_eventhub.example.name
}
```

Creating a consumer group is optional as there is a default consumer group. Note also that having multiple consumer groups does require the standard SKU as opposed to the basic SKU.

As was the case with Azure Event Bus, there are multiple ways to authenticate to Event Hubs endpoints. The easiest way is to use a connection string, as shown in the following example:

```
$ az eventhubs namespace authorization-rule keys list --resource-group mdfranz-eventbus- \
  group  --namespace-name mdfranz-eventhub-namespace --name RootManageSharedAccessKey
{
  "aliasPrimaryConnectionString": null,
  "aliasSecondaryConnectionString": null,
  "keyName": "RootManageSharedAccessKey",
  "primaryConnectionString": "Endpoint=sb://mdfranz-eventhub-namespace.servicebus.windows. \
    net/;SharedAccessKeyName=RootManageSharedAccessKey; \
    SharedAccessKey=jfMUbfQZX8UJglcCKLAeIp5CZVLcwcSGpuKdJX/CMzk=",
  "primaryKey": "jfMUbfQZX8UJglcCKLAeIp5CZVLcwcSGpuKdJX/CMzk=",
  "secondaryConnectionString": "Endpoint=sb://mdfranz-eventhub-namespace.servicebus. \
    windows.net/;SharedAccessKeyName=RootManageSharedAccessKey; \
    SharedAccessKey=gFy7SuuGjw12GfoHXd6UQeZdy5Y0xu/gStZtQUhaxsY=",
  "secondaryKey": "gFy7SuuGjw12GfoHXd6UQeZdy5Y0xu/gStZtQUhaxsY="
}
```

The parameter `EntityPath=mdfranz-eventhub`, i.e.:

```
Endpoint=sb://mdfranz-eventhub-namespace.servicebus.windows.net/;
SharedAccessKeyName=RootManageSharedAccessKey;EntityPath=mdfranz-
eventhubSharedAccessKey=jfMUbfQZX8UJglcCKLAeIp5CZVLcwcSGpuKdJX/CMzk=
```

*must* be added to the connection string, because if you are creating a client using `NewHubfromConnectionString`, the `Send` method does not allow an event grid name to be specified as a parameter, so you need to add an `EntityPath` instead.

# Azure Event Grid

Azure Event Grid was released for general availability in 2018 and is the best of the Azure-offered messaging brokers, as it allows multiple event sources to be routed to a variety of destinations within the Azure ecosystem. Messages can be sent to/from the existing message services we just discussed (Azure Service Bus and Azure Event Hubs) and to additional services and endpoints (shown in Figure 10-16), such as Azure Functions, Webhooks, Logic Apps, and other in-application purposes (e.g., tracking how users interact with the application). Azure Event Hubs is a first-class "serverless" offering in which billing is by the event.

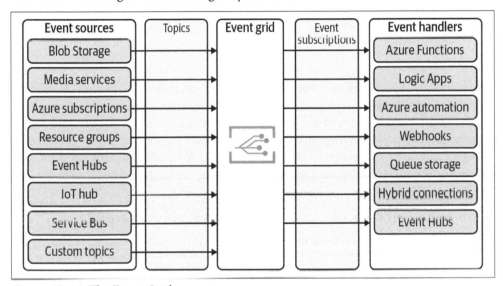

*Figure 10-16. The Event Grid ecosystem*

In Figure 10-16, note the push nature of the Event Grid as opposed to the general push-pull topology we're used to in other systems.

Azure Event Grid uses terminology that slightly differs from the other platforms we've discussed:

*Domains*
> Domains are analogous to namespaces, which separate use cases within the tenant.

*Topics*
> For Event Grids, there are two types of topics: system topics, which come from Azure systems (Event Hubs, Blob Storage, etc.), as shown on the left in Figure 10-16; and custom topics, which can be your own customized scheme wrapped in the Event Grid Schema (*https://oreil.ly/BYRxP*).

### Deploying and using event grids

Azure event grids have a minimalistic Terraform deployment, as shown in the following example:

```
resource "azurerm_resource_group" "example" {
  name     = "example-resources"
  location = "East US"
}

resource "azurerm_eventgrid_topic" "example" {
  name                = "my-eventgrid-topic"
  location            = azurerm_resource_group.example.location
  resource_group_name = azurerm_resource_group.example.name

  tags = {
    environment = "Production"
  }
}
```

You will want to change the name of the topic as it is globally unique across the Azure region you deploy to. Once this Terraform deployment is applied, a new Event Grid topic will be created with the name *https://<event-grid-topic-name>.<topic-location>.eventgrid.azure.net/api/events*; or in our case, *https://my-eventgrid-topic.east-us.eventgrid.azure.net/api/events*. You will be able to find the access key for the topic by running `az eventgrid topic key list --resource-group example-resources --name my-eventgrid-topic`.

Here is a simple producer using the `azure-eventgrid` Python package:

```
from azure.identity import DefaultAzureCredential
from azure.eventgrid import EventGridPublisherClient, EventGridEvent

event = EventGridEvent(
    data={"team": "azure-sdk"},
    subject="Door1",
    event_type="Azure.Sdk.Demo",
    data_version="2.0"
)

credential = DefaultAzureCredential("<access-key>")
endpoint = `https://my-eventgrid-topic.east-us.eventgrid.azure.net/api/events"
client = EventGridPublisherClient(endpoint, credential)
client.send(event)
```

A number of great examples on how to code with the Event Grid are available at the Azure Event Grid client library for Python (*https://oreil.ly/i0SN1*).

# Summary

You have many choices when picking messaging technologies to implement with new or existing applications. As usual, the answer as to what and how to run a piece of technology is often "it depends!" There is significant overlap in functionality across the open source and Azure messaging offerings we discussed in this chapter. Ensuring that you understand your durability, scale, and security requirements before picking a messaging service will set you up for success as you deploy a messaging infrastructure. We will now move to our final piece of infrastructure, serverless computing.

# CHAPTER 11

# Serverless

Up to this point, we have largely focused on taking on-premises concepts and discussing and implementing their cloud-based equivalents. In this chapter, we will take a deep dive into a new type of computing architecture known as serverless, which is rooted in cloud computing. Specifically, we will examine common serverless platforms including Azure function apps, Knative, KEDA, and OpenFaaS.

## Introduction to Serverless Computing

Similar to containers, there is a lot of hype around serverless computing and what can be done with it. This chapter will examine the features and benefits of serverless computing.

### What Is Serverless?

Unlike containers, which largely still contain a number of host-based concepts, serverless abstracts all of that away to the point where you are only worried about being able to run a software function.

Serverless has gained a lot of popularity due to the ability to create applications quickly and run them without worrying about infrastructure management. Furthermore, serverless considers autoscaling as a first-class feature, which means you do not need to worry about anything other than writing code and deploying it using standardized framework deployment mechanisms.

The benefit of serverless is that server maintenance and configuration is mostly not a concern. Furthermore, if you want to run a software function infrequently, serverless functions can be a much more economical option as you pay by the request, not by the reservation of the computing resources (i.e., the compute).

The serverless landscape, as previously mentioned, is a reasonably new space that has innovated quickly. As well as the big cloud providers providing a function platform, other internet companies like Cloudflare, Netlify, and Twilio also provide serverless functionality.

## What Is a Serverless Function?

A serverless function is a small, short-lived program that is run when triggered. Serverless functions can be triggered via an HTTP(s) request, via a timer, or in Azure Event Grid by triggering a function based on a Cosmos DB or Service Bus event.

A function will generally have a single self-contained purpose that is executed quickly and has limited dependencies. Furthermore, it is generally not a high-qps (queries per second) endpoint as performance is a secondary concern of serverless functions.

You may have heard of utilities like *https://icanhazip.com*, which is a service that just returns the public IP address you're connecting from. This can be written and deployed easily as a serverless function:

```
async function handleRequest(request) {
  const clientIP = request.headers.get("CF-Connecting-IP")
  return new Response(clientIP)
}

addEventListener("fetch", event => {
 event.respondWith(handleRequest(event.request))
})
```

The preceding example creates an event listener for a "fetch" type of event (which is an HTTP GET), and when that event is triggered, the `handleRequest` function is called. The function parses an HTTP request header, `CF-Connecting-IP`, which is the IP making the request to the serverless function. The function then responds with the requesting IP address.

## The Serverless Landscape

As mentioned earlier, despite being a new space, the serverless landscape has seen rapid system development. The CNCF Serverless Landscape (shown in Figure 11 1) consists of a number of sections:

*Tools*
> Software frameworks that assist in building serverless software

*Security*
> Software that is specifically designed for securing serverless infrastructure

*Frameworks*
> Software frameworks for building serverless functions

*Hosted platform*
> Public providers that offer serverless functions

*Installable platform*
> Software you can install to run serverless functions

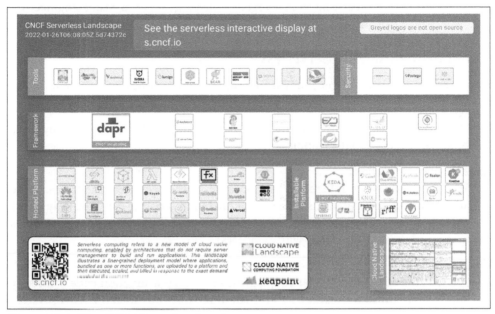

*Figure 11-1. The CNCF Serverless Landscape*

While we won't cover it in detail in this book, beyond the frameworks and primary cloud providers providing serverless offerings, edge-network (or CDN) providers are also offering serverless or "edge-compute" functionality. This has become extremely popular at companies like Cloudflare.

# Benefits of Serverless

When used correctly, serverless can come with major benefits to the user:

*Lower costs*
> You are billed for the number of times or the amount of time your function runs, meaning that you do not have to pay for idle cloud resources.

*Eliminated operational overhead*
> Given the simplicity of the function model and the limited dependencies, the need to actively provision or manage the function is severely reduced.

*Autoscaling*
> The function scales automatically and no additional effort is required to scale the number of function workers up or down.

*Faster development cycles*
> Tying all of the preceding points together helps generate a faster engineering cycle, which can lead to increased developer and operator productivity.

## Potential Downsides of Serverless

Serverless can also have potential downsides that should be considered as well:

*Debuggability*
> When all of the compute is entirely ephemeral and short-lived, debugging your function is exceptionally complex.

*Large number of functions*
> While autoscaling is inherently built into all of the serverless functions, there are a number of side effects to always autoscaling. First, it can adversely affect performance, and second, managing connection pooling downstream becomes more complicated (especially with databases).

*Vendor lock-in*
> A downside of all of the serverless platforms is that your function code is directly tied into the software platform you're running your functions on. This severely limits your portability over time.

Now that we've explained what serverless is and some of the benefits of using the technology, we will look at various platforms on which to run serverless functions.

## Azure Function Apps

Azure function apps are Azure's platform offering of serverless applications. Function apps provide the ability to run either code or containers in either Linux or Windows environments with support for multiple programming languages, including:

- .NET Platform (C#, F#)
- JavaScript and TypeScript
- Python
- Java
- PowerShell Core

An Azure function app will have an associated plan that dictates how your app will scale, the features that are available, and the price that you pay. At the time of this writing, there are three options:

*Consumption*
> This is a basic plan in which the function scales automatically and you only pay when your functions are running.

*Functions Premium*
> This automatically scales based on demand using prewarmed workers. It runs with more powerful instances and allows some advanced network functionality.

*App Service Plan*
> This is for long-running scenarios in which you also need predictive scaling and billing.

You can find more information about each plan on the Azure Functions hosting options (*https://oreil.ly/rqWha*) documentation page.

## Function App Architecture

Azure's app architecture (see Figure 11-2) fits in with the larger suite of Azure offerings including Cosmos DB, storage accounts, and Azure Pipelines. The native integration with Cosmos DB and storage accounts makes it an attractive offering for simple integration with other Azure offerings. While we won't cover it in this book, Azure functions also tie in with the continuous integration/continuous deployment (CI/CD) offering in Azure Pipelines and can be monitored by Azure Monitor.

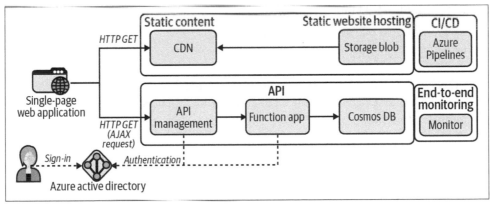

*Figure 11-2. Azure's serverless function reference architecture*

When creating a function app, you must also link a storage account. This can be used for temporary storage. Each app will be provisioned with a public HTTP(s) endpoint at creation so that the function is accessible. It is possible to secure the function app using a private endpoint.

## Creating a Function App

In this section, we will create a function app using the Azure portal:

1. We will start by opening the Azure portal and clicking Create under Function App.

2. Now we will fill out the basic parameters of the function app:

    a. We will create a new resource group called `serverless-test`.

    b. The DNS name of our application will be `ourtestfunctionapp.azureweb sites.net`.

    c. We will run code (a function) instead of a container.

    d. The language will be Python v3.9.

    e. The function app will be deployed in the region East US.

3. In the Hosting tab:

    a. We will create a new storage account called `functionstorageaccount`. As storage account names are globally unique, you will need to pick your own name.

    b. Because we are running Python, we must run Linux.

    c. Finally, we will utilize the Consumption plan for the purposes of this example.

4. In the Monitoring tab:

    a. We will turn off Application Insights.

    b. Then we will click Review + Create.

Now that we have our function app created, we need to create a function. Visual Studio Code has an extension, Azure Functions, which makes it simple to create, test, and publish a function:

1. If you haven't installed Visual Studio Code you can download it from the Visual Studio Code download page (*https://oreil.ly/GjiXf*).

2. Once you've installed Visual Studio Code, you will need to install the Azure Functions (*https://oreil.ly/AZCC8*) extension.

3. Click the Azure icon on the Activity bar on the lefthand side of the screen, which will bring up the Azure Functions window. Click "Create new project."

4. A dialog box will pop up where you'll need to choose a local directory in which to save your code.

5. You'll then be prompted for some project information in separate Visual Studio Code pop-ups:

    a. Select a language for your function project: choose Python.

    b. Select a Python alias to create a virtual environment: choose the location of your Python interpreter.

    c. If the location isn't shown, type in the full path to your Python binary.

    d. Select a template for your project's first function: choose "HTTP trigger."

    e. Provide a function name: type HttpExample.

    f. Pick an authorization level: choose Anonymous, which enables anyone to call your function endpoint. To learn about authorization levels, see the Authorization keys (*https://oreil.ly/00cHw*) documentation.

    g. Select how you would like to open your project: choose "Add to workspace."

    h. Using this information, Visual Studio Code generates an Azure Functions project with an HTTP trigger. You can view the local project files in the Explorer. To learn more about files that are created, see the Generated project files (*https://oreil.ly/osoat*) documentation.

6. At this time, you'll have the skeleton of a project created. Add the following code to the *HttpExample* file, which will return the IP of the client making a request to the function (similar to *icanhazip.com*):

    ```
    import azure.functions as func

    def main(req: func.HttpRequest ) -> func.HttpResponse:
        response = False
        if (req.headers.get('X-Forwarded-For')):
            response = req.headers.get('X-Forwarded-For').split(':')[0]
        else:
            response = "127.0.0.1"
        return func.HttpResponse(response)
    ```

7. Test your function by pressing F5 on your keyboard and then going to *http://localhost:7071/api/HttpExample*.

8. To deploy to Azure, you will need to click the "Sign in to Azure" button in the Azure Functions window.

9. Click the Upload button, which will allow you to upload your function to the app you created previously.

Now that we've looked at the Azure native offerings, let's discuss the function apps deployed with Kubernetes.

# Knative

Knative is a serverless platform built on top of Kubernetes and was an early favorite in the industry given the buzz around Kubernetes at the time of release. One of the advantages of Knative is that the functions are packaged and executed as Docker containers, which makes integration effort into an existing cloud environment minimal.

## Knative Architecture

Knative has two modes of operation:

- Knative Serving (*https://oreil.ly/3L09I*) uses Kubernetes to deploy serverless functions or containers and has full support for autoscaling (including down to zero Pods). It also has an added bonus of supporting cloud networking solutions like Gloo and Istio.
- Knative Eventing (*https://oreil.ly/D7qeV*) allows developers to develop applications built around an event-driven architecture. In an eventing deployment, you can specify event producers (sources) to respond to.

Let's look at how to install Knative on Kubernetes.

## Installing and Running Knative Serving on Kubernetes

In this section, we'll run a basic Knative serving system:

1. Start by installing the custom resources:

   ```
   $ kubectl apply -f https://github.com/knative/net-kourier/releases/download/v0.26.0/ \
       kourier.yaml
   ```

2. Then install the serving components:

   ```
   $ kubectl apply -f https://github.com/knative/serving/releases/download/v0.26.0/ \
       serving-core.yaml
   ```

   If you want to use any of the networking integrations (Kourier, Ambassador, Contour, Istio), you can follow the networking layer instructions (*https://oreil.ly/Fx6MN*).

3. Now you need to create your application. We will use Python's Flask library to create a simple application:

   ```
   Import logging
   import os

   from flask import Flask

   app = Flask(__name__)
   Log =

   @app.route('/', methods=['POST'])
   ```

```
def hello_world():
    return f'Hello world. Data {request.data}\n'


if __name__ == '__main__':
    app.run(debug=True, host='0.0.0.0', port=int(os.environ.get('PORT', 8080)))
```

4. Now you need a Docker image containing your serverless application:

```
FROM python:3.7-slim

RUN pip install Flask gunicorn

WORKDIR /app
COPY . .

CMD exec gunicorn --bind :$PORT --workers 1 --threads 8 app:app
```

5. Build and push your new serverless image using:

```
$ docker push https://myharborinstallation.com/helloworld:v1
```

6. Now define your serverless service in a file called *hello-world.yaml*:

```
apiVersion: serving.knative.dev/v1
kind: Service
metadata:
  name: helloworld
  namespace: default
spec:
  template:
    metadata:
      name: helloworld
    spec:
      containers:
        - image: docker.io/test/helloworld:v1
```

7. Deploy the function using:

```
$ kubectl apply -f hello-world.yaml
```

8. At this time, your serverless function will be deployed. You will be able to find the URL for the function by running:

```
$ kubectl get ksvc hello-world --output=custom-columns=NAME:.metadata.name, \
  URL:.status.url
```

9. Test your function by calling the URL:

```
$ curl  -X POST <URL found from above> -d "My Data"
Hello World: My Data
```

Now that a basic serving function is running, let's look at Knative eventing.

# Installing and Running Knative Eventing on Kubernetes

In this section, we will install Knative eventing components and write a simple eventing system:

1. Start by installing the custom resources:

   ```
   $ kubectl apply -f https://github.com/knative/eventing/releases/download/v0.26.0/ \
     eventing-crds.yaml
   ```

2. Now install the serving components:

   ```
   $ kubectl apply -f https://github.com/knative/eventing/releases/download/v0.26.0/ \
     eventing-core.yaml
   ```

   At this time, you will have the eventing components installed. We are going to reuse our Docker image from the preceding section. However, we will configure Knative so that we can send an HTTP message to a message bus within Knative instead of posting to an HTTP application server. When the message reaches the message bus, it will trigger our Python application server. In a more complicated example, you can set a Kafka topic as a source of events.

3. Create a *knative-eventing.yaml* file:

   ```
   # Namespace for sample application with eventing enabled
   apiVersion: v1
   kind: Namespace
   metadata:
     name: knative-samples
     labels:
       eventing.knative.dev/injection: enabled
   ---
   # A default broker
   apiVersion: eventing.knative.dev/v1
   kind: Broker
   metadata:
     name: default
     namespace: knative-samples
     annotations:
       # Note: you can set the eventing.knative.dev/broker.class annotation to change
       # the class of the broker.
       # The default broker class is MTChannelBasedBroker, but Knative also supports
       # use of the other class.
       eventing.knative.dev/broker.class: MTChannelBasedBroker
   spec: {}
   ---
   # hello-world app deployment
   apiVersion: apps/v1
   kind: Deployment
   metadata:
     name: hello-world
     namespace: knative-samples
   spec:
     replicas: 1
     selector:
       matchLabels: &labels
         app: hello-world
   ```

```
      template:
        metadata:
          labels: *labels
        spec:
          containers:
            - name: hello-world
              image: https://myharborinstallation.com/helloworld:v1
              imagePullPolicy: IfNotPresent
---
# Service that exposes helloworld-python app.
# This will be the subscriber for the Trigger
apiVersion: v1
kind: Service
metadata:
  name: hello-world
  namespace: knative-samples
spec:
  selector:
    app: hello-world
  ports:
    - protocol: TCP
      port: 80
      targetPort: 8080
---
# Knative Eventing Trigger to trigger the helloworld-python service
apiVersion: eventing.knative.dev/v1
kind: Trigger
metadata:
  name: hello-world
  namespace: knative-samples
spec:
  broker: default
  filter:
    attributes:
      type: dev.knative.samples.hello-world
      source: dev.knative.samples/helloworldsource
  subscriber:
    ref:
      apiVersion: v1
      kind: Service
      name: hello-world
```

4. Apply the *knative-eventing.yaml* configuration on Kubernetes:

```
$ kubectl apply -f knative-eventing.yaml
```

This will create a new Kubernetes namespace called `knative-samples` that allows eventing, and a message broker that will pass messages to our Python application server (on events).

5. We will now send an event to our Knative message broker. Here is the response:

```
$ curl -v "broker-ingress.knative-eventing.svc.cluster.local/knative-samples/default" \
-X POST \
-d 'My data'

Event received. Context: Context Attributes,
  specversion: 0.3
  type: dev.knative.samples.hello-world
  source: dev.knative.samples/helloworldsource
```

```
id: 536808d3-88be-4077-9d7a-6a3f162705f79
time: 2021-11-09T06:21:26.09471798Z
datacontenttype: application/json
Extensions,
  Knativearrivaltime: 2021-11-09T06:21:26Z
  knativehistory: default-kn2-trigger-kn-channel.knative-samples.svc.cluster.local
  traceparent: 00-971d4644229653483d38c46e92a959c7-92c66312e4bb39be-00

Hello World Message "My data"
Responded with event Validation: valid
Context Attributes,
  specversion: 0.2
  type: dev.knative.samples.hifromknative
  source: knative/eventing/samples/hello-world
  id: 37458d77-01f5-411e-a243-a459bbf79682
Data,
  My data
```

# KEDA

KEDA stands for *Kubernetes Event-Driven Autoscaling*. KEDA allows you to scale any container in Kubernetes based on the number of incoming events. KEDA is an add-on to Kubernetes and utilizes the Horizontal Pod Autoscaler (HPA) to scale based on a variety of event sources, including Apache Kafka, Azure Event Hubs, and NATS streaming.

## KEDA Architecture

A typical KEDA architecture is depicted in Figure 11-3, where KEDA interacts directly with the Kubernetes API server, HPA, and the configured trigger source.

The KEDA component performs the following roles:

*Controller and scaler*
> The controller and scaler will scale the number of Pods up or down depending on the signal from the metrics adapter.

*Metrics adapter*
> The metrics adapter acts as a Kubernetes metrics server that provides queue length or stream lag information to the agent. The scaler uses this information to scale containers up and down.

You can see all of the KEDA scalers in the Scalers documentation (*https://keda.sh/docs/2.4/scalers*).

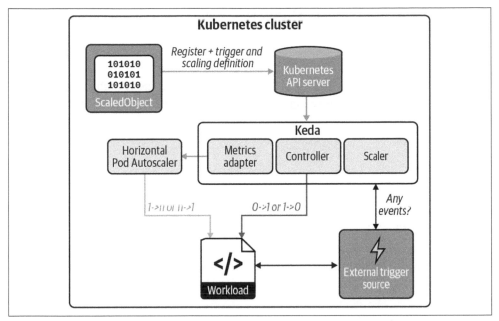

*Figure 11-3. The KEDA reference architecture*

## Installing KEDA on Kubernetes

KEDA is best installed using the Helm operator on Kubernetes. We will walk through this now:

1. Add the KEDA Helm repository:

```
$ helm repo add kedacore https://kedacore.github.io/charts
```

2. Install the Helm chart:

```
$ kubectl create namespace keda
$ helm install keda kedacore/keda --namespace keda
```

After this, your Kubernetes cluster will be ready for function deployment.

In the next example, we will build a proof-of-concept event system with an Azure Service Bus queue. We will produce messages to the Azure Service Bus queue using a Python script and then use KEDA to scale a Python consumption job:

1. Grab your Service Bus connection string using either the manual method described in the Azure documentation (*https://oreil.ly/XpeG3*) or by running:

```
$ az servicebus namespace authorization-rule keys list \
    -n RootManageSharedAccessKey -g <group> --namespace-name <namespace> \
    --query primaryConnectionString -o tsv
```

2. You will need to get the Base64-encoded values of the connection string and the queue name by running:

```
$ echo -n "<connection string>" | base64
$ echo -n "<queue name>" | base64
```

3. Now create a file called *secret.yaml*. Replace the `servicebus-queue` and `servicebus-connectionstring` values with the Base64 strings generated in the previous step:

```
apiVersion: v1
kind: Secret
metadata:
  name: sample-job-secret
  namespace: default
data:
  servicebus-queue: <base64_encoded_servicebus_queue_name>
  servicebus-connectionstring: <base64_encoded_servicebus_connection_string>
```

4. Create a second file, called *keda.yaml*, which will create your ScaledJob. It will be running a Docker image (docker.pkg.github.com/prabdeb/sample-python-keda-service-bus-scaler/consumer:latest) when triggered:

```
apiVersion: keda.sh/v1alpha1
kind: TriggerAuthentication
metadata:
  name: auth-service-bus-sample-job
spec:
  secretTargetRef:
  - parameter: connection
    name: sample-job-secret
    key: servicebus-connectionstring
---
apiVersion: keda.sh/v1alpha1
kind: ScaledJob
metadata:
  name: servicebus-queue-so-sample-job
  namespace: default
spec:
  jobTargetRef:
    parallelism: 1 # max number of desired pods
    completions: 1 # desired number of successfully finished pods
    activeDeadlineSeconds: 600 # Specifies the duration in seconds relative to the
      startTime that the job may be active before the system tries to terminate it;
      value must be positive integer
    backoffLimit: 6 # Specifies the number of retries before marking this job failed.
      Defaults to 6
    Template:e
      metadata:
        labels:
          app: sample-keda-job
      spec:
        containers:
        - name: sample-keda-job
          image: docker.pkg.github.com/prabdeb/sample-python-keda-service-bus-scaler/
            consumer:latest
          env:
            - name: SERVICE_BUS_CONNECTION_STR
```

```
            valueFrom:
              secretKeyRef:
                name: sample-job-secret
                key: servicebus-connectionstring
          - name: SERVICE_BUS_QUEUE_NAME
            valueFrom:
              secretKeyRef:
                name: sample-job-secret
                key: servicebus-queue
        restartPolicy: Never
  pollingInterval: 30                         # Optional. Default: 30 seconds
  successfulJobsHistoryLimit: 100             # Optional. Default: 100.
                                              # How many completed jobs should be kept.
  failedJobsHistoryLimit: 100                 # Optional. Default: 100.
                                              # How many failed jobs should be kept.
  #envSourceContainerName: {container-name}   # Optional. Default:
                                              # .spec.JobTargetRef.template.spec
                                              # .containers[0]
  maxReplicaCount: 100                        # Optional. Default: 100
  scalingStrategy:
    strategy: "custom"                        # Optional. Default: default.
                                              # Which Scaling Strategy to use.
    customScalingQueueLengthDeduction: 1      # Optional. A parameter
                                              # to optimize custom ScalingStrategy.
    customScalingRunningJobPercentage: "0.5"  # Optional. A parameter
                                              # to optimize custom ScalingStrategy.
  triggers:
  - type: azure-servicebus
    metadata:
      # Required: queueName OR topicName and subscriptionName
      queueName: <servicebus_queue_name>
      # Required: Define what Azure Service Bus
      # to authenticate to with Managed Identity
      namespace: <servicebus_namespace>
      messageCount: "10" # default 5
    authenticationRef:
        name: auth-service-bus-sample-job # authenticationRef would need either
          podIdentity or define a connection parameter
```

5. Now you can apply the two files to Kubernetes using:

```
$ kubectl apply -f keda-config/jobs/secret.yaml
$ kubectl apply -f keda-config/jobs/keda.yaml
```

6. Verify that your ScaledJob is ready by running:

```
$ kubectl get ScaledJob
$ kubectl get TriggerAuthentication
```

7. You can test your KEDA deployment by running a test script. First you need to set up the Python environment:

```
$ python3 -m venv .
$ source bin/activate
$ pip3 install logger
$ pip3 install azure-servicebus
```

8. Now you need to create your program that sends messages to the Azure Service Bus queue. You will need to modify connection_string and queue_name:

```
import os
import sys
import time
import yaml
from logger import logger
from azure.servicebus import ServiceBusClient, ServiceBusMessage


def send_a_list_of_messages(sender):
    messages = [ServiceBusMessage(f"Message in list {i}") for i in range(1000)]
    sender.send_messages(messages)
    logger.info("Sent a list of 1000 messages")

def main():
    with open("azure-service-bus.yaml", 'r') as stream:
        config = yaml.safe_load(stream)

    logger.info("Start sending messages")
    connection_string = <FIXME>
    queue_name = <FIXME>

    queue = ServiceBusClient.from_connection_string(conn_str=connection_string, \
      queue_name=queue_name)

    with queue:
        sender = queue.get_queue_sender(queue_name=queue_name)
        with sender:
            send_a_list_of_messages(sender)

    logger.info("Done sending messages")
    logger.info("----------------------")

if __name__ == "__main__":
    main()
```

9. Run *python3 send_message_queue.py*. This will create 1,000 messages and send them to the Azure Service Bus queue.

You can see the messages being ingested and then processed in the Azure Service Bus queue (Figure 11-4).

*Figure 11-4. Azure Service Bus queue*

In the next section, we will look at OpenFaaS, which provides simple, no-frills functions on both standalone systems and Kubernetes clusters.

# OpenFaaS

OpenFaaS is another event-driven function service for Kubernetes that allows you to write functions in any language and then package them in Docker or OCI-compatible containers.

## OpenFaaS Architecture

The OpenFaaS reference architecture (as shown in Figure 11-5) is reasonably similar to KEDA. However, OpenFaaS does rely on metrics from Prometheus to act as an autoscaling signal.

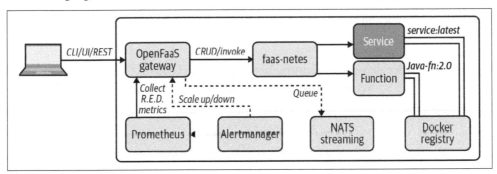

*Figure 11-5. The OpenFaaS reference architecture*

## Installing OpenFaaS

OpenFaaS has three recommended installation methods:

- Using arkade
- Using helm
- Installing with Flux or ArgoCD

To be consistent with the rest of the book, we'll deploy OpenFaaS using Helm:

1. Create the namespaces (one for OpenFaaS core services and one for functions):

   ```
   $ kubectl apply -f https://raw.githubusercontent.com/openfaas/faas-netes/master/ \
     namespaces.yml
   ```

2. Add the OpenFaaS Helm chart:

   ```
   $ helm repo add openfaas https://openfaas.github.io/faas-netes/
   ```

3. Finally, deploy OpenFaaS:

```
$ helm repo update \
  && helm upgrade openfaas --install openfaas/openfaas \
    --namespace openfaas  \
    --set functionNamespace=openfaas-fn \
    --set generateBasicAuth=true
```

4. You'll be able to retrieve your administrator password by running the following command; this will be used for accessing the OpenFaaS dashboard:

```
$ PASSWORD=$(kubectl -n openfaas get secret basic-auth -o \
  jsonpath="{.data.basic-auth-password}" | base64 --decode) && \
echo "OpenFaaS admin password: $PASSWORD"
```

Now that we have OpenFaaS installed, we're going to write an OpenFaaS function.

## Writing Your First OpenFaaS Function

In this section, we will utilize the faas-cli to quickly create and deploy a serverless function:

1. Download the faas-cli by running `brew install faas-cli` on OSX, or by running `curl -sSL https://cli.openfaas.com | sudo sh` on Linux.

2. Create a folder to place your new function:

```
$ mkdir -p ~/functions && cd ~/functions
```

3. Use the faas-cli to create a new Python function project:

```
$ faas-cli new --lang python helloworld
```

This will create three new files:

```
$ ls
helloworld/handler.py
helloworld/requirements.txt
helloworld.yml
```

The *handler.py* file will be where you write your function. The *requirements.txt* file is the same as a standard Python *requirements.txt file*. The *helloworld.yml* file defines some boilerplate for your function.

4. In the *handler.py* file, we will define our function. This function will print "Hello World! You said: " plus the data posted to the function endpoint:

```
def handle(req):
    print("Hello World! You said: " + req)
```

5. Finally, in your *helloworld.yml* file, you will define metadata about your function. *http://127.0.0.1:31112* is the default address of the OpenFaaS gateway/API server:

```
provider:
  name: openfaas
  gateway: http://127.0.0.1:31112
```

```
functions:
  hello-python:
    lang: python
    handler: ./hello-world
    image: hello-world
```

6. Build the serverless image and push it to the Harbor registry you created in Chapter 2:

```
$ faas-cli build -f ./hello-world.yml
$ faas-cli push -f ./hello-world.yml
```

7. Deploy it to the Kubernetes cluster:

```
$ faas-cli deploy -f ./hello-world.yml
Deploying: hello-python.
No existing service to remove
Deployed.
200 OK
URL: http://127.0.0.1:31112/function/hello-python
```

8. The previous step outputs a URL you can test against. Use curl to test it:

```
$ curl -X POST 127.0.0.1:31112/function/hello-world -d "My name is Michael"
Hello world! My name is Michael
```

By default, OpenFaaS uses requests per second (rps) as a mechanism to perform autoscaling. You can find more information about OpenFaaS autoscaling configuration on the Autoscaling documentation page (*https://oreil.ly/xcPFX*).

At this time, you will have a running OpenFaaS function on Kubernetes. You can also run OpenFaaS outside of Kubernetes using `faasd`. There's more information on the OpenFaaS deployment page (*https://oreil.ly/ZZidU*).

Finally, OpenFaaS is built on top of the Kubernetes HPA. You can find out more about how to load-test and autoscale your OpenFaaS function from the OpenFaaS Kubernetes tutorial page (*https://oreil.ly/mpyme*).

## Summary

While serverless is definitely not for everyone, when used in the right situations it can provide significant upsides. The serverless space is still evolving, but the barrier to entry is extremely low, which makes it an exciting technology. In this chapter, we explored four different ways you can run serverless functions on Azure. First we looked at Azure function apps and then we looked at three leading CNCF projects: Knative, KEDA, and OpenFaaS. At this point, we have outlined the major pillars of cloud native infrastructure. In Chapter 12, we will recap what you learned throughout this journey.

# Conclusion

We've come to the end of the book, so let's recap our journey. Throughout this book, we aimed to provide a single resource that you can use to build and run a cloud native infrastructure in Azure. Although Azure has been our focus, you can also apply the same knowledge to build and operate your own cloud native environment over different cloud vendor platforms. Let's go through what you've learned so far.

We began this book by looking back at how the world of infrastructure and services evolved over time with the introduction of the cloud. To take full advantage of what the cloud has to offer, we need to develop solutions that are native to the cloud and not just retroactively adapt them for the cloud. We understood how cloud native is the way to go in order to fully utilize the power of the cloud.

In Chapter 2, we introduced the steppingstones to building a modern cloud native environment using Azure. We set up an Azure account and got started with Ansible, Terraform, and Packer. By employing them as our key tools, we can enable production-ready services in an automated fashion. We used Microsoft Azure as our choice of cloud provider, and throughout the book we used both cloud native and Azure services in conjunction to showcase how modern infrastructure is built and supported.

In Chapter 3, we introduced you to the container and the container runtime, which form the fundamentals of a modern cloud native world. We discussed the layers of abstraction that make up the container ecosystem.

We moved on to the mighty orchestrator, Kubernetes, in Chapter 4 and Chapter 5, and we showcased the nitty-gritty of how this important tool can be used in modern cloud infrastructure to facilitate the platform for cloud native applications. Kubernetes led the inception as well as the adaptation of the Cloud Native Computing Foundation (CNCF) and was the first project to graduate under it. This led to a whole lot of streamlining of the containerization world and higher adaptation of the cloud native ecosystem. We looked into the various components and concepts that make this system operate at scale and learned how to create the Kubernetes cluster both manually and using Azure AKS as a managed service.

At this point, we had covered the basics of what a bare minimum cloud native infrastructure looks like. The next step was to add a way to gain application and infrastructure insights. So, in Chapter 6, we introduced the concept of the three pillars of observability, to give you insights into this massive infrastructure and application stack. By building observable systems, you can have greater control over complex distributed systems that interact over boundaries. In this chapter, we also took a stab at observability and its growing need in the cloud native environment. With the three pillars of observability and an introduction to the preferred ways of doing logging, monitoring, and tracing over modern distributed systems over Azure, we concluded the chapter with a brief look at how Azure offers its built-in solutions to perform some similar tasks with Azure Monitor.

When we talk about boundaries and borders, we are faced with the problem of service-to-service communication in this dynamically changing environment. So, to solve this, we introduced service discovery and the service mesh in Chapter 7 as a means to find services and communicate to them effectively. We also carefully show-cased the need for service meshes and proxies to efficiently control the overall environment where your microservices reside. We introduced CoreDNS as the default DNS, replacing kube-dns, in the Kubernetes environment. We also introduced service meshes using Istio, which uses Envoy as its data plane for getting useful insights on services and provides the full feature set of the Istio service mesh. Toward the end of the chapter, we showcased Kiali, which provides a full management console on an Istio-based service mesh.

In Chapter 8, we moved on to the problem of networking and policy management in cloud native environments. We introduced you to two main tools: Calico and Flannel, which serve as the container networking interface. We also shed some light on how you can enforce policies across the stack using open policy management. We reviewed the CNI standard and how it's the foundation for platforms like Flannel and Cilium. We examined how those systems can be used to provide connectivity and network security to your cloud infrastructure. We also looked at non–network policy mechanisms for managing your cloud infrastructure via Azure Policy as well as policy for applications via Open Policy Agent.

In Chapter 9, we looked at how storage is perceived and designed in cloud native environments using Vitess as a distributed database. We also talked about Rook, which is an extensive storage orchestrator that can help you reduce the burden of managing a distributed storage system by simply doing things like self-scaling and self-healing. In this chapter, we reviewed why it is advantageous to use cloud native data systems in Azure's cloud. We covered four systems: Vitess (relational), Rook (blob), TiKV (key-value), and etcd (key-value configuration/service discovery). These systems are the bedrock of a cloud native architecture that stores and serves online data, and they offer a large upside over utilizing PaaS components.

In Chapter 10, we talked about how messaging and streaming services are built and deployed in cloud native environments using traditional technologies like NATS, gRPC, Apache Kafka, and RabbitMQ.

Finally, in Chapter 11, we explored four different ways you can run serverless functions on Azure. First we looked at Azure function apps and then we looked at three leading CNCF projects: Knative, KEDA, and OpenFaaS.

We hope you have been able to gain a good understanding of how to build and use cloud native infrastructure. You now have the knowledge to build and operate your own cloud native infrastructure on Azure.

# What's Next?

The CNCF (*https://landscape.cncf.io*) Landscape is quite big and it contains a lot of projects that are consistently being built and supported by a lot of great companies (Figure 12-1). These projects are built from the ground up with consideration for scale and reliability.

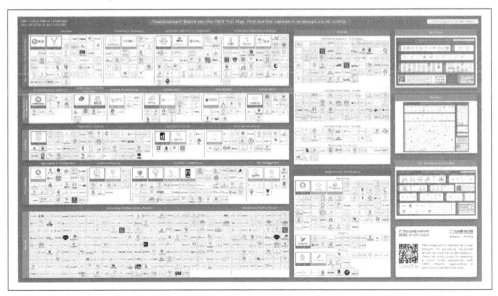

*Figure 12-1. The CNCF Landscape*

We highly encourage you to explore other technologies in the CNCF Landscape to build your cloud native environment according to your use case, and we encourage you to explore the CNCF Serverless Landscape as well (Figure 12-2).

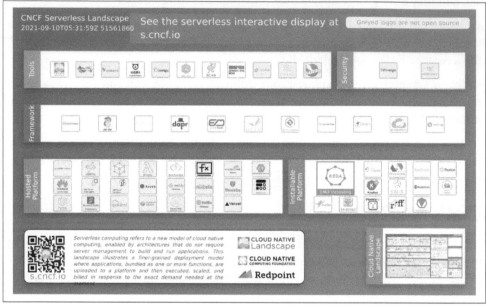

*Figure 12-2. The CNCF Serverless Landscape*

The CNCF (*https://landscape.cncf.io/serverless*) Serverless Landscape highlights serverless computing and the associated programming model as well as message formats. Though serverless computing has been widely available, there is plenty of scope and depth in the development of this approach. You can explore serverless computing if your workload is asynchronous, sporadic, stateless, and highly dynamic in terms of changing business requirements. You can also start using various Azure services and see how they can compare with CNCF technologies.

Most of these projects are open source and are the efforts of many engineers who contribute vigorously to the community. Open source also brings a great amount of quality control to the overall design of these projects. This means cloud native technologies are supported well around the world, and are easily adaptable. It's also important to note that many of these cloud native technologies are the result of difficult problems that needed to be solved efficiently. Hence, it is equally important to venture out at times and ask hard questions in order to gain an in-depth understanding of your systems that will eventually lead you to finding the right solutions to complex problems.

The cloud native landscape continues to grow, and we encourage you to explore it even further to its true potential. We wish you the best of luck.

# Index

## About the Authors

**Nishant Singh** is a senior site reliability engineer at LinkedIn, where he works to improve the reliability of the site with a focus on reducing the mean time to detect (MTTD) and mean time to respond (MTTR) to incidents. Prior to joining LinkedIn, he worked at Paytm and Gemalto as a DevOps engineer, spending his time building custom solutions for clients and managing and maintaining services over the public cloud. Nishant has a keen interest in site reliability engineering and in building distributed systems.

**Michael Kehoe** is a senior staff security engineer at Confluent. Prior to this, he worked on incident response, disaster recovery, visibility engineering, and reliability principles as a senior staff site reliability engineer at LinkedIn. During his time at LinkedIn, he led the company's efforts to automate the migration to Microsoft Azure. Michael specializes in maintaining large system infrastructure as demonstrated by his work at LinkedIn (applications, automation, and infrastructure) and at the University of Queensland (networks). He has also spent time building small satellites at NASA and writing thermal environments software at Rio Tinto.

## Colophon

The animal on the cover of *Cloud Native Infrastructure with Azure* is a Stellar's jay (*Cyanocitta stelleri*), a crested jay found in western North and Central America. Stellar's jays typically reside in coniferous forests but can be encountered in deciduous forests as well.

Named after Georg Wilhelm Steller—the German naturalist who first recorded the jay in 1741—this blue-colored jay is distinct from eastern North America's blue jay, its defining characteristic being a dramatic black crest.

Steller's jays are omnivores; their diet mainly consists of nuts, pine seeds, acorns, berries and other fruit supplemented with insects, small rodents, and eggs.

While the Stellar's jay's conversation status is listed as of Least Concern, many of the animals on O'Reilly covers are endangered; all of them are important to the world.

The cover illustration is by Karen Montgomery, based on an antique line engraving from *Lydekker's Royal Natural History*. The cover fonts are Gilroy Semibold and Guardian Sans. The text font is Adobe Minion Pro; the heading font is Adobe Myriad Condensed; and the code font is Dalton Maag's Ubuntu Mono.

Milton Keynes UK
Ingram Content Group UK Ltd.
UKHW021956160324
439469UK00004B/14